Meanders throug

Meanders through England and Wales

With Small Churches as my Guide

SALLY RIEDER

© Sally Rieder, 2021

Published by Sally Rieder

A CIP catalogue record for this book is available from the British Library.

ISBN 978-1-5262-0920-7

Book layout and cover design by Clare Brayshaw

Front cover image Chesterton Windmill, Chesterton – Wikimedia Commons

Prepared and printed by:

York Publishing Services Ltd
64 Hallfield Road
Layerthorpe
York YO31 7ZQ

Tel: 01904 431213

Website: www.yps-publishing.co.uk

For Robert

Contents

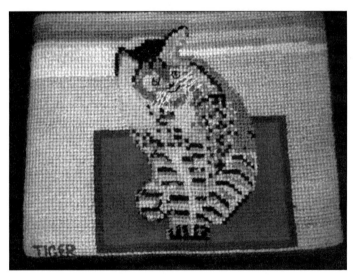

My favourite cat forever in St Mary & St Gabriel's,
South Harting, West Sussex

Introduction

Though born in Leicester my early years were little spent in England. Shortly afterwards my father was posted to the RAF base at Weeze, Düsseldorf in Germany and thereafter time I don't remember in South Africa and years I very much do remember in the then protectorate of Aden. Until the last years of schooling in Hampshire visits to England were short and sporadic followed by a couple of years in Canada and a spell in London before I decided to visit the land of father's birth, South Africa. Little did I know almost twenty years would pass before I returned to the country of my birth of which I knew so little.

One Christmas my son Robert gave me a book which neither of us anticipated would lead me to explore and get to visit and know, superficially but with much pleasure, the wonderfully varied countryside of England and Wales. Sir Simon Jenkins' tome on a thousand best churches of England was an unusual gift from a twenty year old to his mother so I imagine he picked up on something I had mentioned or an interest expressed in a sort of unaware way – maybe the school prize I had won for an essay On Graveyards (what, I now wonder, did a schoolgirl have to say on this subject). For two years this book remained tucked in between others on the shelf until a thought, comment or person – I remember not – caused me to take it on a walking holiday in Somerset. Any earnest intention I may have had to learn all about the architectural and period properties of chapels, churches, minsters and abbeys was soon abandoned. Academic learning is *not* where my interest or capability lies. There are others far better qualified and able to absorb and ponder the evidence and legend as to what happened, how and when, in the history and building of these seats of worship. Besides, exploring the villages and countryside of this country in which I was born but had spent so few of my young years was interesting and such fun in itself – I was easily distracted by another building, country corner, local legend. Instead of seeking out the grand and the great edifices warranting a five star tag, I became instead drawn to the simplicity, charms, quirks and, sometimes, curious tales revealed, of the many rural churches and chapels once the centre of long vanished hamlets – sometimes an occasional medieval dovecote or grand windmill – tucked away down lanes, on hills, in fields. I began to go out of my way to visit churches rated by others with a single star, even no star at all. Many of these churches are no longer surrounded by the community for which they were built in Saxon, Norman or early English times. Sometimes I've driven miles along narrow sunken lanes, passed through farmyards, taken wrong turnings seeking to come across a tiny church. The beauty and tranquillity of the isolated location would more than compensate for the occasional disappointment.

Any feature or legend of these little semi retired churches is as likely to remain in my memory as is the magnificence to be found in their grand cousins. I was a long way off coming to this realisation when I set off on my first explore and, looking back, I have two regrets: that I didn't examine more closely the oddities of churches, sometimes graveyards, to which I'm now unlikely to return; and my then lack of a digital camera. A bonus while pursuing my interest in these little gems of rural life has been meeting people, wandering off subject, and visiting pockets of England I would probably not have otherwise explored. Crawling or cantering, it has been, and will continue to be, such fun. Most important of all is to encourage others to visit these rural delights: so many are now isolated and neglected but should never be forgotten, allowed to go to ruin. They are such a charming part of English rural history to value and cherish. As is the variety and wonders of our countryside.

* * *

C16th dovecote, Willingdon, Buckinghamshire

Somerset

My interest in churches started with those first visited, in this county, as I began to explore England more widely. I have dipped in and out of Somerset on several occasions over the years, the county of hunky-punks and Lorna Doone, significant towers and Ham stone, moors and sea shore and there is one special church I revisited many years later, this time following a quite different route, one taken some two hundred years ago by Samuel Coleridge Taylor.

The Dorset Dawdlers – a collective term for a small group of walking friends – set off one April from Chedington, Dorset to follow the Parrett River (just to confuse, a local village is South Perrott) from its source to Stert, Somerset. Since then, visiting churches and a rural area of interest has often been combined with walks and walking holidays. On this occasion I checked into my allocated cottage two days ahead of the other Dawdlers. Stashed in the car boot with provisions and all necessary walking apparel was a tome (*England's Thousand Best Churches* by Simon Jenkins) destined to accompany me on many subsequent 'crawls'. After breakfast I set off to find my first church, the rather grand St Andrew's, Curry Rivel. It was locked. I could do no more than admire the grotesques (known in Somerset as 'hunky-punks') adorning the exterior. Somewhat disgruntled, I drove on to **St Catherine's, Swell** *(TA3 6PZ),* an enchanting chapel adjacent to a farmyard, set back from a stone wall behind a spreading fruit tree thick with white blossom beginning to shed petals onto a short path leading from a wrought iron gate. Without a tower or roof cross, it had the external appearance of a well-kept labourers cottage. Once inside the porch, a Norman arch dispelled this illusion. It led into a delightfully light, slightly squiffy and simple interior with little to boast of other than worn pews and a bell sitting useless on the floor. Charmed, my good humour was restored.

The next church on the route I had planned is as imposing as Swell is unprepossessing. The tower of **St Mary's, Isle Abbotts** *(TA3 6RH)* is clearly visible from a considerable distance. Seriously tall towers, more often than not a feature of Somerset churches, are constructed from either greyish blue lias or the more costly warm ochre and cream local Ham stone. Intrigued by the complex decorations and the several human forms set into niches, I went inside to find out more about the carvings generally and the creatures protruding from all corners and two centre sides along the bottom line of the parapet. No doubt I missed little delights inside the church but back outside, clutching the church information board, I was gazed up at the 'hunky punks', grotesques which would be gargoyles if a water spout was incorporated to lead rainwater away from the building. Apparently 'hunky punk' is derived from 'hunkers punchy', the old English form of saying 'squatting short legged on haunches'! Only one hunky punk was in human form, a hairy man cheeks puffed with blowing two melody pipes. Five creatures completed the collection, a goat and four dragons, eyes, mouth or tongue exaggerated, all puffing out their chests. The information sheet mentions Westonzoyland and Lyng as having their own hunky punks; they were listed as a person playing the bagpipes, an oriental lion dog, a goat, a dragon, a Chinese dragon, a primitive dragon, a winged lion and a lion. Should I return to this area, I'll certainly renew my acquaintance with these Somerset peculiars. According to the notes on the last Thursday night in October a lantern procession takes place; it was, maybe still is, a west country tradition surely related to Halloween, led by the Punkie King and Queen, when children carry hollowed candle lit swedes and sing something along the lines *"Give me a candle, give me a light, if you haven't a candle, a penny's alright"*.

With a long drive planned for the following day, I returned to my cottage accommodation for an early night, prepared to set off early next morning to find my first church of the day. I remember **Stogumber** – village cottages around a duck pond on which some fancy white ducks with curly tail feathers cruised about – but recall nothing at all of its church, **St Mary's** *(TA4 3TA)*. I re-joined the A358 and continued parallel to the Bristol Channel until I reached **Dunster**, a town on the periphery of Exmoor. The high street has a curious octagonal open sided barn, right in the middle of the high street, which I walked past towards the tall, red sandstone tower of **St George's** *(TA24 6RY)*. Even I, a newcomer to church interiors, appreciated the stunning rood screen and the beautifully carved designs of foliage and green men depicted on the oak bench panels. With still a way to drive if I was to reach both Culbone and Oare that day, time didn't allow me to linger longer. Both St Mary's and such a beautiful medieval town warrant a return visit.

Just before Porlock I turned off towards the coast and the climb to Selworthy Beacon. High up on a bank studded with many headstones **All Saints', Selworthy** *(TA24 8TW)*, overlooks the pretty village below it. White-painted with a stocky turreted tower and, inside, a wonderful wagon roof, the ceiling painted blue and white. The whole interior is light, bright and welcoming. Above the porch a priest's room is accessed by a little staircase leading up through a narrow door next to the south entrance. I would have preferred to enjoy this church on my own but had to share it with a large number of other visitors, either in the church or sitting on a bench outside, drinking in the view.

The road, which I had almost to myself, ascended hilly countryside to the high open space of Exmoor moorland, surely one of the last wildernesses in the country. I had difficulty finding the right track to take me from where I could set off on foot to find **St Beuno's, Culbone** (*TA24 8PQ*). Marker located I headed along a narrow track downhill through deciduous woods. After about a mile, the track and a little stream running parallel to it continued through a short rounded tunnel under the first floor of a sizeable house. A little further on the wood cleared and there was this tubby church, its mini tower reminiscent of a dunce's cap. I fully expected to be the only visitor so was surprised to find a middle-aged couple sitting on a bench. They told me they had come across the church on their honeymoon thirty years before this, their first return visit. They kindly agreed to take a photograph of me leaning against a headstone. Eleven churches in Wales and England are dedicated to St Beuno, a C7th Welsh abbot. This little Culbone church is mentioned in the Domesday Book: it's a mix of Saxon parts, C12th and C13th, Grade 1 listed and possibly once served a leper colony, charcoal burners, even vagrants. According to the church leaflet the total length of the chancel and nave is thirty-five feet with seating, at a squeeze, for thirty-three people. Enchanting. Yet another reason to return to this tranquil corner of England.

By now thirsty and probably hungry, I paused for a while at the Culbone Pub before continuing westward towards **St Mary's, Oare** *(EX35 6NX)*. Far below the hill road on which I approached stretched a wide and very beautiful vista of the moor, a cluster of buildings and, of course, the church made famous as the setting for the death of Richard Blackmore's tragic heroine. *Lorna Doone*, set in the C17th, published in 1869, is based on legend. In his novel Blackmore, a vicar's son, has Lorna shot dead on the altar steps. The church interior is plain with a wagon roof. Disappointment – no blood stains on the steps …!

I managed the drive back to the cottages without a wrong turning to find fellow Dawdlers ensconced in their accommodation and ready to gather for supper at a pub nearby, the same one we would use every evening. Charles had sensibly arranged for a minibus to take us to the starting point for each day's walk, collect us where we ended up and return us to that point the following day. The Parrett Potter, as we named it, is the shortest coast-to-coast walk. For the most part the route passes through beautiful scenery though we were in agreement there was little to excite us about the Somerset levels; especially when hungry and thirsty with no pub in sight they seemed interminable. The monotony was briefly interrupted when Rupert recognised the gentleman tending his garden as a former neighbour in Hampshire when they shared an interest in breeding eels. A truly chance encounter. One day during the Potter we diverted into **Muchelney Abbey** *(TA10 0DQ)*. It has had a chequered history since it was founded 762: destroyed by the Danes, then re-established around 950 to last for nearly six centuries. Our collective less than academic interest was held by blue painted bare breasted topless angels looking down from the roof upon our startled upturned faces.

When we gathered for a last communal meal in a pub at Steart, all but two of us were falling apart: Paul's blisters were causing him huge distress, James was exceedingly unwell – neither able to complete the last mile through saltmarshes to a lookout tower, the 'official' end point – with most of the others about to follow suit. Jenny and I were the lucky ones to escape both injury and sickness.

Next morning, after we had all taken leave of each other, I set off to seek the five churches I had selected to visit during the drive back to Chichester. **St Andrew's, High Ham** *(TA10 9DF)* is slightly north east of where we had been staying, standing, as the name implies, on a mound. The battlements boast hunky punks as weird and wonderfully carved as those at Isle Abbotts and rather easier to examine, being lower down. The very best feature, however, is inside: the staggeringly beautiful and elegant rood screen. The tracery is very fine, fan vaults surmount the shafts and above them is a platform for musicians and choir, accessed by a little doorway next to the pulpit. These were pre-digital days and, to my regret, I had no more film in my camera to record this extraordinary screen.

On to **St Michael's, Somerton** *(TA11 7NB)*, quite a sizeable town. The church roof is another fine example of the intricate work carried out by wood carvers of Somerset in the C16th. Whilst I appreciated the many panels, each filled with a quatrefoil and the anything-but uniform bosses dotted about, I was by then in need of a coffee and a powder room so didn't explore any further. Having attended to both needs I couldn't resist going into one of those interesting antique-cum-junk shops. I bought a little crystal necklace and some fine lawn embroidered cloth destined to become a petticoat, part of the family christening dress hours in the making into which I poured all my love and limited skill.

Stitched round the scalloped hem (albeit a little unevenly!) are the names and birth dates of all my grandchildren.

Holy Trinity, Long Sutton *(TA10 9HS)* was on the way to Martock. As with Isle Abbotts, the building was a mix of blue lias and Ham stone, the result a gorgeous mix of ochre, blue milk and red cream. Nowhere else have I come across such a pulpit – shaped very much like a wine glass – and screen with all the detail of panels, figures and carving picked out in brilliant greens, reds and gold. A happy blaze of colour to lift anyone's heart. Tired from days of walking and socialising and with a long way still to go, I almost didn't stop in **Martock** and only did so as there was a space in which to park the car opposite **All Saints** church *(TA12 6 JL),* the Ham stone rosy red under the late afternoon sun. Somerset churches are known for beautiful roofs. The artistry of the wood carving at Martock was another example, worth cricking my neck to gaze up at over a hundred pierced intricately carved panels divided into six sections under the steeply pitched roof. I didn't look at anything else, anxious to reach **St Bartholomew's, Crewkerne** *(TA18 7HY),* the last church of the day.

Except it wasn't to be. I arrived in the town, legs tightly crossed, so nipped into a pub, intending to use the loo. Feeling I ought to 'pay' for the facility I was about to use, I ordered a soft drink only to find my wallet was missing. I probably spent a penny anyway but then tore back to the car expecting to see my wallet on the passenger seat or even on the pavement next to the car door. No luck. In which case, the only place it could be was next to the honesty box in the church at Martock. I retraced the drive at quite irresponsible speed, arriving just before the door was locked for the night and was amazed, not to say relieved, to find my wallet exactly where I had left it! Sometimes the gods do look after you. Of course, Crewkerne was locked by the time I returned but I didn't mind. The church would still be there another day and my need go home was far stronger than a curiosity to see yet another church.

Five years later, returning home from a visit to Bath, I made an impulsive decision to veer off to visit **St Andrew's, Mells** *(BA11 3PW)*. After coffee in The Talbot Inn, an attractive old pub alongside which is a cobbled alley lined with beer casks, I walked the short distance to the church along New Street – which it is not! – between a perfect row of C17th stone houses. St Andrew's porch is a grand affair with a fan vault ceiling and, above it, a window and a room. I don't remember much about the interior other than a large statue of a horse by Alfred Munnings and a curiously yellow and miserable face set as a roundel in a medieval stained glass window. Outside there was much more of interest. A lengthy avenue of clipped yews leads away from the north side of the church and the graveyard positively abounds with famous deceased. Bonham-Carters, Asquiths, Siegfried Sassoon: they are all there, some of them with headstones designed by Lutyens or Eric Gill.

With a day to myself while staying with Robert and Hannah, I decided to drive down to the city of Wells, visiting a church or two en route. **St James', Cameley** *(BS39 5AH),* not far off the A39, has some delightful quirks. The main body of the church is blue limestone, the tower red sandstone. Immediately next to the porch, an external staircase leads up to a gallery running across the west end and along the south wall. Inside there is a wagon roof, box pews, rows of hat pegs –for top hats *and* cloth caps? On the north wall, a faded rusty pink painting of a crab and some fish leap about in different directions. (It is hard to imagine what a painted crab is doing on a church wall in Dorset any more than the large one carved on a misericord in Durham Cathedral).

Driving through Chewton Mendip I wasn't attracted to its church despite Simon drawing attention to the very tall tower, so I pressed on to visit **St Mary's, Croscombe** *(BA5 3QS).* There I found the nave abuzz with ladies carrying buckets and armfuls of flowers to arrange for a wedding taking place the next day. Feeling rather in the way I didn't stay to admire an abundance of fine wood carving. Before returning to Wells, a helpful woman advised me exactly where to go to park my car at no cost for so long as I needed to be in the city. I could always return to her church another day; in the meantime, I took her advice and found a handy street in which to park. The name of this city, the smallest in the country, derives from wells located in the Bishop's Palace. I guess water in the mini canals which run down both sides of the main street is the constant overflow from those wells. I enjoyed walking round the city centre. It being market day, the square fizzed with stalls and shoppers. On the north side of the Cathedral under a deep arch is the entrance to the mid C14th Vicar's Close, the only remaining intact medieval cobbled street. It continues to be home to the twelve members of the Vicar's choir together with organists and vergers, members of the Cathedral community.

Wells Cathedral is especially beautiful, from the fabulous West Front carved with hundreds of statues to the graceful scissor arches, a medieval master mason's solution to adding support to the towering nave. Colourful against almost black oak choir stalls, green, blue and mustard cushions comfort every seat of the triple rows and tucked next to a column in an aisle I admired an impressive fan shaped oak chest in which the cloak and stole were laid out when not in use. The embroidered 'cope' is fastened across the chest with a clasp or fabric band and worn by a member of the clergy. The cover to the chest looked as though two if not three pairs of hands are needed to lift it up; I expect these days the cope is kept on a hanger behind a door.

Wells Cathedral, scissor arch

In the North Transept is something very special. The medieval clock is one of the very oldest – and most entertaining – original clocks in the world (dated between 1344-1392. High on the wall of the transept, it is apparently the second oldest original working clock in the world (the oldest is in Salisbury Cathedral) and still has its original dials. Twenty-four hours are marked on the outer circle; a gold pointer with a sun indicates which one. A smaller pointer with a star shows the minute on a second circle and then there is a third circle to indicate the cycle of the moon by showing its shape, crescent through to full sphere, through a hole in the centre. Amazing. That's not all. Originally calibrated to appear on the strike of every hour four jousting knights would rush out from underneath a turret above the clock face, and do battle. In 1968 an electric motor was installed to ensure the gaily painted knights astride their black steeds confront each other every quarter hour. Above the clock is a little turret, home to two jousting knights. Every quarter hour they gallop round, the same one being knocked down *every* time for over six hundred years. The clock on the exterior wall of the North Transept, shares the same mechanism: two four foot high knights on horseback, painted and exactly carved from oak, swing out on spindles to strike a bell.

Mortuary Chapel, Smallcombe Vale, Bath, Somerset

Returning to Bath I paid a return visit to **Smallcombe Vale Cemetery**. Robert and I discovered this quaint corner of old deaths and neglect during an exploratory walk soon after he moved to the city. Tucked away on a slope on the periphery of Bath by Widcombe Hill it is a most curious, creepy churchyard. The nonconformist mortuary chapel – opened in 186l, long closed, Grade II listed in 2011 – is most unusual: the walls form an octagonal, the slate roof resembles a semi-collapsed umbrella. A narrow belfry sits atop the locked porch extended off one wall, complete with its own baby buttresses. A toy church. We walked on up the slope past yew trees, rotten trees, trees grown fat around headstones, trees choked with brambles, headstones tilted, headstones fallen, grass choked graves, crosses, angels, table top tombs, with just a hint of pathway threading between the wood and the stone. And then, another dying church, dwarfed by surrounding trees but not as pretty as the toy chapel. The autumnal chill added to the Gothic atmosphere. As we walked out past gate-posts without gates, I noticed the front door knocker of the lodge next door: a grimacing gnome with bulbous nose, an obscenely oversized tongue flopping out, ready for the grasping.

Robert and Hannah introduced me to Two Tunnels Greenway. These tunnels, originally constructed to bring quarried stone from Combe Down to Bath, had long fallen into disrepair until in 2010 someone had the brilliant idea to restore them, creating a cycling and walk way circuit. Emerging from the atmospheric underlit gloom of the second tunnel fitted with sensors to trigger 'mood' music as one passed by, we pealed off towards Monkton Combe. Next to the churchyard path is the family grave of Harry Patch (17.6.1898 to 25.7.2009), the last of the soldiers to survive The Great War. Spotting Harry was an unexpected bonus to a very different and enjoyable walk.

The oldest church in use so near to Bath is **St Mary's, Charlcombe** *(BA1 8DS)*. During a weekend Paul, Joan and I spent with Robert and Hannah, we went for an eight mile walk, swinging across to Upper Weston, following alongside the race course to return through Lansdown from where we descended a deep steep lane to Charlcombe. Grade II listed, Norman in origin, tiny St Mary's underwent Victorian restoration. It is built of limestone with a natural stone roof and two huge buttresses indicate there has been movement down the years. According to the information paddle inside, the square squat little tower resting on the roof ridge and west wall is a bell-cote rather than a bell tower; what the precise difference is I do not know. Inside there are two fat arches and a deep squint (*hagioscope*) cut into the wall between the nave and chancel. The smooth stone pulpit, lined with wood and plain but for a simple cornice, is unusual, built onto the south wall. The Norman font is a single piece of stone shaped like an eggcup. Carved onto some of the modern pews is a wee mouse, the traditional feature of every piece carved by Robert Thompson and descendants. I was surprised to see Thompson mice far from the Yorkshire family's home ground. The churchyard is delightful, more wild garden than graveyard, abundant with shrubs, flowers and ancient headstones; an underground spring feeds a holy well where baptisms may take place. Shortly after we continued on our way down the lane, we noticed the following words chiselled into a wall plaque:

We took a charming
Walk to Charlcombe
Sweetly situated in
A little green valley
Jane Austen 2 VI 1799

I always intended to make a return visit to this simple ancient church in-a-garden-in-a-valley but couldn't possibly have anticipated the circumstances which brought me back to this rural outskirt of Bath so many years later. The tree sheltered graveyard overlooked by the bell-cote at the west end of St Mary's, a place of flowers and tranquillity, is where rests my beautiful granddaughter who died peacefully in sleep after seventeen months of her so much loved life.

St Culbone, my second visit

The Somerset church to which I returned is **St Beuno's, Culbone** *(TO24 8PQ),* one of the eleven dedicated to this C7th Welsh abbot. This time I parked Ruby, my red Mini, in Portlock Weir *(TA24 8PB).* An attractive and no doubt usually peaceful coastal village, that afternoon it was teeming with noisy beer and ale enthusiasts rocking to a group of oldies belting out oldies. I left the merry rockers behind to follow a steep path snaking its way up, up the hillside through mysterious woods devoid of birdsong, the sea occasionally visible far below. This was the path followed by Samuel Taylor Coleridge in 1797; though I find it puzzling that this little church with its Noddy hat of a spire allegedly inspired his poem 'Kubla Khan'.

> 'But oh! That deep romantic
> chasm which slanted
> Down the green hill
> Athwart a cedarn cover!

A savage place! As holy and enchanted
As e'er beneath a
Waning moon was haunted
By woman wailing for her demon-lover!'

Inside the nave glowed red, orange and yellow from clusters of harvest bounty: apples, pumpkin, sweet corn, beech leaves filled and spilled over deep window recesses. St Beuno was no less magical on this second visit.

On this same 'crawl' not far from Selworthy, hidden on an inland hillside, I eventually found **St Leonard's Chapel, Tivington** *(TA24 8SU)* built by an important local Member of Parliament in 1340-60. Obscured from the lane by the cottage incorporated into the west end after the reformation – a door behind the altar leads directly into the sitting-room which is used as a vestry – for a while this charming 'chapel-of-ease' with its wheaten reed thatched roof and generous open fireplace centred on the north wall, became a barn, then a 'dame's school' run by a good woman for the benefit

St Leonard's Chapel, Tivington fire place

of poor local children. It was returned to service in 1896, thanks to the founder of the Central Council for the Care of Churches who arranged for repairs to be carried out in 1940. In 2002 ownership transferred to the National Trust, owner of the cottage and Holnicote Estate. Services are still held in this atmospheric little chapel. On a winter day surely the best seat in the house is on a pew next to the fire.

Lured by mention of 'hunky punks', I passed by **Kingston St Mary** *(TA2 8HR)*. It was closed for renovation. No matter as I could just make them out near the top of the tower, including a rather alarming depiction of a woman giving birth to a large baby.

Wales has the crooked church of St Martin's, Cwmyoy; Somerset has the leaning tower of C14th **St Saviour's, Puxton** *(BS24 6TF)*. The westward lean of this otherwise sound C15th tower is pretty startling to see. Sunk into soft ground, it is rather more than a slight and barely noticeable misalignment. I wandered into a whitewashed interior simply furnished with Georgian box pews across the aisle from C16th benches below the octagonal pulpit. On the wall an iron frame which once held the congregation's friend, an hour-glass to guard against long winded sermons.

St Andrew's, Holcombe *(BA3 5FR)* wasn't exactly on my way back to Bath or easy to locate and, when I did find it at the end of a long drive through fields, a note on the locked door said the key could be obtained from The Holcombe Inn. A further search up a lane beyond the village led me to the Inn from where I collected the original outsize church door key. I'm glad I persevered for this small C12th church, now in the care of the Churches Conservation Trust, has charm in abundance. In 1348 The Black Death decimated the local population. Cottages around the church were demolished and buried which, according to church notes, explains the lumpy bumpy contours of the churchyard. Inside the plain Georgian interior, disturbed bats in the chancel soon returned to roost while I explored the simple interior, furnished with paint washed box pews, a musicians gallery and a row of hat pegs along the north wall opposite the pulpit. Outside I was directed to two memorials. Capt. Robert Scott's family moved from Devon to Somerset: his remains are forever in the Antarctic where he died in 1912, but here rest his parents and brother. The other poignant memorial, a stone carving of five lambs huddled together, is for five young children from two families: they fell through thin ice and drowned in December 1899. I set off to return the key before driving back to Bath, passing what I had thought to be an empty field but was, in fact covered, not with a flock of grazing Brent geese but hundreds of shifting, waddling Mallard ducks.

* * *

Dorset

After many years spent in South Africa, I exchanged vast and varied landscapes and huge skies – diamonds scattered on black by night, sunlit blue by day – for the intimacy of Sussex and the beauty of ancient countryside littered with farms, villages, towns, ribbons of road, lane and track. The Jurassic coast of Dorset, most of which is owned by the M.O.D., the National Trust and private estates, has escaped much of the blight the South Coast has suffered from poor town planning and the indiscriminate hands of developers. After many visits over the years as a member of the Dorset Dawdlers – a group of friends who walk together – the magic Dorset holds for me has in no way dimmed. How can one not feel glad to be alive to walk along a broad ridge under a big sky, and look, down over the green of spreading fields and valleys, and beyond, to the south, grey blue sea extending to meet, but seldom match, the sky.

Jen and Charles live in Winfrith Newburgh, not so far from **Moreton** *(DT2 8RH)*. The reason Jen took me to **St Nicholas** one May was twofold: to visit the nearby grave of T.E. Lawrence and to delight in the beauty of Laurence Whistler's fourteen engraved glass windows. We walked to the far end of the sadly neglected graveyard situate on the other side of the road from the church to read the inscription on the headstone, noting we happened to be standing there on the very date, 19th May, of Lawrence's birth or death day, I forget which. However, this was a side show to the glory of St Nicholas' windows.

Whistler's windows illuminate the interior of this late C18th church – probably the only church in the world with all windows engraved glass, designed by Laurence Whistler (etched by the London Sandblast Company craftsmen (1955-1984)) especially when sunlight streams through the glass. The soft blue of walls, bosses and shields decorating the roof and finely carved and patinated pews are a pleasing backdrop to this treasure tucked away in rural Dorset. Whistler's first brief was to replace glass in the five bomb damaged windows in the apse. The central and two outside triple pane windows all depict beribboned candles as well as, respectively, a Cross, a Christmas tree and a leafy tree. Nineteen years later private donations paid for the Seasons window in the north aisle, each season delicately etched within a glass bauble. Another donation made possible the completion of three tall engraved windows in the north aisle: a bejewelled cross extends across the centre window which is flanked to the left by the Light Window glowing with lit candles, to the right by the Dark Window, the candles snuffed. Memorable is the window in the Trinity Chapel, 1982, funded by an anonymous donor. The story of an RAF pilot shot down in 1940 is shown in minute detail: his Surrey home, Salisbury cathedral near his base, the English Channel, the French coast, birds, butterflies and, by no means least, his crashed 'plane on the propeller of which are etched the dates of his one year marriage. A truly beautiful work of art commemorating one life cut short. The engravings for the west window twinkling with a profusion of stars, and the vestry window on which the Frome and Piddle rivers are shown as forks of lightning, are dated 1984. Three years later the last two small porch windows were installed. I'm not sure if the engraving in a semi-circle of glass set in wood is Whistler's work: " *1910-1989 Remembered Gratefully, Betty Friend and her Generosity to the Church she Loved*".

Over some twenty years Dorset has been a frequent destination, either to join the Dawdlers for a Thursday coastal walk or to spend the weekend with Paul and Joan near Broadmayne. When Mary and Neville lived in Tarrant Kynston, I would call in for breakfast on my way down, croissants in hand until they relocated, lock, stock and ninety Aberdeen Angus, to farm near Gillingham. Too far for breakfast but an easy detour en route to or from Bath. Of the thirty-something churches visited – some intentionally, others happened upon during the course of a Dawdle – there are only a few I recall beyond, say, one feature or even a tree as in the Martyrs' Tree of Tolpuddle under which the first trade union was formed in 1834. The redundant shell that is Whitcombe Church sits in a field near Broadmayne; Paul took me to see it as he has a relative or two buried within the stone walled churchyard. Churches I particularly associate with Dawdles are those of Steeple, Studland, Chideock, Kingston, Wareham. Most memorably, of the hamlet that is Corton.

Not far inland from Kimmeridge and the nodding donkey we paused our coastal walk to step inside **St Michael & All Angels, Steeple** *(BH20 5NY)*, home to a most colourful 1858 barrel organ. On another walk Norman grotesques carved along the exterior walls of **St Nicholas, Studland** *(BH19 1HU)* lured me up the path to peer round the door into an interior so gloomy and drear I went no further.

Much more interesting to explore was the Roman Catholic **Church of Our Lady Queen of Martyrs & St**

Ignatius, North Chideock *(DT6 6LF)* visited while on two Dawdles and, on both occasions, we all spent time to take in the history of the church and little museum adjacent to it. The Mandeville and de Chideocke families were the first of only four families who have owned the Manor since the Norman Conquest. When Catholicism was banned the then owners, the Arundell family, kept the faith, gave refuge to priests and allowed villagers to attend Mass held secretly in a barn. Ownership then passed to the Catholic family, Wells of Lulworth Castle. Thomas Wells turned the barn into a chapel, his son Charles later transformed it into the church it is today, a memorial to priests and laymen cruelly martyred for their faith between 1587 and 1642. Left of the grand west entrance next to a grubby door in a deep recess, a sign indicating 'Lavebo' seems ill placed. Inside, all is Italian Romanesque but with a light touch. Light streams in through clerestory windows under which there is along both sides a row of portraits of both martyrs and family members. Next door, in the museum room, there are all sorts of memorabilia including two vicious iron contraptions labelled 'man traps'.

One semi-rural Dawdle started from the High Street, **Wareham**. After an excellent café lunch, Charles went off to obtain the key to the Anglo-Saxon **St Martin's-on-The-Wall** Church *(BH20 4AG)* situated at the high end of the street. It is single cell, with C12th wall paintings, rush seat chairs, a curved modern beech altar rail and an effigy of T.E. Lawrence. Delightful. We then set off single file on what was rather a dull, urban walk, passing a graveyard in which Charles had come across a headstone on which was inscribed under the name of the deceased the words 'How much?' A Scot, maybe…?

While everybody was booting up for the August Dawdle 2009, I tried, unsuccessfully, to open the door to **St James',**

Kingston *(BH20 5LL),* south of Corfe. As the tower was only open once a year on the day of the village fete, Joan and I returned to this substantial late C19th church to climb the tower for what should have been a magnificent view. Unfortunately, heavy grey sky and mist restricted visibility to the parapet and then the heavens opened.

En route to visit schoolfriend Mary I was running late when I stopped off at **St Mary's, Charlton Marshall** *(DT11 9HZ),* to find the nave stewn with greenery and flowers, pails of water asking to be knocked over and many good ladies preparing for a service at which they were going to raise money for Madagascar. They received my early donation and I left with time only to notice a gold pelican in its piety atop an outsized tester over the pulpit. Another golden pelican, I remember, forms the lectern in an otherwise dull church sitting at the crossroads in East Stour.

Neville was home alone with his Aberdeen Angus herd when I arrived at the farm. While waiting for Mary to return from walking her black Labrador, chatting over a welcome pot of coffee, I was persuaded their church was worth a look. A little way along the lane I left Ruby in a layby next to a way marker pointing the way through two fields to *Judge Wyndham's Tree.* Blackface sheep, face and legs splattered with black markings, grazed round about the immense bulk of an ancient oak tree known as the **Wyndham Oak**, so named after Sir Hugh Wyndham (1602-1684), famously loyal to Charles II whose six-hundred mile escape route from Worcester to Shoreham is mapped as a footpath known as the Monarch's Way (I thoroughly enjoyed reading Charles Spencer's account of this escape, *To Catch a King*). The Judge's remains lie a little further west in the churchyard of St Andrew's, Trent but 'his' tree was right there, alive, twisted branches knotted, gnarled, its huge girth hollowed at the

Judge Wyndham oak tree, Silton

base, a wonderful survivor of at least nine centuries. It was well worth my admiration and a short diversion. I followed a man whom I took to be a churchwarden, or possibly even the vicar in civvies, through an immensely heavy medieval oak door into **St Nicholas', Silton** *(SP8 5PR)*. If only he had been! He was, in fact, a fellow visitor of churches except his mission was to 'tick off' every single church in Dorset. He volunteered he wasn't an Anglican; I foolishly volunteered I didn't subscribe to any 'club'. O, woe is me. He quite spoilt my enjoyment of this church as he tailed me, urging me to 'join up' while there was still time! Despite, or perhaps because of, my obvious lack of enthusiasm, he would, he declared, include me in his prayers, consumed with concern there was little time left for me to 'see the light'. I was rather more interested in the towering monument to Judge Wyndham and the Victorian stencils. No surface – from smooth plastered walls to magnificent barrel roofs, from gilded bosses to organ pipes – escaped decoration in warm shades of umber, rust and brown. The effect was charming, homely. Pugin would have been impressed.

2001 was the year Foot and Mouth spread with alarming speed and destruction. The West Country was especially badly and sadly affected. One sunny chilly Saturday in April, guests, invited to the marriage of my godson Ben to Sophie, mustered on the green at **Worth Matravers** *(BH19 3LN)*. We filed aboard one of those old buses with a snub nose and large chrome radiator grille before setting off towards the coast. Where road became track we stopped and someone, possibly the vicar himself, sprayed all the wheels with strong disinfectant before giving the driver thumbs up to rumble on our way, navigating humps and bumps. The old bus rolled to a halt in front of the square, squat shape of **St Aldhelm's**, the only chapel in England with no east wall as the corners are compass points. The bleak cliff top setting is perfect for this plain Norman chapel; I could imagine it being chosen for a romantic rendezvous with *The French Lieutenant's Woman* as imagined by John Fowles in his novel. This was not the occasion to drop in to 'The Square & Compass' as we have done before and after Dawdles. This quirky pub with a hatch but no bar and limited menu – Cornish pasty or veggie Cornish pasty – is hugely popular with visitors, locals and, of course, stone masons.

By now I realised I was becoming ever more drawn to the small, modest and quirky. That said I thoroughly enjoyed visiting **Milton Abbey** *(DT11 0BZ)*, **Sherborne Abbey** *(DT9 3LQ)*, and **Wimborne Minster**, stunning buildings in completely different settings. In C18th, the Earl of Dorchester decided to destroy the village of Milton Abbas, leaving the Abbey to dominate the rural landscape in which it sits. The interior is vast but, unlike Abbey Dore, it feels welcoming. There are some beautiful monuments and, perched on a ledge, is a quaint stone bust of St James of Compostela, patron saint of pilgrims and the church in Milton Abbas. The left hand was lost, found, and restored thanks to the generosity of an old boy of the school. The huge south window designed by A.W.N. Pugin depicts the Tree of Jesse. Milton Abbey School next door and a small chapel were both rescued from ruin and restored by Baron Hambro, the Danish merchant banker.

Sherborne Abbey is in the centre of town. The amazing fan vaulting is well worth cricking one's neck and don't miss the glass reredos in the Lady Chapel, engraved by Lawrence Whistler.

Another memorable visit was to **Wimborne Minster** *(BH21 1HT)*. The astronomical clock, adorned with two bugle blowing angels on top, doesn't quite compare with the one in Wells Cathedral but the Minster is home to the second largest chained library after Merton College, Oxford, including over two hundred ancient first editions. Hereford Cathedral has an impressive chained library as has the Royal Guildford Grammar School. The Minster's library is housed in a room reached by a 600 year old spiral staircase. I entered the room as the devoted custodian of these books was explaining to an American couple the ancient method of ensuring books were available to read but not to remove. Americans really do exclaim 'Gee whiz' and 'Golly Moses'!

Sometimes the location outshines the church as is almost the case with **All Saints, Chalbury** *(BH21 7EY)*. It sits atop a hill, one of the highest points in the county, from where, so says the church leaflet, the sea can be seen on a clear day. In 1588, a chain of bonfires from London to Plymouth was lit, one on this hilltop, to warn of the Spanish Armada. This delightful church is enchanting, pretty as a picture inside with the original Georgian box pews, gallery and pulpit. A note pinned to the door informed that the number of people on the Electoral Roll for this parish in April 2010 was fifty. Here are some of the entries in the church's book of accounts for the C17th. There are many entries listing payments for pest control: *'a grey's head 1s'*; *'stote's head 2d'* and *'one dusden of sparos' heads 1d'*. In 1702 the cost of *'fetching of 6 thousand of bricks and six score bushels of lime, £3.0.0.'* The village doctor was paid for painting the church but the amount wasn't noted! In 1791, the church paid Robert Well £13.8.6d for the new bell and 2s 6d was a regular entry as *'allowance for the Rector's dinner'*. Not to forget, in 1777, it paid *'1s for Prayers to be read in the church for the safe delivery of the Queen.'*

Wandering around the churchyard, my eye was caught by a particular gravestone for Bessie Eliza and Frederick Henry Cake who both 'passed over' in 1960. My memory was jogged back to **Tyneham**, the Dorset village tucked into gorgeous, still unspoilt countryside between Corfe and Lulworth. It was appropriated by the M.O.D. in 1943 to become a ghost village in the midst of army training country, only open to the public during August when we dawdled through the ruined village. Tumbledown cottages are almost all that remain of a once thriving community, charming village. Still in a good state of repair is the church – I regret I didn't then pay it much attention – and the village schoolhouse comprised of a classroom and vestibule. The shoe lockers and coat hooks are still there, as are little faded name cards for the children. One of them read 'Violet Cake'. Why I don't know, but I started to wonder about Violet and what became of her. I was to find out. The father of Paul and Joan's neighbour was at school with Violet and still then living in Dorchester (he died shortly after his hundredth birthday). They arranged for me to meet Violet's elderly classmate who, despite being frail and hard of hearing, was perky and welcoming. I think we were a rare event, visitors other than his attentive sons and care workers and, we soon realised, a rare opportunity for him to relive his war. He talked of his time in the desert, of the loss of his good friend 'Slasher Jim', and how at times he was so scared his knees *shook in time to the Bofors gun'*. We gently steered him round to the subject of his old classmate but he knew little of what became of Violet or the name of her husband other than this poor man had no roof to his mouth and was an 'eff-cropper'. This is a Dorset expression to describe someone who lived off the heath, who foraged and sold what he cropped. I can only imagine Violet's life cannot have been easy.

(I wasn't aware of the other 'ghost' village until several years later. The lost village of **Imber** is on Salisbury Plain, a couple of miles east of Warminster and only a few miles off the much travelled A36, my route to Bath when visiting my son and his family. Unlike Tyneham open for the whole month of August and some weekends and is a joy to wander through, Imber is open to visitors but three August days a year. Such is its popularity crowds arrive by the busload and by car: not only those with a military connection but civilians, three generation families and curious others like myself. Unaware I could drive Ruby to the village, I sat upstairs on a packed No 23A double decker Routemaster as it trundled along the ridge high above a deep vast valley dotted with houses, paddocks and livestock onto the 'business' area of the plain, scattered with warning notices and battered, rusting tanks. All that remains of Imber is a scattering of stripped out utilitarian buildings and a restored church in the care of the Churches Conservation Trust: of pretty cottages and gardens, village shop and post office there is no sign. In the distance a group of soldiers on exercise in camouflage gear milled about between tall mellow brick walls under green and red pitch roofs. I made a beeline for **St Giles' Church** alone on a knoll, my gaze drawn to a rare fifth pinnacle atop the C13th tower. Inside I found myself almost unable to move for visitors, display boards, tea tables, even the odd dog. My stay was brief).

To return to Dorset. These last churches were such a pleasure to visit. School friend Mary, while still living in Tarrant Keynston, directed me to **St Mary's, Tarrant Crawford** *(DT11 9HU)*. I followed a track for some way through farmland before arriving at the west tower of this redundant pretty church, standing quite alone in a completely rural setting. A steep pitched roof rising above the crenulations of the tower is unusual and quaint. The C12th chancel is the oldest part, the C13th nave slightly younger and entered from the north side. Inside, one wall still bears faint evidence of medieval wall painting. Wild flowers in a jam jar on a sill. It was a perfect place and time to take Rudi, my 'god-dog', for a short walk along a stream and round a few fields.

Joan accompanied me to search for **St Andrew's, Winterborne Tomson** *(DT11 9HA)*, which we found, with some difficulty, quite literally in a farmyard. We both fell instantly in love with this C12th single cell apsidal Norman chapel with a top-knot pretending to be a tower and pale oak Georgian box pews under a simple barrel roof. Restoration was funded by the sale of a Thomas Hardy manuscript which I'm sure would have pleased the local lad! Another tiny Norman single cell apsidal church I have yet to visit is St Swithun's, Nately Scures *(RG27 9PH)* in Hampshire. One day.

St Andrew's, Winterborne Tompson

Not far out of Yeovil on the way to Dorchester there are two very small churches, one either side of the A37, both reached along dirt tracks and tucked out of sight. Even driving slowly it would be easy to overshoot the insignificant marker pointing left to **St Edwold's, Stockwood** *(ST2 0NG)*. The car bumped along a grass track through a field, a farmhouse visible through trees. A small wooden gate led to a path and bridge over a stream and beyond, all but hidden by surrounding trees, what is alleged to be the smallest church in Dorset. It is also the only church dedicated to this little known saint, the younger brother of St Edmund, the unfortunate king of East Anglia who was slain and beheaded by the Danes in 869. A plain single cell building, restored in both C15th and C17th, now redundant, it has one odd feature. I beg to differ from Psvsner's somewhat harsh description of the *"delightfully naïve bell-turret round, with* *a cap on four stumpty columns and a big grotesque face"* – I saw not a face but a pretty crown. **All Saints, Sutton Bingham** *(BA2 29QP),* is also well hidden off a country road dissecting a large reservoir some way off the main road. I lurched up an uneven dirt track, skirting a car crouched under some branches, its occupants far too 'busy' to notice me squeezing past. Despite the scruffy state of the graveyard, Sunday services are still held in this charming C12th church. According to church notes the roof was once thatched, altered in C13th and C14th. Wall paintings, hidden from Puritans under a layer of paint, were revealed when the porch was added in the C19th. I know nothing at all about medieval church wall painting but for aficionados these, one being the death of the Virgin Mary, are interesting, distinct and well worth the detour. I liked the windows too.

Apostle on the roof of St John's, Bere Regis

I usually drive through **Bere Regis** *(BH20 7HQ)* long before the town wakes up so it was some years before, on a gorgeous spring afternoon, I took this daytime opportunity to visit **St John's** Church. The churchyard sparkled with spring flowers and hummed with the sound of a mower steered between headstones for the first cut of the year. An unusual and attractive combination of stone, flint and brick, although quite large the church has a jolly rather than intimidating atmosphere. The *pièce de resistance* is the nave roof. Unique and extraordinary, the original roof constructed in the late C15th, was the gift of a local church worthy, John Morton (1420-1500). It is his stern face on the single centre bosse. According to church notes there are *oak trusses, tie beams, corbel springers, 'cusped and braced arches', 'rafters at ridge and purlin positions', not to mention corbels and painted bosses!* To the lay person – me – those components are merely the backdrop and support to twelve carved and painted full length figures lying horizontally face down. Between 1774 and 1978 written opinions vary as to whom they represent. Are they the Apostles dressed in C15th costume? Or merely friends of the patron? The current theory supposes they are saints arranged in alphabetical order: Andrew, Bartholomew, James, two Johns, Judas, Lebbaeus, Matthew, Philip, two Simons, Thomas. Under the chancel roof ten painted angels. The local lords of the manor from the C13th until they died out in the C18th were the Turbervilles, their vaults under the church floor; the family name was perfect for Thomas Hardy to 'disguise' as D'Urberville. Also of interest is the squint with an iron grille, perhaps to prevent the unclean or undeserved from climbing through? On the corners of two capitals are some quirky carvings: a moustachioed gentleman clutching his head; an anguished man suffering from toothache; a bear baiting a creature. The oldest stone in the churchyard is dated November 22nd 1676. How poignant are these barely legible inscriptions on two headstones:

In Memory of Tom Lockyer aged 7
Died October 18th 1858
Also Mary Lockyer aged 2
Died October 19th 1858
Also John Lockyer aged 15
Died October 30th 1858
Also Ann Lockyer aged 3 months
Died November 6th 1858
Also Alfred Lockyer father of the
Above children died November 18th 1868
Aged 53 years
Also Mary Ann Lockyer mother of the
Above children died December 15th 1869
Aged 49 years
1858 – the long hot summer – Cholera & Typhoid when London and
Parliament ordered sewers to be inspected

and

In Memory of Thomas, son of Thomas and Ann Fry, who was killed by the
over-thro of a dung cart June ye 12th 1722 in ye 11th year of his age

Walking with Paul and Joan across the heath and through Thorncombe Wood near Dorchester, we passed by Max Gate, a cottage in the trees where Thomas Hardy spent most of his life and where he died. Another day Joan and I followed the river from Lower Bockhampton to **St Michael's, Stinsford** *(DT2 8PT)*. The Hardy family already had connections with this small C13th church prior to Thomas's birth in 1840. It has been much restored, revived and rearranged over the centuries. An appealing feature of its interior is the displaced plain choir stalls aligned along the walls and the attractive chairs which replaced pews in 1911, red-brown wood glowing with polish, backs rounded for comfortable support. Apparently the font was discovered in pieces in the churchyard by Thomas Hardy and restored a few years before he died. According to the church notes, the marble font in which Hardy was christened is now in a church near Winchester. Buried in the long, narrow churchyard are Hardy grandparents, parents, aunts and cousins and, at the top end near the main gate, the grave containing Emma and Florence, Hardy's wives. Hardy's wish to be buried with them was partially realised. When he died in 1928 his ashes were placed in Poets' Corner, Westminster Abbey but his heart, placed in a small casket, was buried next to Emma. Nearby is the grave of another wordsmith, Cecil Day-Lewis, Poet Laureate, whose wish to be buried close to the writer he most admired was fulfilled in 1972.

One Dorset day we woke to a cold world, painted white by Jack Frost, a clear sky promising an ideal day for walking. We left the car not far from Broadmayne and set off westward along the ridge in the general direction of Portisham. Sooty faced sheep scattered as we passed by, wool heavy bodies lurching on ridiculously skinny legs. Ragged remains of stone walls divided cropped green fields from the rich red earth of those recently ploughed and beyond them, the sea. Glorious Hardy country! After a while we descended through a gap in the hills and looked down on the cluster of stone buildings that is Corton: farmhouse and outbuildings, a few cottages and a tiny chapel, surrounded by a picket fence and grass littered with snowdrops and crocus. We had come upon **St Bartholomew's, Corton** (DT3 4EP), some years ago while Dawdling. On that occasion curiosity led us inside and for one of the men to look up the last hymn on the board. As he began to sing 'All Things Bright and Beautiful' the others spontaneously joined in, their tenors filling the chapel with song! A natural response, perhaps, to the intimate atmosphere of the small interior (35ft by 23ft) with its green painted roof beams, rough cut strips of carpet along the length of each pew, cross-stitched cushions, flowers on the sill and sunshine pouring in through the south door by which we had entered. During this second visit, information sheets informed of the chapel's eventful life since its beginnings in the C13th. In 1765 when digging for chalk nearby, a number of skeletons unknown were disturbed, buried alarmingly close to the surface together with items of pottery. The C13th chancel and rare stone altar have survived the centuries but the nave fell into disrepair and St Bartholomew was deconsecrated, restored then re-consecrated in 1897. Between the two world wars the church went into service as a saw-mill and, as agriculture declined and population drifted away, some cottages in the hamlet were razed, the rubble buried. Just beyond the farmhouse the ruined remains of a stone *pigeonnier* still stands, long deserted by doves and pigeons so valued for meat, manure and feathers throughout many centuries.

St Bartholomew, Corton

Ann, owner of the farm and devotee of the chapel, had been told of my interest in the chapel and hamlet. As a result of a telephone conversation with her, some months later Charlotte and I made our way to Corton to spend a morning in the farmhouse kitchen of this delightful, young and sprightly octogenarian. While we had coffee and ate her irresistible shortbread, she showed us faded old photographs of chapel and farm buildings as they once were. There was no sign of an organ in the chapel. Ann told us their organist peddled and puffed away on an ancient harmonium until this was recently exchanged for a keyboard. We were charmed. Drawn both by church and octogenarian, the following year I decided to attend the special service held in St Bartholomew's every Easter Monday. It was still dusky dark when I set off on foot along the ridge before dropping down to Corton. A flock of Jacob's sheep scattered as I walked through the field behind the church, in front of which heat radiated from a blackened cauldron of glowing coals! I thought its purpose was to warm hands before the congregation gathered inside; in fact it was intended to act as a beacon in the pre-dawn gloom. Only just a latecomer, I sidled through the door to receive both a lit candle and a welcoming beam from the 'vicaress' before taking my place behind the other twelve singing members of the congregation. I spared them a vocal contribution of my own. For reasons unknown, on this occasion musical accompaniment was provided by a violin; this was unusual enough as was the solo piece the elderly musician played for our extra 'enjoyment'. It was such a sweet scene: golden candles flickering under the green barrel roof, daffodils in a jam jar on the stone altar, lusty voices raised in song. The service ended with an announcement we all applauded: coffee and croissants would be served to all in The Turkey House nearby, a kindness extended by Ann. We went from chilly church into cosy kitchen and the warmth of Ann's Aga, hospitality and friendly chatter of strangers. Afterwards I walked back up on to the ridge under a bright, warmer sky.

My least favourite Dorset Dawdle route follows the coastal path around **Portland**, an island but for Chesil Beach extending from the mainland, until the causeway was built in 1839. The grass reminded me of a balding man's pate, thin on the ground, a skimpy layer over the famous stone. The route, above bleak, wind-battered cliffs, led past the prison block safe behind security fencing, a hideous visitor centre and a huge quarry littered with enormous blocks of stone. There's nothing soft or gentle about this scenery. Team Leader chose The George Inn as our lunch venue prior to our third (for me, definitely last) walk round **Portland**. Across the road, in the middle of a large and neglected graveyard, is **St George's Church** *(DT5 2JP)*. Impressively large and gloomy grey, a fancy steeple and saucer dome behind its Georgian façade added interest to this edifice. Paul, Joan, god-dog Rudi and I, arrived ahead of the gang – time to look inside and let Rudi have a wander round the headstones. Building commenced in 1754 and was completed in 1766 when it was, and remains to this day, consecrated even though few services are still held and the church is looked after by The Churches Conservation Trust. Long may they continue to do so as the austere, simple interior is as built: *two* pulpits, numbered box pews and twin graceful, curling stairways leading up to the gallery running round three sides of the nave. On the wall a plaque, reminder of a shameful event: *To the memory of the Following Islanders who were shot by the Press Gang, its unlawful raid on the Royal Manor of Portland on wha was known as the Easton Massacre on April 2nd 1803: Alexander Andrews, Quarryman, Richard Flann, Quarryman, William*

St George, Portland

Lano, Blacksmith and Mary Way who died later of wounds received in the same raid. Everything, walls, ceiling and furniture, is painted soft green and cream. The unkempt graveyard, full of long forgotten bodies under headstones, some plain others decorative, could do with a flock of goats to trim the grass tussocks back to neatness. The wording on one headstone read as follows:

> *Sacred to the Memory of Mary, Daughter of John and Mary Way,*
> *Who was Shot by some of a Press gang on the 2nd of April 1803*
> *And died of the Wound the 1st day of May the same Year*
> *Aged 21 Years*
> *"Here, In mortality with beauty lies*
> *Lifted from Earth to kindred skies,*
> *Her life was short, her Death severe,*
> *Stop Reader, think and shed a tear."*

* * *

Sussex

Living as I do in the county, it's not surprising over the years I have visited more churches in Sussex than those in other counties. There is much of interest: small Downland chapels in deep countryside, oozing charm and antiquity from every flint and brick; tapsell gates, unique to the county; rural retreat of the Bloomsbury set; Jewish symbols etched on the east window of an Anglican chapel; Tiger, the most apologetic cat ever to grace a hassock.

Long before I visited, let alone developed an interest in small churches and while I was still living in South Africa, my mother, soon after moving to Park Farm, Milland 'discovered' **St Mary's, Chithurst** *(GU31 5EU)* and introduced me to this simple place of worship about which little seems to be known. Only just visible from the lane, this very small Norman church sits atop a mound in an untidy graveyard with the River Rother flowing below, charming in its location and simplicity. Rather better known is the Buddhist Monastery, a little further up the lane; walking in nearby woods you are quite likely to glimpse the saffron robes of monks perambulating through the trees.

We came across a number of Downland delights on Saunters as we criss-crossed the Downs. On the other side of the A272 **Didling** is little more than a cluster of houses, barely a Sussex hamlet let alone a village. Look beyond these houses towards the South Downs and you'll see to the side of a dirt track climbing through hedged fields, almost hidden under the skirts of an ancient yew, **St Andrew's** church *(GU29 0LG)* known locally as The Shepherds' Church. Still in my teens, I happened to be in the car when my mother was showing her visiting American cousins the rural beauty of Sussex. How they enthused over the antiquity of the "darling little building", its Saxon font and Jacobean furniture. In the 1800s a villager walked by, fortuitously in time to stop some axe wielding fellow from felling the huge churchyard yew. I remember the tranquility of the surroundings, sheep of course, and a sense of almost believing for a moment I was living in a different age.

The start of a circular route I never tire of walking is just off the Chichester to South Harting road. The steep path flanked by 'young' yew trees – new centenarians – leads to the top of Kingley Vale nature reserve continuing through the glory that is a cathedral of beech trees before descending a path between fields of a wide valley, flanked by slopes of yews to one side, beach the other, leading to the village of **Stoughton**. During the autumn months the bellows of rutting deer, invisible in the yew woods, resound and bounce off the slopes of this bowl. I usually call in to the excellent village pub for some sort of refreshment before the long return climb to the Devil's Humps, four rounded bronze age barrows on the ridge top. The stubby bell tower of **St Mary's** *(PO18 9JQ),* the mainly Norman village church, is just visible from its raised position above the village. The interior, though quite large, is inviting. The nave is lit by a double row of handsome brass hanging lamps converted from gas to electricity; red and white sallies of the six rope pulls form huge loops under the bells above in the south transept; tapestry wall hangings depict village scenes. Best of all, this is the home of my favourite hassock. I don't like cats but I love 'Tiger'. His shape doesn't make sense: he sits on a red mat, is round shouldered, squiffy, impossibly coloured, has curly whiskers, ears of different shapes and size and his expression is curiously humble, even apologetic. Several years later I met at a gathering a former resident of Stoughton from whom I learned Tiger's backstory. As a small kitten he was heard mewing in stinking heap of silage, given a thorough wash by the rescuer, licked clean by her cat and named Silage before being adopted and cherished by Polly, an elderly lady then living in the village. She changed her pet's name to Tigger and ensured his posterity by cross-stitching a 'likeness' of him to adorn a hassock. The misspelling of his name only adds to his charm.

All three Marden churches are enchanting, perhaps **St Michael's, Up Marden** *(PO18 9JR)* especially. Walking from Compton through field and copse to a collection of houses that is the hamlet, the path takes you past an all but tumbled down barn behind which is a small church. Maybe the addition of a modern porch was sensible but all else is of a long ago time and place. There is still no electricity to light – and warm – this simple chapel embraced by thick walls and furnished with wooden pews, old red brick flooring and pretty wrought iron candelabra, indigo-painted and ceiling-hung. Following the footpath from the graveyard diagonally through a field we completed our circular walk back to Compton. **St Peter's, East Marden** *(PO18 9JE)* is neither in a field or a farm yard: it stands right on the very small triangular village green in the middle of which is a thatched well with, so I've read somewhere, a square wheel! Until 1924 the sole source of water for this hamlet was drawn from the well. A gentleman was playing the organ when I arrived; he happily interrupted himself to tell me the organ once belonged to

Prince Albert and came from St James's Palace donated by a Mrs Penn. How she came by it no one knows! He also said Bertrand Russell lived in Battine House between 1928-1931 where he started a school which later moved to the much larger Telegraph House nearby. End of local history lesson.

St Mary's, North Marden *(PO18 9JD)* stands in a farmyard to one side of the road running along the Downs between Chichester and South Harting. The beautiful Norman doorway made of Caen stone leads into a single cell and apse. A parishioner was arranging flowers for the Sunday service when Gai and I called in. Church organist as well as florist, she kindly gave us an energetic few bars on an elderly harmonium, her little feet pumping furiously beneath the keys.

From the gentle wooded slopes and chalk paths of the Downs to the coast, farmland and bird reserves bordering Pagham Harbour. Walking the promenade from East Selsey towards the harbour I turned inland along the lane leading to the tiny **Chapel of St Wilfrid, Church Norton** *(PO20 9DT),* all that is left of a medieval church removed mid C19th to be rebuilt in Selsey town. The chapel may be small but the surrounding graveyard is extensive with row upon row upon row of headstones. On the spring day I went the scene was a sea of pinks and yellow, daffodils, tulips and primroses growing in between graves, on many of which had lay bunches of fresh flowers. The faded red door opened into a single cell furnished with a dozen worn oak benches on a floor of coffin slabs, above modern stained glass windows. My eyes went to a framed illustrated copy of Rudyard Kipling's poem *'Eddi's Service'*, one of several in *Rewards and Fairies*, a book of short stories by Kipling with historical themes set in Sussex. Kipling lived in Sussex for many years; St Wilfrid (633-709) who was born in Northumbria and is buried in Ripon Cathedral, lived in Selsey for six years from 681to 687 when he built the original probably wooden church of St Peter.

Eddi, priest of St Wilfred in the chapel at Manhood End,
Ordered a midnight service for such as cared to attend.
But the Saxons were keeping Christmas and the night was stormy as well,
Nobody came to service though Eddi rang the bell.

"Wicked weather for walking," said Eddi of Manhood end,
"But I must go on with the service for such as care to attend."
The altar candles were lighted – an old marsh donkey came,
Bold as a guest invited and stared at the guttering flame.

The storm beat on at the windows, the water splashed o the floor,
And a wet, yoke-weary bullock pushed in through the open door.
"How do I know what is greatest, how do I know what is least?
That is my Father's business" said Eddi, Wilfred's priest.

"For three are gathered together – Listen to me and attend,
I bring good news, my brethren!" said Eddi of Manhood End.
And he told the Ox of a Manger and a Stall in Bethlehem,
And he spoke to the Ass of a Rider that rode to Jerusalem.

They steamed and dripped in the chancel, they listened and never stirred
While, just as though they were Bishops, Eddi preached them the Word.
Till the gale blew off on the marshes and the windows showed the day,
And the Ox and the Ass together wheeled and clattered away.
And when the Saxons mocked him, said Eddi of Manhood End,
"I dare not shut His chapel on such as care to attend

In the care of The Churches Conservation Trust the chapel is much loved and cared for by its Friends and volunteers who prepare it for weddings, funerals and touring theatrical productions and fund raising events. Given its history, charm and idyllic setting little wonder it is much used and attracts so many visitors.

Apsidal charm on the South Downs,
St Mary the Virgin Upwaltham

To return to the Downs, another apsidal church in
the area is **St Mary the Virgin, Upwaltham** *(GU28 0LX)*
perched on a hillside above the road winding its way
through the undulating landscape between Chichester and
Petworth. I walked up an uneven track behind the church
through a garden gate into what was more daisy meadow
than graveyard with a heavenly view beyond. This small,
narrow church with high, fat walls appears little changed
since it was built some nine hundred years ago with the later
addition of a porch over the south facing door. The interior
is plain under a burgundy red plastered ceiling. At the west
end of the nave, resembling a truckle of mouldy cheddar
cheese, squats a plain tub font as old as the church. On the
south wall is a memorial stone, dated 2009, inscribed with
the names of fifteen airmen: in February1944 a Lancaster
Bomber, Dambuster Squadron, came down near the village;

exactly a year later a Dakota of the U.S. Army Air Force met the same fate. I think it is rather wonderful that, years later, parishioners raised the funds to commemorate the lives of those airmen from America, Australia, Canada and Britain.

St Andrew's, West Stoke *(PO18 9BN)* is special to me because my son Robert's marriage to Hannah took place there in May 2009 on probably the only good weather day of the month. It's a small church – the pews could only just accommodate seventy something guests – and on that day the charm of the interior was delightfully enhanced by simple white and green floral arrangements. I wonder how many guests noted an intriguing small relief directly opposite the south door (which is peppered with gunshot) of an unknown bearded bishop whose ears are significantly different in size?

I often walked my god-dog Rudi from Fishbourne church following the harbour path to and from Dell Quay. You can't walk along this route without noticing **St Mary the Virgin's** *(PO20 7EF)* church tower and shingled bell cote. The first time Rudi and I walked alongside the field towards it the magnolia next to the approach path was white with flower. This little church serves the hamlet of **Apuldram**. Apulder = apple, hamm = enclosure in old English, shortened to Apuldram which could almost mean (apple) orchard. I was rather taken with the interior of this church. There's a beautiful three part oak screen in front of a tiny chapel and a couple of grey wrought iron candelabras designed with an excess of curls and whirls extending some eighteen inches from their wall mounting.

The Saxon tower of **Holy Trinity, Bosham** *(PO18 8LY)* indicates its prime position by the harbour edge, a hop and a skip from the village hub and pub, The Anchor Bleu. The church is forever linked in history and myth to King Knut's hopeless command to the waves to retreat. Only eight years old when she died, allegedly his daughter is buried in the nave near the crypt entrance by the south door. The chancel doesn't quite line up with the nave, further adding to the charm of this delightful church.

I have driven through **South Harting** on numerous occasions, always aware of the bright copper broach spire of **St Mary & St Gabriel's** overlooking the village street. Every time I am reminded of the unusual wooden spiral staircase in the nave to the left of the chancel arch, made in 1852, which winds its way to the clock room and bell chamber. Also memorable are the many and varied kneelers and local sculptor Philip Jackson's Archangel Gabriel 'floating' in front of a south window.

Tucked away close to Chichester I came across two very different little buildings: one a restored Estate chapel, the other a Saxon church. A few miles to the west is Stansted House and Estate – owned by the Bessborough family until the 10th Earl formed a Charitable Trust – in the grounds of which is a chapel with an interesting story to tell. Lewis Way (1722-1840) was a clergyman, born in Denham, Buckinghamshire. In 1800 he came to know of two deeply religious ladies living in Exmouth. They felt passionately for the Jewish people; it is alleged their wish was an oak tree planted near the chapel they built in their garden '*should not be cut down until the Jewish people returned to the Promised Land.*' The Rev. Way decided to devote his time and considerable inheritance to do what *he* could to restore them to Israel. He purchased **Stansted** Park in 1804 whereupon he restored the chapel to include a singular stained glass window behind the altar. The design and symbols are entirely Jewish so, in this corner of Sussex, is the only window Jewish in design in a Anglican place of worship. A rainbow glows across the top part of the window. Beneath are depictions of items inside the Tabernacle including a menorah and gold Ark of the Covenant. Incidentally, the walls of the chancel are painted rosy raspberry pink and blazing blue linked by generous quantities of gilding. Most jolly! In 1817 Rev. Lewis Way travelled to Russia. He obtained an audience with the Czar so as to plead the Jewish cause and ask his help to buy land in Palestine to create a homeland. The newly restored chapel at Stanstead was reconsecrated in 1819; John Keats, who died two years later, attended the service. It is sad to think such a gentleman, so devoted to the plight of the Jewish people, was eventually committed to an asylum for the insane in Warwickshire where he died in 1840. One hundred and eight years later, after the Balfour Declaration, Israel became an independent state.

St James', Selham *(GU28 0PW),* is on the periphery of this tiny hamlet between Midhurst and Petworth. Both the church and its rustic surroundings are so pretty I'm surprised we haven't seen it on television, venue for a wedding or funeral in a period tale. Apart from various repairs and inevitable additions down the years this is a still very much a Saxon church, its best feature being the chancel arch with stunning capitals either side. There is a tubby Norman font – perfect – and Victorian stained glass windows, the history of which is interesting even if they seem out of place in this context. There have been many changes of ownership until, in 1613, Richard Taylor, Fellow of Brasenose College, Oxford, gifted it to his college. The college remained responsible for the living until 1900. From then until 1978 it came into the gift of Lord Cowdray. It is currently in the joint care of Lords Cowdray and Egremont who now take it in turn to appoint incumbents.

Among the many attractive buildings *in* Chichester there are several of which I'm especially fond. Originally a hospice, refuge for the sick and paupers, **St Mary's Hospital** in St Martin's Square is, I think, one of the most beautiful buildings. For most of its length the pitch of the high tiled roof sweeps almost to ground level. The heavy oak main door in the Square opens onto a broad central passage to one side of which are alms apartments which today accommodate the indigent elderly. At the far end of this passage is a rood screen beyond which is the barrel ceiling of a chapel, home to ten fine misericords and a pair of ornate poppyheads. Outside a substantial walled garden lies alongside the sweeping roof, a quiet area in which the inhabitants may potter and perch.

Also notable, the remains of the church in Priory Park, an empty yet still imposing shell and **St John's Chapel**, a rare C19th preaching house which is redundant yet still in regular use for concerts and events: the elegant interior boasts excellent acoustics. Seated uncomfortably on long bare pews, shoulder to shoulder with others, rapt or dozing (Chichester is a hive of bus passes and walking frames and sticks), I remember a range of speakers: from Roy Jenkins to Ann Widdecombe, Amanda Foreman to Giles Brandreth. The raked surround gallery is supported on narrow fluted columns. The impressive triple pulpit (from which more than one cleric may have once enjoyed declaiming) is centrally positioned, all the better to see and be seen.

Last and almost least – considering its size and access to worshippers only on one day of the year, the 24th August, St Bart's saint's Day – is **St Bartholomew's**. This tiny stone-built, whitewashed chapel is squeezed between four adjoining almshouses and approached through a walled courtyard just off the busy road to Midhurst. They, chapel and almshouses, were built in 1625-6 by William Cawley

(1602-1666), Member of Parliament for Chichester and one of the judges who signed the death warrant for King Charles I in 1659. Curious to see inside the chapel, I had to attend an annual service. For several years I managed to miss that specific day of the year until 2012 when I was in town, aware of the date *and* learned what time the service. As I sidled into a side pew at the rear, bobbing respectfully to the red-robed cleric beaming away, I was convinced the scattering of elderly ladies and two gentlemen recognized me as the imposter I felt myself to be. While bowing my head, voicing responses and even attempting the one hymn set in a sensible key, I looked about me. Oak paneled walls, smooth surface and honey tone of worn side and box pews, a plain altar and reredos, uneven stone flagged floor: a simple house of worship, happily still in use albeit solely on it's saints day.

Churches visited over the years to the east of Chichester have either been the focus of an outing or, more usually, en route to or from an event or visit to a friend. At the foot of Duncton Hill some way down a lane, is **St Mary's, Barlavington** *(GU28 0LG),* the churchyard separated from a busy farmyard and buildings by a low stonewall. Two curious grey wrought iron coronets hang either side of the aisle; no candle cups so no the reason for them other than ornament. The position is *so* rural. I sat for a while on a seat carved from the stump of an old tree, enjoying a view extending far over fields and woods. Another old stump, similarly carved, had had time for vigorous leafy shoots to bush densely round the sides and back.

The little church at East Dean has need of a hungry goat in the graveyard.

Although I have driven past the turning to **St Mary's, Sompting** *(BN15 0AZ)* many times, eyes always drawn to its famous Saxon steeple, a rare example of a 'Rhenish helm' –

also known as a 'Dutch cap' – I have yet to break my journey. Beyond fields of grazing alpacas en route to a performance of *L'Elisir d'Amore* at Glyndebourne, I did stop and go into **St Mary the Virgin, Glynde** *(BN8 6SX)*, a relatively small C18th church, Palladian in design; my only recollection is of walls covered in patterned hessian. In deep countryside on the other side of the A27, not far from Monk's House, Rodmell, once owned by Virginia and Leonard Woolf and much visited by the infamous Bloomsbury Set, is one of three churches in Sussex with a round tower. The plain interior of **Southease** *(BN7 3HX)* is appealing; the chancel arch curving from centre to sides without returns, fragments of paintings on white washed walls, and deep splayed windows. Perched on a hillock with trees behind overlooking a triangular village green with long field view beyond, this essentially Norman is a picture.

One birthday Robert suggested a mini church crawl. First stop was **St Botolph's, Hardham** *(RH20 1LB)*, a stone's throw from the A29 south of Pulborough. Originally Saxon, small and plain but for the wondrous array of medieval paintings, all dusty reds and creams, covering the walls, some subjects more clearly visible than others. It is astonishing these almost complete early C12th paintings, recently restored and conserved, have survived the eight hundred years. Outside we wandered round to the south side and sat for a while in the sunshine on a bench facing across the churchyard to meadows beyond. From there we set off to find **The Holy Sepulchre, Warminghurst** *(RH20 3AW)*, possibly because it was sort of in the area and Simon mentions it in his book. We didn't easily find this redundant little red sandstone church. I'm glad we did for the interior was peaceful, its box pews, pulpit and screen bleached pale and pleasing.

The Good Shepherd, Lullington

I first heard of **The Good Shepherd, Lullington** from Robert and Hannah. They came upon this smallest of churches when walking in the area. I approached by car along winding lanes. A little brick footpath leads through trees to a clearing at the back of which sits this tubby little flint and tiled place of worship capped with a white clapboard belfry. Double doors lead into a space so small there is just enough room for twenty-two chairs, the altar, bible and pedal organ. No sounds or trappings of the modern world intrude upon the bucolic scene and looking towards Alfriston in the far distance that peaceful summer afternoon, I would not have been surprised to see a rose cheeked milkmaid appear wearing a mop cap, across her shoulders a yoke balanced with pails brimming with fresh milk.

Instead of returning to the A27 the way I came I decided to drive on to **St Mary & St Peter, Wilmington** *(BN26 5SL)* and found another treat. The church sits high above the lane. To the right of the path is an enormous and truly ancient yew tree estimated to be older than the church itself: I counted nine sturdy logs positioned to prop up heavy sagging branches. The gloomy interior is rescued by two modern stained glass windows both by Paul San Casciani. For the west window he designed a Tree of Life to mark the new century. In 2002 a fire claimed the original Bee and Butterfly window in the north transept. Casciani's Butterfly replacement window is very different from the original. Both are exquisite.

Not far from Wilmington is **St Michael & All Angels, Berwick** *(BN26 6SR)* which being but a field or two away from Charleston has close links with the Bloomsbury Set. While Paul, Joan and I were staying with Kate and her husband the walk Kate had chosen led us to Charleston Farmhouse, home to Duncan Grant, Vanessa and Quentin Bell. Riveting though the interior is we all found it a tad claustrophobic and left, happy to continue our walk to the church to be greeted by a riot of colourful, though not exceptional, murals and a jolly floral pulpit.

Some years later on my way to visit Kate in her 'new' (C14th) home, I allowed time to make a detour to **St George's, West Grinstead** *(RH13 8LR)*, not far from Partridge Green. Turning off the A24 I then followed a country lane for some distance before coming to the vicarage. Further along what seemed to be a private drive St George's Church came into view. The weathered stone, moss greened roof tiles and little pointy shingled spire above the tower rising in the middle of the church, presented a charming picture with the promise of interest inside. Before entering on the north side through the attractive late medieval porch under some attractive Saxon herringbone stone work, I wandered in the extensive churchyard, densely populated with lichen-mottled

Farms of a lost era, St George's, West Grinstead

headstones in various states of topple that no lawnmower was likely to navigate. Dominating an area to the west is a giant of an oak, its arrow straight trunk branch free to about twenty metres from which point horizontal branches extend wide and even to form a huge canopy. Simply magnificent. The original small C11th building with, historians speculate, an external bell tower, has been extended over the centuries to incorporate the tower into the nave. My tour around the chaotic churchyard completed, I found the church interior to be as untidy as the churchyard: chairs, wardrobes, cupboards, watering cans all dotted about a south aisle as the nave. Squashed into the chancel is the oldest working organ of the Hull firm Forster & Andrews *'who built 1,378 organs world wide between 1843 and 1956'* and, round the corner, under the tower, a pretty chamber organ circa 1785 which can be wheeled around the church on a trolley. Most memorable and captivating are the pews. What is unusual, if not unique, about these simply carved and numbered dark oak C16th-17th pews are the names spaced above every prayer ledge, four to a row. According to the church notes these were local farms of which I counted sixty plus two illegibles and two blanks! Such is their charm, variety and oddity I couldn't resist noting them all:

Wincaves; Bletchendean; Grinders; Pratts; Allens Cottage; Shop House Jolesfield; Sharps; Whitefoots; Clothels; Sunt; Copy Bold; Allens & Griffins; Painters; Great Tuckmans; Fullers; Tuckmans; Joles; Place Farm; Small Ham; Little Champions; Dial Post; Priors Bine; Pinland; Posbrooks; Well Land; Conies; Freezers; Blanches; Ivories; Champions; Lancasters; Hobshors; Figland; Bright: Westlands; North Fening; Patching; Plats Green; Haynes; Buchells; Rook Cross; Sherwoods; Bassells; Goveland; East-Rith; Cottage; Dunstone; Whiting Wick; White Soan; Courtland; New Lodge; Lindfield; Fosters; Thistleworth; Bowshott; Potthill; Highlands; Denmans; Sands; Woodmans

How many still exist? Around four to six. How times have changed.

Next day it seemed only polite to agree to a peek inside **St Michael & All Saints, Withyham** *(TN7 4BA)* just because the route Kate had chosen for our walk from Hartfield through field and wood passed by this rather large church. I was unaware of its famous corner, the Sackville Chapel, or of the monument to young Thomas Sackville (1662-75) and his parents, the Earl and Countess of Dorset. This extraordinary monument was created for a fee of £350 by a Danish sculptor, Caius Gabriel Cibber (1630-1700). The boy is depicted lying down, his hand on a skull *'showing he had pre-deceased his parents'* who kneel in grief opposite each other, partially obscuring the figures of their other children along each side of the tomb: six daughters and six sons. Charles, the eldest, was the antecedent of Vita Sackville-West whose ashes, along with many other members of the Sackville family, are entombed in this chapel.

Should I too become an octogenarian, may I be as interested in people, places and events beyond my own small world as is Gai. No sooner had she learned of my interest in small churches than she determined to introduce me to five churches well known to her through living and walking in the area between Pulborough and Storrington. Come the August day of our jaunt Gai made it clear who was in charge. "We'll go in my car because I know the route – anyway, you drive too fast." To protest was pointless; besides, it was a rare treat for me to be a passenger. Feasting my gaze on sweeping Sussex scenery glowing under a late summer sun, instead of concentrating on tarmac unfolding under the wheels as we drove along, was a pleasure in itself.

The first church on Gai's chosen route was **St Richard's, Burton Park, Duncton**. Shortly after descending Duncton Hill on the road from Chichester to Petworth we turned between tall wrought iron gates into Burton Park to follow the road winding its way through fields of grazing sheep and horses towards the imposing house. The original Tudor house, owned by the Goring family for generations, was burnt down twice then rebuilt in 1826. The Estate was sold in 1904 since when various residential properties have been built around the house, one of which was Gai's home for several years. **St Richard's** is best described as stubby: it is only twenty-nine feet in length and there is no height to the belfry above the west door through which we entered. The exterior, a charming muddle of materials, dates back to Norman times, then rebuilt in 1636 since when it has been left alone, happily. No Georgian improvements or Victorian restoration. The Gorings were recusants, Catholics loyal to the Pope, and staunch royalists. This is evidenced by biblical scripts all over the walls and on the south wall is a rare coat of arms of Charles I proclaiming *Cristo auspice regno. (I reign* *under Christ's Authority*). A scroll depicting John Goring's heartfelt plea *Delicta juventut meae, et ignorancias meas, ne memineris Domine* (*Remember not the sins of my youth, nor my transgressions; according to thy mercy remember thou me for thy goodness sake, O Lord)* made one wonder how naughty he had been. Beyond the C15th rood screen recessed in the chancel wall is a simple monument to a little girl; on the aisle floor two bold monuments to various Gorings; an ancient bible rests on another monument against the north wall, backed with brass segments, and next to it an unusual brass lectern. A rather smart harmonium, simple stone font and well worn pews complete the furnishings. St Richard's was a delightful church with which to start our 'tour'.

Gai turned right onto the winding A283 which we followed through Fittleworth but not quite as far as Pulborough. We drew up outside the church of **St Mary the Blessed Virgin, Stopham** *(RH20 1EG),* a hamlet nestling close to the River Arun. Even before entering the churchyard my eyes went straight to the huge girth of an ancient yew and half toppled headstones under its spreading branches. How old? Surely a thousand years have passed since it first pushed through the grass. The interior of this not-so-little church, originally early C12th, built of grey stone rubble with a slate roof, is quite plain but for the many brass effigies dating from 1428 of at least twelve members of the Barttelot family which to this day owns the Stopham Estate. It has been in its possession since 1296. To the front a horseshoe shaped pew, carpeted, cushioned and dotted about with quirky hassocks; to the rear, we were startled to find a sleeping ginger cat curled up on a cushion behind the vestry curtain. Was it breathing? Was it stuffed? A toy feline was the only explanation. No threat to church mice! (Several years later I entered the village shop in Abbots Ann, Hampshire, and there on the floor was 'our cat'! Noting my interest the helpful assistant informed me a switch underneath would cause the flanks to gently rise and fall. So our cat was 'breathing' after all.)

Gai was keen to show me **Wiggonholt** church *(RH20 2EL)* deep in gentle countryside where she had often walked with her husband. We strolled under the pretty, almost dainty, lych gate along a path leading more through flower meadow than churchyard to the charming grey stone church, little and dumpy. To then find the oak door locked was so disappointing, especially for Gai. Further down the road **Greatham** church, also without a dedication, was open. We walked a short distance through a field to the walled churchyard surrounding this little C13th building with a modern perky spiky spire atop its pitched roof. The single cell interior is delightful, simply furnished and devoid of electricity. Light poured in through clear glass to reflect off whitewashed walls. Peaceful.

The last church Gai wanted to show me that day was **St Peter's, Parham**. Years ago I had been round Parham House and garden, probably quite unaware of the church some distance away in the park. Attached to the west door was a hand written notice: *Important. Deer and sheep droppings are a problem so please be careful to wipe your feet.* Which we duly did! Inside all was whitewashed and bright, the box pews stripped of varnish and honey coloured with a lovely patina. Just inside the double door is an unusual font: a small decorated lead 'drum' with highly polished wood cover atop a tall stone column standing on an octagonal plinth. Also unusual is a large rectangular family pew, complete with fireplace, which explains the chimney. I was interested to read in the church notes that an entire village used to surround the church but was demolished in 1778-9 as it *was regarded as a source of infection!*

Gai had treated me to a lovely day out.

The oriental madness that is The Royal Pavilion is a fine reason to visit **Brighton**. So too is **St Bartholomew's** *(BN1 4GP)*. Unusually, due to the site available it is aligned north-south instead of east-west as with most churches. Sadly today it is surrounded by hideous office blocks; they rather detract from the impact of the brickwork. I wandered into the vast, astonishing interior and was overwhelmed by the height of the nave – over one hundred and thirty feet. The style is very much Arts & Crafts and the general feel is High Church. Several confessionals stand at intervals along the sides and a huge organ sits in its own gallery facing the highly ornamented altar, pulpit and font. From the menu of regular musical settings I imagine solemn high mass on Sunday is as much concert as religious service. Maybe I'll attend one day.

On the way home I diverted myself to **Coombes Church** *(BN15 0RS),* one several friends had long been urging me to visit. No wonder. It is *so* special. I was lucky with both the time of year and the weather that day. I followed lanes from Shoreham through glorious countryside to park next to a sloping field, a farm yard and a wooden sign indicating the church visible at the top of the field from within the embrace of trees. The bucolic setting was like something out of a Thomas Hardy novel: a pergola covered in yellow flowers framed a gate into another field, the tapsell gate into the churchyard next to 'squeeze posts', flowers in the grass, sheep in the field, and overlooking this beauty a small stone church, still essentially C12th and C13th. The interior is no less magical: rough stone white-washed walls, sections of rusty red early paintings; C12th plain arch into a tiny chancel; old brick and tile floor; deep splayed windows. Outside an old man was seated on a bench. I joined him. We exchanged not a word, content just to be there, quiet in so tranquil a setting.

Tapsell – or Tapsel – gates are an example of simple design, its intention obvious and practical. Invention is attributed to John Tapsel, born in the mid C18th into an old Sussex family of rope makers and bell founders traced back to 1577. Made from hard wood, the gate has a central iron spindle upon which it rotates in either direction through ninety degrees with a stop post at each end, a latch on one. Centrally balanced, the problems of heavy gates hung with side hinges are avoided and, just as young John intended, his gate makes for the easy passage of coffins, great for pallbearers. The gate into Coombe's churchyard is one of only three original gates left; there remain four others, two replicas, two modern. I was curious to see them all, so one brilliant April morning Charlotte and I set off on a gate hunt.

We took the scenic route east via Amberley, along the valley road parallel to the South Downs on our right, through Storrington before rejoining the main road and traffic at Shoreham to head for the church furthest from home, in the village of **East Dene**, just short of Eastbourne. The Tiger Inn, well known to Charlotte, faces onto a triangular village green, to one side of which a small flint cottage boasts an unusual blue plaque: allegedly this was the home of Sherlock Holmes in his retirement! For me the charm of **St Simon & St Jude** *(BN20 0DL* was all in the approach: swinging through its original tapsell gate along a tidy path to the porch planted on both sides with a climbing rose. The interior disappointed, a hint of very old with an obvious overlay of new in the form of a C20th extension. We retraced our route to park Ruby in a layby between a rustic pond and **St Mary the Virgin, Friston** *(BN20 0AK)*. This original gate is framed by yoke shaped wooden lintel with lantern, the path leading to another rose

St Mary the Virgin, Friston original tapsell gate

framed porch and so much more to delight us. Charlotte was my perfect companion for the day, this area being very much her old stamping ground. Her mother's ashes were scattered in this very churchyard; a more peaceful, rural resting place you couldn't wish for. In sight over the stone wall enclosing the churchyard the sea was visible blue beyond the wide view over layers of fields and Downs. Gorgeous. Five grand gravestones and a memorial cross, home to one local family, have been cordoned off behind iron posts and rails; elsewhere a higgledy-piggledy scatter of graves. Three oak boards ranged along the far boundary wall displayed little metal tags engraved with the name and date of death, some barely legible, of those cremated, one hundred and forty-four per board. According to church notes most of the nave dates from Edward the Confessor to William the Conqueror, the chancel slightly later, and the little font, origin Puritan, is made of "winkle stone". The stunning feature of St Mary's is the nave and chancel roofs; from tie beams, wall plates to struts they are original timbers and quite beautiful. Look up and behold.

Somewhat reluctantly we continued on our way to **St Andrew's, Jevington** *(BN26 5QE)* where we expected to find a restored tapsell gate with stile incorporated. The Saxon west tower looks over another stunning landscape but sadly the south façade of this church has been despoiled by the addition of a hideous porch. Inside a Saxon sculpture of Christ, excavated in 1785, looks a tad incongruous displayed on the north wall. A flint wall towers behind St Andrew's and alongside it a dirt path leading from the churchyard. The stile once part of the tapsell gate is no more.

After a less than memorable lunch in Alfriston we drove beyond Lewes to **St Pancras, Kingston near Lewes** *(BN7 3PD)*. The church didn't excite either of us, the gate a modern copy of the original design; after a cursory visit we continued on our way to the delightful Shepherds' church, very much as built in the C12th & C13th, **Church for Transfiguration, Pyecombe** *(BN45 9FR)*. Perched on the edge of a hilltop village, right on the South Downs Way, the sound of unrelenting traffic on the A23 spoiling the peace of an otherwise rural spot, this little flint church has charm: from the twin pitched roofs of the north porch and vestry to the few tilted headstones dotted about in tuffty grass, more field than churchyard. This tapsell gate is quite different from all the others: it pivots on a wooden spindle, two sets of diagonal cross posts support slats *a la* picket fence, and on the post above a latch is a decorative iron shepherds' crook. The interior is simple, the aisle floor a mix of bricks and memorial slabs, both worn under centuries of footsteps, in the chancel a modern cartoon drawing of a monk leading a very small canine wearing a brandy barrel proclaiming itself to be a mountain rescue dog. The tub lead font is one of only three in Sussex.

Turning south off the main road to Storrington, we wound our way along narrow lanes through farmland scarred and defaced to the north by sprawling ruins of a defunct chalk quarry, otherwise beautiful under the soft early evening light. Our penultimate church – and gate – was **St Botolphs Church** *(BN44 3WB)*. Close by the vicarage, this tall, slim Saxon church stands otherwise alone in the landscape. It's a puzzle why a decision was made to add a porch so small and compressed it was hard to enter through the church door into an interior as charming as that of The Shepherds' Church. While I was admiring the south door, clearly dated 1630, Charlotte was thumbing through a paperback edition of John Betjeman's church poems, one of a jumbled pile of books for sale. Remember *Diary of a Church Mouse* who spends his days *"behind this Church of England Baize"*, and *Blame the Vicar,* he who *"after all, is paid to keep us bright and undismayed"*. I couldn't resist, £1 well spent. The tapsell gate is a modern replica of the one at Friston, complete with yoke lintel.

When Charlotte expressed an interest to see the church which triggered our 'gate hunt' I was more than happy to pay a return visit. Framed by trees perched on a rise above farm sheds, **Coombe Church** *(BN15 0RS)* was just as I remembered, little changed from its medieval birth, and the original C18th gate as designed by John Tapsel. Since then I have learned there exist three similar gates nowhere near East Sussex, variations of his original design. The name 'tapsel' was given to the gate leading into the churchyard of St Leonard's, Heston, Hounslow – this one includes a wheel, chain and counterweight. All Saints, North Cerney in Gloucestershire has a simple version; St Wilfrid's, Burnsall near Skipton in Yorkshire – which I intend to visit when I go church 'crawling' in and around York – includes a pulley system in the design of its gate.

I had been living in Sussex more than twenty years before, as urged by one enthusiast, I set off one shower splashed day to **Goring-by-Sea** to visit a purpose built church. I did so reluctantly for this Catholic church is anything but small, medieval or part of a rural landscape. It has one extra ordinary feature: a painted ceiling like only one other. In 1771 when the land around was all fields and hedges, crops, grazing cattle and sheep, and Compton Avenue not even a twinkle in a town planner's eye, a barn was built for a local farming family, the Jupps. Rural became urban and in 1952 the council bought the barn to become the parish church. By 1970 the parish had outgrown the attractive old building so replaced it with a purpose built church. Tim Tom Tom navigated Ruby along residential streets of this plain coastal town to the forecourt of **The Catholic church of English Martyrs**, *(BN12 4UE)*. My little heart sank. I looked up at the presumably west end façade of something resembling an aircraft hanger. At least there is symmetry: three sets of windows either side of the central double width doors set within grey pebbledash cladding under a huge area of glass beneath a pitch roof, the whole cheered up with bright red fascia boards and a plain cross. Entrance is midway on the long side of the building leading first into a sort of corridor before the body of a vast interior. Sweeps of modern beech wood pews on a carpeted floor, central altar, windows on the far side made up of shards of bright coloured glass; under the pitched roof at the east end plain glass etched with figures of eight martyrs; at the west end a glass expanse, blues and greens forming a modern 'picture'. None of this moved me at all. Then I looked up at the vast rounded ceiling. In 1986 a local sign writer, Gary Bevans (1954 -) travelled to Rome, a member of a parish pilgrimage. Noting the shape and size of the convex ceiling in the Sistine Chapel was not dissimilar to that of his parish church, he felt called by God to replicate Michaelangelo's monumental work. Permission to do so was granted by the Bishop, funds were raised to pay for all paints and materials, and over the next five and half years, 1987-1993, aided by his photographs and video camera footage, Gary worked on the church ceiling in his spare time – evenings and weekends – outside of full time employment as a sign writer. Visitors travel from afar to view and admire this astonishing labour of love and achievement. They no doubt take full advantage of the several tea trolleys placed along the central aisle: each one has a mirrored top tray and wheels so no need for cricked necks!

* * *

Chichester Cathedral, Nativity
(black labrador in attendance!)

Surrey

Although just up the road so to speak, it was some years before I made time to explore small churches in a county to which I wasn't particularly drawn. Surrey churches bring to mind a poignant headstone, the 'man mushroom' and big fat yew hedges and arches. Hampshire has its own unique building in the form of Sandham Memorial Chapel, home to the stunning and poignant mural panels by Stanley Spencer; Surrey has two such singular chapels.

Compton lies just off the A3 between Guildford and Hindhead. The long village street is familiar to me from years ago when my Uncle Paul and Aunt Elizabeth shared their home with a pet jackdaw in Field Place which is close to **St Nicholas, Compton** *(GU3 1EG)*, Losely House and the ever popular pub, The Withies. The first time I went into the church was when Vanessa and I met up for a little gallery-cum-church crawl. A striking Arts and Crafts house is to the left of the cobbled approach to this beautiful Norman church. Looking up from the approach path two dormer windows add to a sense of house as much as church. The building beckons and the interior does not disappoint. There are quirks aplenty and, above all, a rare double sanctuary. We climbed a wooden staircase to peer down over a unique richly carved Norman balustrade. I've popped in several times since then and after one such visit I found a tiny pink enamel pig in a bric-a-brac shop across the road. I wore it suspended on a fine chain round my neck for years until one day it was there no longer! I was désolée, inconsolable for weeks afterwards.

At that time the G.F. Watts Gallery was still in a state of dilapidation and the tea-room didn't appear to have been altered or modernised since the 1950s. Not one table, chair, tea-cup, tea-pot or table cloth matched with another, the date and walnut cake was tasty though lacking any sign of date or walnut, framed and faded photographs of the village of yesteryear hung aslant on the walls. One could imagine Kenneth Moore and Kay Kendal wandering into this tea-room of their era! We loved it and I rather hoped Health and Safety wouldn't discover its existence as surely, looking into the 'kitchen' behind the counter, they had yet to do so. Since then both the Gallery and Limnerslease, Watts' house and studio, have been completely and sympathetically restored, which is wonderful, and the café would now bear any kitchen inspection! Nearby, in crucifix form though the building appears to be round and is rich with design details and Celtic symbols, the unique **Watts Memorial Chapel** *(GU3 1DN)* built in the Arts & Crafts style by Mary, the widow of Victorian artist GF Watts (1819-1904) and the villagers in memory of her husband, has benefited hugely from resurgent interest in all things Watts. It sits on a knoll atop a brick path flanked by yew trees planted by Mrs Watts. I expect many jaws drop when they step inside the interior space to gaze upon walls covered with densely painted and decorated gesso, the whole beyond easy description. Peacocks, owls, pelicans, and eagles in their pairs adorn the round exterior walls. Behind the chapel the cloister and gravestones in the Watts Cemetery are all also in the Arts & Crafts style; here you'll find the artist's grave as well as one containing various members of the Huxley family including Aldous who was born nearby in Godalming.

Lower Kingswood bell tower

The Church of the Wisdom of God, Lower Kingswood *(KT20 7DH)* is no less extraordinary than the Watts Memorial Chapel. One barmy March day I drove the considerable distance from Chichester without first checking this Grade I edifice would be open. It was of course locked but thanks to the kind response of a key holder I was able to telephone, my journey wasn't in vain. While waiting for the good lady to arrive I stood by the oak west door set with iron studs – 1400 years old, it was a gift from Turkish priests – gazing up at the unusual bell tower. Set back at right angles to the church, it's a copy of a tower in a Bulgarian village: six steps set into a concrete plinth lead up to a narrow door between wooden clapboard sides underneath a solid wood frame supporting a single bell beneath a domed lead roof. Scalloped edges and weird crocodile-cum-serpent heads extend down from each corner. Bizarre! The key holder led the way into the astonishing interior of this rectangular church. Designed in the style of a basilica and completed in 1892, it was sponsored by two Victorian gentlemen living in Kingswood who employed a local architect and firm of builders to create the only Byzantine church in the country. Dr Freshfield and Sir Henry Orme Bonsor designed a nave and apse filled with complex mosaics and marbles in greys, green, yellow, pinks, red and white from Greek, Italian and Egyptian quarries; antiquities from Italy, Turkey and the Middle East; an ebony pulpit inlaid with mother-of-pearl; two huge wooden candelabra the size of cartwheels; two eggs, an ostrich one suspended over the superb alabaster font and a porcelain egg delicately painted in blue hanging above the chancel; and many other treasures from around the world. Well worth visiting but remember to arrange access in advance. If only this unique church could be transported from its suburban plot yards from the A217 to a more gracious setting....

St Peter & St Paul, Chaldon, Mural

Before returning to Sussex I did as the friendly key holder suggested and drove a little way just north of the M25 to see a special doom mural. **St Peter & St Paul, Chaldon** (*CR3 5AL*) stands alone at the end of a lane high on the North Downs surrounded by rolling fields. I wandered past a smattering of snowdrops towards this tiny Norman church crowned with a perky little C19th spire. Inside I admired a handsome oak pulpit dated 1657 – carved during and despite of austere Cromwellian times – before spending the next twenty minutes trying to take in the myriad details of the stupendous doom mural extending over the original Saxon west wall. Dated to be C12th it is as early, complete and well preserved as the wall paintings in St Botolph's, Hardham in West Sussex. Five metres wide and over three metres high, glowing with rusty yellow and red ochres, it teems with goodies and baddies, some conscripted to hell below a bisecting cloud, others attempting the ladder leading up to salvation, and in one corner the tree of life with a serpent entwined round a branch. Comprehensive church notes describe in full the demons, biblical creatures, symbolic descriptions of envy, gluttony, sloth, lust and the rest. Wonderful.

One spring day Sue and I met up outside The Three Horseshoes in **Thursley** to set off across the heath for a circular walk which brought us back into the village through the church graveyard. I walked into **St Michael & All Angels** *(GU8 6QQ),* and straight out again. It was close carpeted throughout, pale green with a motif! However, in the graveyard are several interesting headstones and a curious tubby sort of tomb sitting on a pair of fat feet at each corner. One headstone is inscribed with these poignant words:

In Memory of
A generous but unfortunate Sailor
Who was barbarously murder'd on Hindhead
On Sept. 24th 1786
By three Villains
After he had liberally treated them
And promised them his further Assistance
On the Road to Portsmouth.

When pitying eyes to see my Grave shall come
And with a generous Tear bedew my Tomb
Here shall they read my melancholy fate
With Murder and Barbarity complete.
In perfect health and in the Flower of Age
I fell a Victim to three Ruffians Rage:
On bended Knees I mercy strove t'obtain
Their Thirst of Blood made all Entreaties vain.
No dear relation or still dearer friend
Weeps my hard Lot, or miserable End:
Yet o'er my sad Remains (my Name unknown)
A generous Public did inscribe this Stone.

There are two other headstones designed by Edwin Lutyens for members of the Lutyen family, Charles and Derek. Neither of us had known Lutyens grew up in this village. Apparently his very first commission was for alterations to The Corner, a house on the village green close to the 'Shoes and our lunch.

A few years later during a still wintry March day, I visited five more Surrey churches. Returning home from London very much earlier in the day than anticipated, I decided on impulse to turn off the A3 and follow the road to Albury and Shere. I drove through the village of Albury, pausing before a house crowned with twelve tall Elizabethan chimneys grouped in four stacks, each standing half the height of the house again. Why such intricate brickwork, why so tall? Distracted, I followed a 'To the Church' marker to find myself before the 'wrong' St Peter and St Paul, the modern parish church built in 1842. **The Old Parish Church of St Peter and St Paul, Albury** *(GU5 9BB),* the one in which I was interested, was within Albury Park. Beyond park gates open land is dotted with huge ancient chestnut trees their deeply scored bark twisting up stocky trunks to leafless branches. I followed the drive until it forked: to the right, the mansion, to the left, in a dell behind a grey stone wall, the old church.

An attractive late C15th timbered porch on the north wall leads through a wonderful C14th oak door, complete with original hinges, latch and *uber* sturdy lock, into an interior quite bare yet friendly, inviting. The warm brickwork of original Saxon-built nave and chancel walls, strengthened and broadened by the Normans, has escaped the plasterer's handiwork. A simple slate wall plaque tells us that William Oughtred 1573-1660, Mathematician and Tutor to Christopher Wren and Rector of Albury for 50 years 1610-1660 lies buried in the ruined chancel. Church notes inform us he wrote a standard mathematical textbook, is credited with selecting the "X" sign for multiplication, and invented an early type of slide rule.

By way of complete contrast to the antiquity of the chancel is the locked mortuary chapel created by the erstwhile landowners at the east end of the south aisle. I peered through lattice panels set within a carved wood screen at an interior, the opulent Victorian décor of which could only have been designed by Pugin (1812-1852). Every surface blazed with colour and repeat designs. Squares of brilliant royal blue dotted with gold stars shone down from the barrel ceiling; a linear pattern of eagles, wings outstretched and crowned with halos linked with pink and yellow ribbons, soar across two walls. The remaining wall area dances with a red, green and gold geometric design and, on the floor, terracotta and yellow tiles in a variety of designs ensure a colourful background for the odd brass memorial. Let me not forget the stained glass: apostles depicted in two side windows, the south wall dominated by a large one, all three teeming with every vibrant colour of the spectrum. As with St Giles, Cheadle, not an inch was spared Pugin's hand.

Someone went to considerable trouble to write a lengthy history of the Grade II listed 'Tupper Vault' in the graveyard. I rather glossed over that but was amused by a reference to Mr Anthony Devis (1729-1816) known to local children as the *'man mushroom'* for he habitually carried a wooden-ribbed white umbrella. Such a thing was quite unknown in the area at that time as only recently had the contraption been widely introduced to London society by James Hanway, traveller, on his return from the East. Umbrella, parasol, *parapluie*: surely the last of those three descriptive nouns would have been the most apposite, considering the climate of our green land.

The helpful person who redirected me from new to old parish church was sure I would be interested in a small church nearby, **St Michael's, Farley Green** *(GU5 9ER)* known locally as The Barn. The reason for its nickname became clear when I found it up a grassy farm track. It is a barn. In the vestibule two jolly red lidded fire buckets, on one wall a framed poem written in 1942, author unknown, simply titled In Praise of St Michael's:

Seven long miles in a little brown bus,
Bumpity, bump all the way,
Past the corner where the kingcups grow
And the lovely Jerseys stray.
One comes to a spot at the end of the earth
Where there's neither shop nor pub,
Just a lovely green and some old fruit trees
And a rather nice little club.
There are winding lanes where one sinks in sand
And a black little baby cow;
There's a tiny place which was once a barn.
You may go to church there now;
There are charming people, friendly and kind
And the sweet smiles I've seen
Belong to the folk you will surely find
If you come to Farley Green.

All the same, it was just a barn with little charm.

St James's, Shere *(GU5 9HG),* didn't excite me either. A framed notice described the provenance of a tiny bronze mother and child figurine placed in an equally small niche: *"Bronze Madonna and Child, dug up on Juniper Hill, Coombe Bottom, Shere, by a dog belonging to Mrs Oliver née Forehead in 1880. It is said by The British Museum to be C13, one similar except for a slight difference in the hair being in their possession, but with not particulars as to where it came from. It is thought to be an ornament from either a Grazier or the top of a pilgrim's staff."* Both squint and anchorite's cell had been filled in. However, I liked and admired the many hassocks, green and gold, beautifully stitched with rural scenes and pretty patterns.

The following month I decided to return home from Guildford via Hascombe and Dunsfold, visiting the church in each village. Everything about that little rural pilgrimage was so enjoyable. Separated by lanes twisting between banks under beech branches bursting with new lime green leaves, two very different churches with one notable feature in common: both churches are approached through ordinary wooden gates all but hidden embedded in a deep, dense and immaculately trimmed tunnel of yew. Impressive! There is little I can add to Simon's informative description of St **Peter's, Hascombe** *(GU8 4JD)* other than to enthuse about the exuberance of the Victorian painting covering the entire chancel, woodwork and panels of the exquisite 500 year old oak screen, restored in 1898. The nave walls are covered with a motif in soft blues through which 'swim' 153 fishes! There is decoration too on the stone pulpit, around a rather grand squint and on the walls behind and beside a narrow spiral staircase twisting its way to the bell tower. Outside, an impenetrable neat yew hedge borders the churchyard dotted about with some interesting tabletop monuments. A group of five is constructed with seven courses of red brick under weathered stone tops and, round the corner, clumped close together presumably for members of the same family, are four huge stone monuments on double plinths, each corner inset with carved urns. The side of one of them has lifted noticeably. Grandpa's ghost wishing to escape perhaps?

St Mary and All Saints, Dunsfold *(GU8 4LT),* is in a different place, literally and figuratively. I drove some distance off the main road and through a modern housing development before parking next to the church gate and another second neatly clipped yew arch. A pity about the modern houses close by but the view of fields and trees falling away beyond the churchyard is a peaceful setting for this charming church. Before entering through the ancient south door – an interesting construction of four wide oak planks, two huge iron hinges and several iron stays – I paused before a magnificent yew tree with a wide split in its considerable girth. A see-through-with- a-view tree! Inside this church all is simple and so special with beautifully shaped bench ends and rare C13th benches as old as the church.

Before returning to the car I followed a track leading down to a small river and the healing well set inside a small enclosure and protected by an oak frame under a pitched roof of small moss green tiles. A prayer referring to the holy water of the well tells us: '*Thou shalt sprinkle me, O Lord with hyssop and I shall be cleansed, Thou shalt wash me and I shall be made whiter than snow.*' Too chilled to be cleansed, I picked wild garlic leaves to add to my evening meal.

* * *

Hampshire

Unusually many of the churches in this county I visited were in the company of friends, either during the course of a walk, a weekend visit or with Vanessa who also keeps a copy of Simon's book in her car. Coming across the snake catcher of Brockenhurst was an exception, as was the day I spent exploring churches of the Test Valley.

Soon after arriving in England I read an article enthusing about a Hampshire treasure. Not sure what to expect I suggested to Vanessa we meet up for a pub lunch and include a visit to **Sandham Memorial Chapel, Burghclere** *(RG20 9JT)*. Our lunch was incidental to this unique memorial to the dead of The Great War. The plain brick building is home to wonderful Stanley Spencer murals, painted in oil between 1927-1932: they were commissioned by the Behrends family in memory of one of their own who died at the end of the Great War. No description could do justice to them. Astonishing works of art, scenes of the soldiers' lives in the field, they need to be seen, not on the pages of a catalogue but standing before them. I have journeyed up the A34 to see these paintings several times over the years and would do so again.

In the mid spring month of March I drove to **Steep**, a small village west of Petersfield once home to the poet Edward Thomas, to join Vanessa and other members of the

Edward Thomas Society to participate in a commemorative walk marking the poet's birthday. Enthusiasts of the poet's work the group may have been but not enough to tackle the steep climb where there is a carved stone in his memory atop of Shoulder of Mutton hill. (Thomas moved from Kent into Berryfield Cottage in 1906, spent five years in The Red House and finally moved to Yew Tree Cottage in 1915, two years before his death.) The walk was interrupted several times when the group stopped to listen to an actor reading one of the poets poems, memorably 'Aspens' while standing in a lane before....an aspen.

> And it would be the same were no house near
> Over all sorts of weather, men and times,
> Aspens must shake their leaves and men may hear
> But need not listen more than to my rhymes....

Lunch was preceded by a talk on Thomas delivered in **All Saints** *(GU32 2DF)*, the fine village church. A narrow window, designed and engraved by Laurence Whistler in 1978 marking the century of the poet's birth was pointed out to us. (Also engraved in the poet's memory is an earlier, larger window in St James the Greater, Eastbury, Berkshire, made 1971). There is more than an etched window to admire in this handsome church the origins of which date back to the early C12th. Although the interior is a tad gloomy (minimal light penetrates through tiny lancet windows) All Saints today is a pleasing mix of medieval and modern. The mellow cream exterior is handsome; roof, tower and C19th wooden spire an interesting mix of tiles and wooden framework. Close to the south porch is an enormous and no doubt ancient yew tree with a deep hollow cleft in its trunk, a perfect hidey-hole for a bored child.

If you continue west from Steep, a little way before the village of Ropley a lane to the left is signed 'West Tisted'. The narrow lane winds ever deeper into and through farm land, passed a scattering of large and architecturally interesting houses, until a sign announces West Tisted. The hamlet came about on land originally owned in the C12th by the Tisted family followed by a succession of other wealthy families. Even today, perhaps because of the imposing manor house, large farm and rural isolation, there is a feudal feel to **West Tisted**. **St Mary Magdalene** *(SO24 0HJ)* was built by Tisteds in the grounds of the manor. Apparently once upon a time both manor and church were surrounded by a moat – today the bridge on the path leading to St Mary's extends over little more than a ditch with an excuse of a stream. Of the original church only the tall narrow nave remains: the C14th bell tower, Victorian chancel and charming C15th porch are later additions. The woodland setting is delightful, the churchyard mildly untidy rather than unkempt and to the left of the south door, *the* reason for my visit. For once it was not the church so much as the churchyard yew. It is the most magnificent, extraordinary giant of a tree. On the floor of Kingley Vale, a reserve on the South Downs just west of Chichester, below slopes dark green with 'young' one hundred year old yew trees, is a sprawling group of thousand year old yews with huge girths, wandering boughs snaking under dense canopies: stroll among them at dusk, imagine faces on their trunks and be a little afraid for there is something about them of Grimms' fairy tales, even the ocult. Those ancients are characters but this one tree has to be king. A copy certificate on the porch wall confirms its age to be around one thousand three hundred years old. What a tree.

On a gorgeous June day after a pub lunch at The George, Finchdean, the Saunterers walked to a tiny church we could see way down below us, standing all alone in a field. When the Portsmouth to Waterloo railway line was built in the mid C19th, the then lord of the manor was so appalled by the despoiling of *his* view, he had his home dismantled and rebuilt way up on the ridge: today only the extensive walled garden, stables and coach house remain. We all fell for tiny **St Hubert's, Idsworth** *(PO8 0BA)*: it was originally dedicated to St Peter, then rededicated to St Hubert who went on to became Bishop of Maastricht & Liege (died 727). A grass path, for the use of which an annual peppercorn rent is paid to Winchester College – so a gentleman wrestling with a lawnmower informed me – leads to this delightful church. We entered under the C18th porch through the west door with a feature I've not seen before or since: an opening, height and width enough to allow passage of a large dog, blocked with vertical iron bars and screened on the inside with a drop down wooden panel. What could possibly have been its use? The interior is simple and charming. Box pews and skinny benches in the nave and above the chancel arch, spanning the entire width, a colourful old style mural commissioned to celebrate the millennium showing Christ surrounded by contemporary scenes. An early C14th mural on the chancel wall is very well preserved, figures and landscape all still clearly discernable. Look over the hedge across the grass to the back of St Hubert's to see the lack of symmetry: no roof line, window or wall is where it should be. Quaint.

Other churches were less admired, less explored, maybe too medium-sized! One April Saunter we lunched at The Selborne Arms; unusually for me I ordered the *soup de jour* just because of its name – 'complex' soup (another name for left-over soup?) was memorably delicious. Before setting off on the Saunter we paid a short visit to **St Mary's** *(GU34*

3JH), still very much as built in the C13th, burial place of the naturalist and curate Gilbert White (1720-93) whose fame put **Selborne** on the map. Close to the entrance of this substantial church is a humungous stump, a forlorn reminder of the great age and size of what was once an ancient yew tree dated 1140 with a girth of 26', felled during a storm in 1990. Known as the Selborne Yew it is recognized as one of the fifty great trees of the land. St Mary's is anything but small and humble but it is full of interest: including a working clock dated 1678, a Jacobean dark oak desk and a charming memorial window dedicated to White made up of three vertically placed roundels showing a fox above a tortoise above a hedgehog and weasel. However, we were here to walk so cut short a further wander round the interior to head for the start of our climb up onto the Selborne Hanger, the zig-zag path famously cut in 1753 by Gilbert White's brother.

A favourite walk to which I've introduced various walker friends includes **All Saints, East Meon** *(GU32 1NJ).* It's a long walk, usually longer than it need be as I always manage to take a wrong turning somewhere along the way. We would set off from Ye Olde George Inn's car park after lunch to walk through the churchyard up onto the ridge to walk anti-clockwise around and above the Meon Valley. The countryside and huge views all along the way are quite wonderful. Towards the end of the walk the broach spire of the church appears below us and from a field high above the village a steep path descends to where we started, in the graveyard. I know there is an unusual black font in this church but, leg sore and weary, we lingered not but retreated to the inn for a restorative drink! The black limestone font imported from Tournai, Belgium, one of four in Hampshire, still beckons…..

One gorgeous day in May Saunterers and their canines gathered for a very jolly lunch at The Hawkley Inn. As we left, I put my head round the door of **St Peter & St Paul**, **Hawkley** *(GU33 6NF)*, before setting off on the Saunter. I found this to be the gloomiest of interiors, dulled rather than lit by hideous Victorian glass but it does boast one redeeming item: a small engraved window by Simon Whistler, 2000. The spire, a four-sided pyramid designed to prevent heavy snow from settling, is known as a 'Dutch Cap' or Rhenish Helm, as is the C14th spire of **St Mary's, Sompting** *(BN15 0AZ)* in east Sussex.

Years later, the day of Andrew's funeral, 13th November, dawned wild and wet. Deciding not to risk driving along the A27 I drove cross country towards Braishfield, Andrew's village. Beach trees lined the route. Even the dismal grey day couldn't diminish the flaming autumnal colours of shivering leaves. Shreds of thin plastic, brand names and logos barely legible, sagged from high branches – these are 'witches knickers', limp reminders of broomsticks flown too low! Despite arriving three quarters of an hour before the service began I was too late for a place in the church. Dawdlers and many others filled the adjacent church rooms while very latecomers huddled outside under umbrellas, listening to the service relayed to us over a less than perfect sound system. What an amazing turnout and a wonderful compliment to the most genial, warm and gutsy friend that he was to the very end. While the committal was taking place we Dawdlers stole away to a pub chosen by Rupert as being sufficiently far away to distance ourselves from other mourners with the same idea. Andrew would have approved of our merry lunch and toasts to him. Taking a slight detour off the A272 on the way home to pop into **St Mary's, Avington** *(SO21 1DB)* seemed appropriate to the day. Georgian built, late C18th, very red brick exterior, wonderful mahogany box pews with rounded corners and two almost homely family box pews complete with carpet and cushions.

A month later on the 8th December it was the turn of old Mrs Sunter whose funeral I attended in **the Abbey Church of St Mary & St Melor, Amesbury** *(SP4 7EU),* a much altered C12th church with an air as grand and stately as was that of the grand old lady I had known for many years. The church is in the main street, within walking distance of the superb garden of the old age home where this family friend comfortably spent her last years. I walked to and from the service with her family: this was not the occasion to explore the interesting interior.

It's always fun staying with Jenny and James whether before or after a Hampshire Hobble or after jaunts, one to the sculpture park at Roche Court, another to Jenny's home city, Salisbury. We spent some time in the Cathedral where I bought a CD of Karl Jenkins' 'The Armed Man' to which Jenny had recently introduced me, since when I have played it again and again. If I have any special request for my own funeral, should I be given one, it would be for my friend cellist Benedict to play the *Benedictus* from this oeuvre. On then to St Thomas and its astounding C15th 'Doom', a huge and complete mural over the chancel arch and the Rector's stall, telling a predictably gloomy tale, showing goodies on the left, baddies on the right. I paid a return visit to the Cathedral one Christmas specially to see the magnificent font designed by water sculptor William Pye. Three metres across, a child could be totally immersed in water trickling without cease off two opposing points of the gently curved cruciform. I stood at the east point looking down the wide space of the nave to the towering and glittering tree precisely lined up with this mesmerizing font and in that brief moment

I was able to photograph the composition without a single person intruding. On the water surface a perfect miniature reflection of the tree, on my face a big smile of pleasure.

Three special churches are all sort of on my way to dawdling in Dorset. **St Michael and All Angels, Lyndhurst** *(SO43 7BD)* is a very large church in a medium sized town. The building of it commenced in 1858 and went on for ten years. In those days, an average Victorian church cost £3,000. Not surprisingly, given the extravagant structure and interior, this church cost £9,000 including a donation of £300 from the Queen herself. Nearby **All Saints, Minstead** *(SO43 7EX),* a quirky kirk, had rather more appeal for me. The exterior is confusing in that it looks quite like a house with a tower on top of which an odd mini spire just peeps out from behind the castellation. Inside, a fun mix of family pews, separate rooms with fireplaces, a two tier gallery for musicians and the poor, and an odd wooden reliquary next to an early Norman font. When I visited there were men running about with instruments and equipment, busy with preparations for a concert later that day. I know Conan Doyle is buried in the churchyard but I was too cold to search for the headstone.

Drawn to **St Nicholas' Brockenhurst** *(SO42 7UB),* on the outskirts of the village by what I had read about the churchyard, I found the C11th church, red tiled roof and cream washed stone exterior bathed in weak winter sunshine. A stubby brick tower, an unfortunate Victorian addition, is all but hidden by the vast girth of a thousand year old yew tree. A wooden bench framed by a pair of yews forming an arch invites rest and contemplation of this charming building and rural scene. The door into St Nicholas was locked which was disappointing. I walked under trees through which sunlight filtered onto the extensive hillside graveyard sloping steeply away from the church, hedged fields and the village in the distance. Along the east boundary are rows of simple headstones: ninety-three New Zealanders, three unknown Belgians, three Indians. In 1915, because of its proximity to Southampton, Brockenhurst became the hospital centre for the war wounded. Between 1916 and 1919 the hospital treated 21,000 New Zealand soldiers. In 1927 the Anzac Memorial cross was erected behind those gleaming white headstones since when an annual service is held on the Sunday nearest to Anzac Day, 25th April. In such a beautiful setting those soldiers surely rest at peace. Nearby is another headstone, notable for the carving of an old man beside a woodland hut above the inscription. Harry "Brusher" Mills, a former farm labourer, (1840 -1905) lived for over nineteen years in an isolated, well hidden charcoal burner's hut in the forest near Brockenhurst. The cricket club paid him to sweep the pitch between overs – hence his nickname – although he became widely known as the Snake Catcher. London Zoo paid him well for the several thousand snakes he supplied over the years as food for larger reptiles. Apparently he caught a snake simply by nipping finger and thumb behind the head, moving quickly to avoid being bitten, then dropping it into one of several cans dangling on strings from his waist. If bitten by a viper, he treated himself with a homemade potion. His possessions and wardrobe were simple and minimal: lunch bag, bottles, tins, string, scissors and stick complemented a battered felt hat, one of two jackets – from the pockets of which snakes would quite often protrude – vest, trousers, thick gaiters and heavy boots *which never had any knowledge of such a mundane thing as polish"*. Although he lived as an eccentric hermit, he was well known locally, popular with tourists, and held in great affection. He frequented The Railway Inn for his tipple of rum and moved into one of the outbuildings attached to the Inn after his hut burnt down, and there he died. The village constable organized his funeral, a hat was passed round the village to raise money for his headstone and the inn renamed The Snakecatcher.

St Nicholas, Brockenhurst Anzac Memorial

Rupert, a fellow Dorset Dawdler, thought I would be interested to visit **St Mary's, Abbots Ann** *(SP11 7NR)* in the Test Valley. The church was bought in 1710 by Thomas Pitt, a forbear of William, and rebuilt in 1716.We approached up a tree-lined drive, the bricks of the church pink in the sunshine, and entered through the west door. Another door opened under a gallery above into a large and airy nave. On either side of the central aisle are tall, dark oak box pews with, unusually, worn ledge seats projecting into the aisle from each door. The font, positioned immediately in front of one of four rotund wooden columns supporting the gallery, is also unusual: it is very small, made from wood in 1726, the lid with lathe turned decorations about one hundred years later. Made in 1933 a not dissimilar wooden font is in the 1903 built thatched church of **All Saints, Little Stretton** *(SY6 6RD)* in Shropshire. Wooden fonts are rare: the only one I came across one other than St Mary's was in St Michael's, Efenchtyd, hewn from a single piece of oak.

As rare is St Mary's unique collection of paper 'bonnets. Around three sides of the nave, well above the windows, runs a sort of picture rail spaced along which are simple wire hooks. From most, but not all, of these hooks hangs a frame decorated with paper flowers. Gloves are also attached to some of them. Behind each 'bonnet' or 'garland' is a very small plaque on which is written the name, age and date of death of the person in whose memory the garland was dedicated. Where the hooks are empty the names remain but the garlands have disintegrated. An illustrated notice tells us of a then widespread custom: "the ceremony of this ancient burial rite takes place at the funeral of an unmarried person who has been born, baptised, confirmed and died in the parish" and further "such persons must also be of unblemished reputation". It goes on to say "the garlands were held above the coffin by young girls as it processed to burial". These garlands, made with ribbons, paper rosettes and flowers, were sometimes accompanied by a glove or kerchief. If, after hanging temporarily for three weeks no one had cause to besmirch the deceased's name, the garland was given a permanent hook in the church. Of the forty-nine garlands, now depleted in number, thirteen were for men. The oldest garland still hanging is for John Morat, died 1740; the most recent is for Myra Annetts, died 1973. Lily Myra, Charlotte, Florence Jane were all in their seventies and died 1921-1973, presumably still maidens. There are few other maidens' bonnets still in existence. Six paper garlands, dull, dusty and drained of original colour but nevertheless intact are suspended from pegs on the gallery wall in C17th church, **Holy Trinity, Minsterley** *(SY5 0BE):* One such maid was Hannah who drowned crossing a river on the eve of her wedding, 10th May 1709. Holy Trinity Church, Ashford-in-the-Water and St Stephen's, Fylingdales, Robin Hood's Bay, Yorkshire boast four each; St Giles', Matlock and the tiny church of All Saints, Trusley, Derbyshire each has one. In 1792 Ann Seward of the Peak District wrote:

> 'The gloves suspended by the garland's side,
> White and snowy flowers with ribbons tied,
> Dear village! Long these wreaths funereal spread,
> Simple memorials of thy early dead.'

St Mary's, Abbots Ann bonnets 2

I promised myself a return visit to the Test Valley. I chose a crisp spring day during April 2014 – the month of yellow flora. While consulting my map at Cheesefoot Head, overlooking a wondrous valley bowl, I watched a large man and a small boy as they released homing pigeons from two wicker baskets. I learned they were young birds in training for a race to Paris later in the year; this flight was a mere thirty miles back to their loft in Aldershot. Route decided I crossed over the motorway and drove west towards the river. With some miles to go and not even a pond or puddle in sight, I gave Mother Mallard, purposefully leading a string of cheeping brown-yellow feather balls along the road, a wide berth and wondered if she too had a strong 'homing' instinct?

Before reaching the river myself, I drove through rapidly greening countryside to find two very small and ancient gems. **All Saints', Little Somborne** *(SO20 6QT)* and **St Mary's, Ashley** *(SO20 6RJ),* are separated by a few fields, both in the care of the Churches Care Trust, and both are my idea of gorgeous. Bright daffodils swayed and curtsied on the grass apron in front of All Saints'; cowslips, daffodils and primroses glowed on the bank between road and St Mary's.

Still Saxon in shape and in part, **All Saints'** creamy yellow exterior is interrupted in the middle of its length by south and north doors (the latter full of holes and cracks and blocked by a small table) facing each other across the narrow nave. The whitewashed interior is dominated by a criss-cross of roof beams and trusses above narrow lancet windows set in Norman built walls at least two feet wide. On the altar, a jam jar of tired wild flowers. No such flower arrangement adorned **St Mary's** early C12th narrow, disproportionately long chancel. There is a tired harmonium, an exquisite alms box – it is thought Elizabethan – and a curious five-sided porthole window, the glass etched with writing to commemorate the life of one Henry McCay 1881 to 1975. Outside: a floral carpet, a narrow lane, a peaceful village.

I wasn't sure about visiting **St Peter & St Paul's**, **King's Somborne** *(SO20 6NX),* a large village with the Test and rills running through it. However, I was there, parking was easy, and though this church is neither small and simple nor wondrous grand, it proved memorable for its needlework! Evidence of the industry and expertise of nimble fingers is everywhere. Cushions, cloths, curtains. Tapestry, embroidery, quilting. Themes and scenes, homilies and dedications. Colour coordinated cushions and hassocks ensured comfortable seating and kneeling on and before every pew. Most impressive is the much-folded banner embroidered with the names of all couples married in the church since 1993. Is there anyone in this parish who doesn't sew! I remember too the stone pulpit with a huge, no doubt saintly, head carved in relief on each of three sides; a worn, forlorn and headless stone effigy on the chancel floor, and five dangling *sallies,* instead of red white and blue, bright green and yellow.

More usual red, white and blue *sallies* loop above the west door entrance to **St Andrew's, Mottisfont** *(SO5 10LL).* An earnest little sign apologizes for any bat droppings one may come across and, propped on a ledge is a rather wonderful black and white photograph of a Victorian wedding group. Further into the nave, on a broader ledge, is a beautiful wood sculpture of hands in prayer on an ugly base of iron, heavy enough to deter anyone with light fingers.

I had looked forward to visiting **St Andrew's, Timsbury** *(SO51 ONE)* a little further south of Mottisfont. How shocking then to look up at the charred remains of the turret and a patchwork of blue and green plastic sheeting secured over the blackened remains of roof trusses and beams. Inside a man was busy boarding up the undamaged chancel. Responding to my shocked 'What happened?' Colin said it was thought this fire, like so many others, was caused by an electrical fault. As I drove away from the wounded church I saw two old girls chatting over their garden gates. I brought Ruby to a stop and wound down the window to commiserate with them about the fire. "Would 'ave been worse" said one, "if 'er Ivor – tipping her head towards her neighbour – 'adn't got up to feed 'is 'ens at 7.30 Sunday morning, 9th March. It was 'er Ivor who saw the flames and called the brigade." The parish is surely indebted to Ivor's chickens. Several years later I made a detour through Timsbury en route home, delighted to find medieval St Andrew's restored as 'new'. A genial gentleman rested on a bench, three golden retrievers slumped around his feet. Encouraged by his smiley greeting I enquired after Ivor's chickens and asked if the church was open. Robin, as he introduced himself, said the chickens were long gone and the church door locked – "them days of door always open is over". He then led me to the star attraction of the churchyard, a headstone probably hidden under detritus

St Andrew's, Timsbury,
Thelwell headstone

or plastic on my previous visit. Near by the south door lies Norman Thelwell (1923-2004), illustrator extraordinaire of naughty fat little ponies and their diminutive riders, at rest next to his wife Rhona. Etched on either side of the headstone are two tubby ponies, tails and manes a-flying, their mini riders' little legs akimbo as they send a bugle fanfare to the heavens. Gentle levity to the end.

I confess the only reason I set off to **St Margaret's**, **East Wellow** *(SO51 6DR)* is because this is where Florence Nightingale (1820-1910) is buried. There is a bed of roses named for her planted in 2006 to commemorate 150 years since her return from the Crimean War, and inside much for a Nightingale pilgrim to see and read, including a little rusty cross made out of shrapnel. I was amused to see in the quire stall two curious cushions – one depicting all the Telly Tubbies, the other an excited Tigger pouncing on a spider – juxtaposed to a pastel Dove of Peace and Lamb of God. The clergy showing a light touch.

I followed looping lanes through stunning countryside before parking on grass between a field and the churchyard of **St Winfrid's**, **East Dean** *(SP5 1HD).* The long south church wall with stumpy bell turret above lies at right angles to post and rail fencing leading to a garden gate where I paused to read *Tired Gravestones:The gravestones in the churchyard are old and tired, They may collapse if read too vigorously, Take Care* before entering through the most beautiful 600 year old door hung under an unusual yoke shaped lintel. The interior of this very small ancient church exudes charm, warmth and quiet; white paint, oak beams, a little gallery and staircase, pews to seat a capacity congregation of about sixty-five and a harmonium to accompany their song. The pews may be 'ordinary', the cushions on every one of hem are not: every colour on the spectrum has been included into rag worked cushions and kneelers. Surely an indication of the affection the villagers have for their delightful unprepossing little church. I'm beginning to wonder if Hampshire is the County of Needlewomen.

I almost bounced along over the churchyard grass surrounding **St Nicholas**, **Leckford** *(SO20 6JG),* so thick and springy surely a few grazing goats should be more effective

St Wilfrid, East Dene altar kneelers

than a lawn mower. Whereas the little church of East Dene exudes care and love, this interior is somewhat worn and feels a little neglected. No needlework here, merely carpet offcuts on box pew seats and hassocks covered with shabby grey leather. Huge wood posts support the bell tower, nearby an Italian chair, a crude box pew and two full buckets of water. For church going dogs maybe?

St Nicholas is across the road from the offices of the 4,000 acre Leckford Estate, owned by the John Lewis Partnership. John Spedan Lewis (b.1885, d. in Romsey 1963) became a partner in his father's business in 1907. In 1928/29, after the death of his father and buying out his brother, he became sole partner, founded the John Lewis Partnership and purchased the estate, the church excluded, the village of Leckford providing housing for his workers. Four years before John Spedan was born, Wallace Wyndham Waite was born in 1881, the son of a civil engineer. For family reasons he had to start earning his living aged eleven. After taking up a three-year apprenticeship to a grocer in Pontypool, he moved to London in 1904, determined to start his own business. To do this he teamed up with Arthur Rose and, for a short time, David Taylor. The first Waitrose store opened at 263 Acton High Street and soon afterwards it became a private limited company. By 1923 Wallace Waite was sole owner and on 16th October 1936 Waitrose, with its staff of 164, joined the John Lewis Partnership. There is an interesting, somewhat crackly BBC recording of John Spedan Lewis as an old man in 1957 describing his vision for the business.

I digress.

From Leckford I pottered off in the direction of Bullingdon along lanes over hung with branches of beech dressed in leaves still sharp lime green. Sadly the door into St Michael & All Angels *(SO21 3RE)* was locked. I could only stop and admire the mature avenue of pollarded limes leading from the church gate. On to **St Michael the Archangel**, just beyond the village of **Quarley**, curious to see its bell, the remaining one of three housed and hung at ground level outside the north wall. The C13th bell is rung from the vestry by a rather crude contraption involving a rope running through the wall, under its own little housing, to the 'bell house'. Inside, on every chair a blue and yellow hassock stitched in a variety of designs; on the wall four 'ladders' each made up of three quilted scenes – a wishing well, a maypole with dancing children, a cenotaph and poppies, rats among headstones, a man and his dog out walking. More imaginative examples of needlework.

By now I was more than ready for tea (not cider!) with Rosie so made my way to Long Parish, a short distance from where I was to spend the night with Jenny and James. The next morning I set off to find, with some difficulty – I took a wrong turning, again! – the *crème de la crème* of churches visited on this crawl. I'm so glad I persevered. If there is only one church to see in Hampshire, above all others, for me it is **St Mary & St Michael, Stoke Charity** *(SO21)*. It has everything. A double row of posts and rails flank the approach from village road between fields and cottages. Through a double gate into the churchyard dotted with daffodils, beyond a towering yew tree, willow trees dip tapering branches into a lake. I found two headstones especially touching: a small rough stone for *Charles Lampton died 2-2-48 aged 10 months*, and a simple stone pot filled with sweet smelling pinks for *David Clark aged 11 years died May 5th 1956*. Pinned to a board in the porch a sensible notice:

> *While fresh flowers on graves are much encouraged, unfortunately our large rabbit population tends to eat them all the year round before they die leaving bare stalks, and in winter frost kills them.*
>
> *The Church flower arranging team members have been asked to remove all dead flowers from beside graves. Empty vases or bowls will be stored at the back of the church, next to the water butt.*
>
> *Families are respectfully asked not to place plastic or artificial flowers on graves as they very soon become shabby.*
>
> *We suggest that bulbs are a good solution as the rabbits leave them alone.*

Other churches could take note. The interior of this delightful church, glowing with light, is as memorable as the location. Two wide arches lead from the Norman nave into the Saxon north aisle, each has its own altar, both visible through an unusual double squint on the north side of the chancel arch – two churches in one! Everywhere there are magnificent memorials and wall plaques; corners and ledges with interesting carvings; extraordinary floors. Such a special church with which to end my day exploring the Test Valley.

A few months later while staying with her, Christine interrupted my visit to whisk me off to two nearby villages on the River Itchen to show me two little oddities. We approached **St Margaret's**, **Candover Preston** *(RG25 2DN)* through a churchyard much in need of a flock of grazing sheep, tucked a little way from the village. The tiny building, its east end marked with a flint cross, is a chancel, the quaint remains of a church demolished after fire, nestling in a quiet corner overlooking farmland. Rather more interesting is what remains of **St Nicholas the 'Buried Church'** of **Chilton Candover**, a mile or so away. We turned into a private driveway, parked the car and walked across a field, through a garden gate into a walled enclosure, once upon a time a churchyard. Four shallow stone steps led up to a tarmac surface sealing what was once a C14th church demolished in 1878 some years after it ceased to be used for worship. In 1927 an old man, William Spiers, remembered playing as a boy in what he thought to be a crypt. The then rector decided to excavate and in 1929 the crypt, part of the earlier C12th church, was rediscovered. Christine and I followed steps down to the left of the tarmac and rather cautiously pushed open a decrepit, faded red door. Peering into the spooky darkness we could see a simple C12th font at the far end of a double cell with barrel roof and, set just level with the ground, two skinny barred windows recessed in deep, crudely fashioned stone walls. Not my idea of a playground.

Despite being some distance apart I planned to visit two churches on the same day crawl. One grey sky day I drove from Sussex to the north of Hampshire curious to see a perfect Norman church in a farmyard. Just off the A30 I turned right to follow the drive up to Manor Farm. It appears to be a sanctuary for donkeys and ducks. I paused to watch several small donkey foals careening between their placidly grazing parents before parking next to a pen filled with a variety of vociferous young ducks, feather wetting in a shallow tray. Farm buildings, sheds, next to a house screened by an unusual number of mature yew trees, the apsidal east end of **St Swithun's, Nately Scures** *(RG27 9PH)* was just visible. Framing the north door the arch decorated with chevrons could only be Norman; at the bottom of the arch on the left a mermaid is carved into the capital. Church notes explain the legend: a sailor had a love affair with a mermaid and left her to return home. He then fell in love with a lady from Nately Scures and was set to marry her but the mermaid swam up the Thames and other rivers, arrived at the church and stole him away on her back. The mermaid was carved supposedly to act as a warning to young men who might dally with a young ladies heart. **St Swithun's** – 30' long, 16' wide – the smallest medieval church in Hampshire, is delightful. To the right of the door a narrow stair leads up to a small gallery and organ above white washed walls of the single cell under wooden beams supporting the pitched roof; on the walls a number of plaques four of them unusual being in the shape of card suits. Outside I wandered around a graveyard dotted with almost more mature yew trees than headstones several of them indicating various Barons, Lords and Knights. I loved the proximity of church to farm; as I walked back to Dusty this was underlined by the unmistakable sound of a donkey braying.

Considerably further south I turned off the A272 to descend along near empty lanes to **Corhampton** *(SN32*

3ND) where the Saxon church celebrating one thousand years since it was built. The church is perched on a mound, just visible from the road, the car park isn't. After two wrong turnings and enquiring of passing locals I found the near hidden dirt track leading off another road to a parking area in woods behind the church. A short single file path led to the porch over the south door almost obscured by the canopy of a towering yew tree; its enormous gnarled girth measuring twenty-three feet indicates it is the same age as the church. It was locked. A note advised open days and hours: Sunday, Monday, Tuesday 10am to 4pm. It was Thursday. After the joy of St Swithun's it was disappointing to have to content myself peering through windowpanes into a typically Saxon interior, tall, narrow, plain. Three weeks later, accompanied by neighbour Stephen, we walked past unusual arched brick graves into the Victorian porch beneath early C17th oak roof beams high above the white washed walls of the nave at the west end of which a stunning Saxon arch leads into the chancel furnished with an altar stone and medieval stone chair. Church notes refer to C12th wall paintings on the south wall as a 'great glory'; once glorious and bright, today the colours illustrating the legend of St Swithun are muted and incomplete. The gallery cross the west end, built during general repairs carried out mid C19th, is home to the chamber organ.

From the prayer books and papers, notices and flowers Corhampton church feels well loved and attended which is excellent for both church and community yet its almost cosy interior meant – for me – the loss of an almost mystical sense of being not in our time but in a long lost time in our history. For that feeling of being transported back in time I later found in the Saxon church in Escomb, County Durham and St Peter-on-the-Wall, Bradwell-on-Sea overlooking the salt marshes of Essex.

A wonderful Hampshire treat is to visit the almshouses of **The Hospital of St Cross and Church, Winchester** *(SO23 9SD)*. After a swift half and sandwich at the eccentric (under statement!) Black Boy pub, I strolled alongside a stream running through meadows towards medieval buildings beautiful beyond description. Grandson of William the Conqueror, Henry de Blois (1101-1171) was knight, monk and politician, appointed Bishop of Winchester at the young age of twenty-eight and founder of the Hospital. It gave sustenance to the very poor almost without break until the end of the C19th. The charter of the foundation promises: *Thirteen poor men, feeble and so reduced in strength that they an scarcely or not at all support themselves without other aid, shall remain in the same Hospital constantly; to whom necessary clothing, provided by the Prior of the establishment, shall be given, and beds fit for their infirmities: and daily a good loaf of wheaten bread of the weight of five measures, three dishes at dinner, and one for supper, and drink in sufficient quantity....And besides these thirteen poor men, one hundred other poor persons, as deserving as can be found an more indigent shall be received at the hour of dinner...*

Henry du Blois, keen to ensure financial security for St Cross, put it into the hands of the Knights of Hospitallers of St John of Jerusalem. Unfortunately they redirected funds to the Holy Land. Even when control was restored dishonesty, greed and misappropriation of funds continued to plague the Hospital. Francis North, Earl of Guilford, Master from 1807-55, was the worst culprit: he almost succeeded in bringing about the demise of the Hospital and was the inspiration for Trollope's novel The Warden. Today the purpose and atmosphere of St Cross is much as du Blois envisaged. From the Hundred Men's Hall to the Ambulatory, from the Master's Garden to the Kitchens, the Brothers' Quarters to the Church there is no corner of these remarkable buildings without atmosphere, beauty and serenity. To visit St Cross is food for the soul.

* * *

Gilbert White memorial window, St Mary's, Selborne, Hampshire

Cornwall

My only holiday spent in England as a child was near Camelford. A return visit to this county was long overdue so I jumped at friend Kate's suggestion to explore churches in Cornwall as an extension of my first visit to Devon. There I found Bling in Blisland, followed a tourist tarnished traipse through Tintagel, crossed a golf course to John Betjeman's favourite church-in-the-dunes and came across an unexpected reference to Chichester cathedral.

After passing through Devon on my first visit to that county en route to see Kate in Cornwall I hurried back to the A30 from Brentnor on towards Bodmin Moor. **St Nonna, Altarnun** *(PL15 7SJ),* is a pretty grey stone church, rebuilt in the early C15th, its tower decorated with pinnacles, approached over an old footbridge at the end of the village street. St Nonna was St David's mother – the holy well of St Non is near St David's Cathedral, the small rosy red stone cathedral at the western tip of Pembrokeshire. Inside, various fruits and vegetables had been placed at the foot of a large Norman font carved with a rather grumpy man's head at each corner. Beyond, there is a wonderful collection of seventy-nine solid oak bench ends all carved by a Robart Daye between 1510-1530. The bench ends of St George's, **Dunster**, are memorable for the superb carving but these are fun. The miracle is they survived the Reformation, The Civil

War, even the heavy hand of Victorian restoration. Some designs are multiple: pomegranates are repeated thirteen times; some twenty variations of tracery design; only four Green men; three angels above the stigmatic wounds; quite a few dragons and grotesques; and St Michael stamps on the Devil twice. The individual designs are especially charming: the jolly jester with baubles all a-dangle; the serious visage of a viola player; a cleric stirring holy water in a cauldron; grazing sheep; a stylish gentleman holding his bagpipes, tiny dog at his feet; and the single modern detailed carving of the church by Mr Doug Edward, circa 1970s.

St Catherine's, Temple on Bodmin Cornwall

I continued along the A30 until the next exit then drove over the moor, aware of moorland ponies with their tendency to wander nonchalantly across one's path. The grey stone of the little church of **St Catherine's, Temple** *(PL30 4HN),* appeared nestled below a sloping field at the edge of a wood. Allegedly this church became notorious as a place where marriages could be performed without banns or licence. Descriptions of that time read: *'lying in a wild wastrel, exempted from the Bishop's jurisdiction where many a bad marriage bargain is yearly slubbered up'* and *'a lawless church....where are wonte to be buried such as wrowght violent death on themselves.'* Such marriages were declared illegal in 1752 so the church fell into disuse and, over one hundred years, it became derelict until the 1850s when restoration work was undertaken. Services are now held regularly and at the time of writing this more than one member of the congregation arrives on horseback.

Tim and Penny suggested a visit to **St Protus & St Hyacinth, Blisland** *(PL30 4JE)*. I'm not sure what I thought of this little church with a distinct Catholic flavour. The screen dominates the whole interior. Above the fine tracery of the lower part extended across the nave are six framed square panels at the centre of which a large cross bearing Christ is suspended from the roof. Every surface is so painted or generously gilded I noticed nothing else but could well imagine bells and smells. For the bling of the screen alone, this church was worth a peek. I was even more pleased to pop into the village shop, which doubles as a tea room, just in time (before the hot water urn was switched off) for a refreshing cup of tea and Kit-Kat to sustain me until I reached Abigail's house in Tregony on the Roseland peninsula.

Kate's family once owned a cottage across the water from **St Just-in- Roseland** *(TR2 5JD)*. Kate was keen to show me the gardens and waterside position of this church which otherwise is unremarkable. I remember the pink-red stone of the walls and, nearby, a small tree covered with labels all a-dangle! I guess this is a curious, slightly New Age-y way of sending a prayer. Into St Mawes for a warming coffee before we jumped onto the ferry to chug across to **St Anthony-in-Roseland** *(TR2 5EZ)*. As Kate and I stepped off the ferry we grinned at each other, aware we were both thinking the same thing: not only did our ferryman have a wondrous dark chocolate voice, he was rather delicious too. Giggling like schoolgirls, we followed a path through woodland, the broach spire of restored and redundant church visible above the trees. It is adjacent to a large house, Place House. Although large and soulless, I quite liked the interior. There is a simple depiction of the Lamb of God on one of the Norman arches, rescued from a priory, which frames the entrance door that someone thought to paint pale blue. Leaving churches well behind, we set off along the coast path, the ever-present sea swelling and breaking below us. Trewithian, where we had left my car, was rather further than Kate realised so, when we arrived in the village, we were more than ready for lunch-at-tea-time.

Much to my surprise Kate was happy to spend the next day 'crawling' with me. I, of course, looked forward to her company and her TomTom taking us directly to our intended destinations made a welcome change from my less than successful map reading. Trevalga is on the north coast above Tintagel. Even with the TomTom it proved hard to find St Petroc, tucked down an unmade track between farm buildings and the sea. We found nothing appealing about the church, so wound our way along the ridge to Tintagel. **St Materiana** *(PL35 0DJ)* should have appealed to me – out of town, isolated and high above the sea. Instead, I found it stolid, dark and of course teeming with tourists. My mother always advised against returning to a place of good memories after many years. The ship in which she travelled to Egypt during the war stopped over in Durban for six weeks. Billeted in the fire station, she was enjoying an *affaire* with the ship's doctor at the time, leaving her with romantic memories of walks on the beach by moonlight and dancing until dawn on the lawn of Caster House up on The Ridge. She returned to Durban in 1971 to find the fire station demolished, rubbish blowing over the sands, and Caster House converted into a nursing home! Similarly, I have happy memories of the only family holiday we spent in England when we were children. We stayed on a working farm near Camelford and I remember our day trip to King Arthur's wild, rocky corner of the land. The beach on which we played and built sand castles was far from crowded. A picnic with our beloved step-father was always the same, whether in a field or on a beach: we sat on a rug with mother, he sat at a folding table covered with a white cloth, gin and tonic to hand, a plate of food in front of him, with a large white napkin tucked in to protect the tie he *always* wore! As a gesture to informality, though retaining his jacket, he did agree to roll up his trousers and paddle cautiously along the waters edge. He was so very old school! Such a good memory for me so I'll air-brush the disappointing visit Kate and I made to a much changed **Tintagel**.

We popped into **St Endelienta, St Endellion** *(PL29 3TP)* before crossing the road for a bowl of soup. Our enjoyment of the spacious and light interior with pale grey walls and light oak benches was somewhat spoilt by one man pontificating to his friend, his bellowing voice intruding on the quiet and our ears.

Disregarding the drizzle, Kate set course for a church I had been longing to visit: **St Enodoc** *(PL27 6LD),* near Trebetherick. This chapel among the dunes is pretty much synonymous with our much loved poet, John Betjeman, author of a collection of church poems with a special affection for this dumpy little edifice, and well known for his successful mission to save St Pancras station from demolition and ensure its listed building status. Kate, reassured by hardy golfers wrapped in wet weather gear and huddled under multicoloured umbrellas that no one would be out clamping that day, overcame her understandable anxiety and parked on the golf course near a sign warning unauthorised vehicles would be clamped. Off we tramped up the 13th fairway. St Enodoc's squiffy little dunce cap spire tantalised us from behind a high tamarisk hedge. We approached under the lych gate still adorned with blue and white posies from a very recent wedding. The same white and blue flowers framed the porch door and inside there were charming flower arrangements everywhere. A C13th church with a modernised interior, it is the location and story of St Enodoc that is so memorable: the hedge was planted to protect the church from the dunes so never again would it disappear beneath the sand which covered it until the mid C19th when it was 'excavated' and restored for services. No wonder John Betjeman was inspired to write his poem, *Sunday Afternoon Service in St Enodoc Church*. This little church was more than worth the wet and windy walk.

I had hoped to treat Kate to a full blown Cornish tea at Jamie Oliver's restaurant which overlooks the beach at Westgate Bay but it was closed so the poor girl had to make do with take-away builders' tea from a kiosk on the beach which we sipped while ogling the muscular rubber-suited surfers as they swung past, boards tucked under their arms. The tide was way out, the bay stretched wide in both directions, sun replaced grey – stunning! Tim TomTom took us unerringly to our very last church of the day, **St Mylor** *(TR11 5UG)*. We parked near the grand yacht club and bustling marina, then walked up the path through a jungle of a graveyard, passing a really tall stone celtic cross by the south door. The detached bell tower looked too new and didn't seem to belong. The interior arrangement was something of a hotch-potch. We were drawn to the priest's chair, a really eccentric piece of furniture apparently presented to the church in 1948 in memory of one Thomas Tregenza's daughter. The Irish bog oak frame has Norse carvings and is dated as being one thousand years old whereas the panelling is a mere five hundred years old. You would not fall asleep on this chair.

Here ended Kate's church tour. What a brilliant day.

Old Kea, Cornwall

Sarah, a Cornish girl in Sussex, said **Old Kea** *(TR3 6AN)* would be well worth a visit so I decided to go in search of it the following morning after thanking Abigail and Kate for their hospitality and before heading back to Sussex. I think even Tim TomTom would have had difficulty in locating this very small church perched in a wood by the waterside. Through the suburbs of Truro, on and on along narrow lanes, I did eventually come to a dead end in front of some dilapidated farm buildings next to which was a large car with a stout lady sitting behind the wheel. As we were both heading for the same place, out of sight in the trees, we greeted each other. I learned she was over from Australia, her name really was Sheila, and she was trying to track down her forebears. Finding no evidence of them in or outside **Old Kea**, with a shrug and a wave she returned to her car. I wonder if she read the inscription on the stained glass window just inside the door: *'In Memoriam FA Packer RMA, Organist St David's Cathedral, Tasmania.'* Saint Kea was a lesser known Cornish saint, birth date unknown, death date October 495. The original, rather more substantial church of St Kea was built in the late C13th, the adjacent tower two centuries later. By the beginning of the C19th, the church was a ruin and replaced with All Hallows at Kea, near Truro. Old Kea, as it is known today, was rebuilt and reopened in 1863 since when bequests have ensured its maintenance and, presumably, paid for the hassocks, stitched to designs based on those in Chichester Cathedral! I sat a while in the churchyard. A place of perfect tranquillity on which to end my Cornish crawl.

* * *

Devon

I visited Devon churches in three bites so to speak: one September en route to Cornwall; during a visit to Kingswear in March; staying in Eggesford during December floods when I came across a trend for knitted nativity scenes and the village where the first Jack Russell dog was bred.

When Kate suggested a few days in Cornwall during September while she was down there staying with her daughter Abigail, I thought it would be a fun opportunity to visit some Cornish churches as described in the previous chapter. It made sense for me to drive down following on from the September Dawdle after spending the night chez Paul and Joan. Before meeting up with the Dawdlers at Sturminster Newton I set off to find **St George's, Langham** *(SP8 5DP),* tucked away down a lane out of Gillingham. This small, thatched church in a field, surrounded by fields, is 'new'. It was built in 1921 in the Arts & Crafts style, over the graves of Alfred and Elizabeth Manger, as a result of their dream before The Great War to erect a place of worship for local residents and workers. Tragically their son, son-in-law and nephew were all killed and they both died shortly afterwards. I was disappointed to find it locked.

The next day I did go into a thatched church or, more accurately, the **Loughwood Meeting House, Dalwood** *(EX13 7DU).* It was built in 1653 on the Dorset/Devon border as, at that time, Baptists were persecuted so, should a warning be received of police approaching while an *illegal* meeting was in progress, the preacher could nip over the border into the next county and safety! According to church notes, three steps lead into a baptismal pool hidden underneath floorboards in front of the pulpit, where total immersion would have been in water fed from a nearby stream. The room itself is very plainly furnished with box pews, gallery and clear glass windows. It was quite sweet and I liked the stable built to shelter worshippers' horses.

I went on to pay a second visit to **Ottery St Mary. St Mary's** *(EX11 1DJ)* is a large church with a really beautiful interior, full of colour and monuments, spectacular fan vaulting and a quirky carving of an elephant's head on one of the capitals! The C14th astronomical clock is one of four in the West Country – the others are in Wells, Exeter and Wimborne. After my first visit to Ottery St Mary I met up with a friend for lunch at The Normandy House across the square, remembered ever since not for the meal but for my visit to the Ladies' Room. No bog-standard cistern in this powder room but an aquarium complete with bed of pebbles, fronds and little crayfish which didn't seem at all fazed by the rise and fall of the water whenever the chain was pulled. I was disappointed on my second visit to this small Devon town to find this quirky arrangement is no more.

To continue. Follow a small road north of the A30 and you'll come to whitewashed and thatched cottages and the handsome grey tower of **St Andrew's, Sampford Courtenay** *(EX20 2ST)*. The pale grey interior, tall and spacious, has a light feel to it. A local couple were pointing out various features to friends visiting from overseas. They encouraged me to join 'the tour' during which the husband pointed to the medieval roof bosses, amongst them a stunning 'green man', his mouth full of foliage. I was particularly excited to see a carving of three hares sharing three ears, a trinity I had only come across before as a roundel set into a window in the church at **Long Melford, Suffolk**. I cannot pretend I would have spotted those hares without direction from the 'tour guide'.

I continued a long way down a narrow lane devoid of dwellings and was about to turn back when **St Mary's, Honeychurch** *(EX20 2AE),* appeared on the right. A tiny, simple stone chapel with worn floorboards and a pretty wagon roof, I conjured in my imagination the congregation of days gone by: the farmer, farm labourers, the milkmaids and all their families seated on five hundred year old pews, bleached and worn with time and use. I dropped a coin into the unlocked reliquary, probably the only one posted.

I returned to a road leading across moorland. It turned and it twisted, on and on, until I reached the car park at the foot of the tor from the very top of which **St Michael's, Brentnor** *(PL19 0NP),* looked out over countryside below. On with walking boots and off I went, taking the most direct steep route. I expected to have the church and the summit all to myself. Instead, scrambling up the last rise, I came face to face with a wedding party filing out of the chapel. A small group for, when I ventured into the rather dreary, dark interior, I counted seating for only thirty-six. Incidentally, had I approached from the far side the ascent is a gradual slope and no doubt was the one taken by the wedding party. This chapel was only about location.

This was not the first wedding I have happened upon. I stayed with well-meaning friends who insisted on taking me to their less-than-interesting local church in Westerham, Kent. We arrived just as a bride, clutching a large plastic bottle of water in one hand and her groom in the other, stepped through the porch followed by bridesmaids in matching strapless, purple frocks. Wedding guests wearing varying degrees of finery drifted out, and among them, little flower girls, price tags dangling from the hem of their lilac dresses. We stepped inside just long enough to be waylaid by the organist who was still in deep shock from seeing a bride walking up the aisle to join her future husband at the altar carrying a bouquet *and* bottled water.

SA church, van Reenan's pass

While visiting my daughter and her girls thousands of miles away in South Africa, en route to Lesotho we followed the N3 from Kwa Zulu Natal, through the Drakensberg Mountains. Before crossing into the Free State, Tok stopped the car at the top of **Van Reenan's Pass** for us to admire the spectacular views below and all about us. She also knew, hidden among blue-gums and willows, there is a very small Roman Catholic Church which would be of interest to her mother. We walked along a sand track to a tiny brick building behind a stone-wall with a single bell in the belfry above the arched west door. No sooner had I emerged from the dark, decorated interior with seating for maybe twenty worshippers, than a bright yellow two-seater vintage car drew up by the entrance gate. More beetle or bumble-bee than car, it was decorated with white ribbon and bouncing balloons. Seated next to the chauffeur was a stout, hatted and suited, middle-aged bride. This explained the presence nearby of a lady with an important looking camera and a priest in conversation with a gentleman whom we supposed to be the groom. A second car drew up with the best man, flower girl and two guests. For a moment we also felt like guests. An unexpected and charming interlude before we continued on our way.

Devon beckoned twice two years later not including driving down in September solely to walk the eleven mile coastal path from Brixham back to Kingswear. Mid March Charlotte and I decided to ignore both weather of the day and the forecast and set off from Chichester to Devon in the chilly grey before dawn to spend a few days in her charming end-of-terrace fisherman's cottage in Kingswear, across the water from Dartmouth. We arrived in Exeter and made straight for Bill's Café and breakfast. No sooner seated than we were each given a hot water bottle to hug and to hold – such a thoughtful, warming and most welcome touch. Braced by a good breakfast, we decided to explore Exeter before continuing on our way. In the Cathedral we tagged on to a group trailing in the wake of a twinkly, articulate guide with pendulous breasts and billowing skirt, a fount of too much information to retain. We popped our heads around the doors into three tiny city churches, **Saints Martin, Petrock** and **Stephen**, all squeezed between post-war buildings, none of them memorable. Saving the best to last we explored the ravishing, newly furbished and absolutely memorable Royal Albert Memorial Museum on Queen Street. My favourite room? Possibly a small one in which someone had thought to juxtapose three items: a stuffed elephant, towering male giraffe and antique harpsichord.

From Charlotte's cosy cottage eyrie overlooking the marina and River Dart we set off in biting cold along coast paths for a potter through Dartmouth. The light poor interior of **St Petrox**, built on a promontory at the mouth of the river, is hardly uplifting with brass monuments lined up between flagstones, the walls well covered with many memorials to sailors and war dead, but close by a charming memorial garden, cheery with primroses and windflowers, lifts the spirits. Set into a wall there is a poignant memorial to a child who died on 25th May 1819 aged five months:

> *Short was his little stay*
> *He came not as a guest*
> *He tasted life and fled away*
> *To his eternal rest.*

St Saviour's, Dartmouth *(TQ6 9DL),* is altogether a different place and space. There really is little I can add to Simon's enthusiastic description of this church which elicits an involuntary gasp as you enter through the medieval door covered with figurative ironwork, including a tree of life and a lion. The interior is dark yet somehow not at all gloomy and it teems with interest: a magnificent red, green and gold screen, intricately carved; tulip shaped pulpit similarly decorated and painted; beautiful bench ends, choir stalls in the aisles, a barrel roof and a gallery at the west end. We left, shivering with cold but not complaining. Besides, Charlotte knew just where to find a bowl of hot soup.

St Saviour,Dartmouth Door

If only the following December was as cold as March had been, with hoar frosts decorating foliage like icing on cake. Instead it was unseasonably mild. As the month wore on, heavy rains and gale force winds created havoc, saturating the earth, bursting rivers, upending trees onto roads and railway tracks. The weather forecast promised a small lull when I set off in the pre-dawn, destination north Devon. The lull was indeed short. By the time I drove into Exeter to pause for a leisurely breakfast, it was raining and high winds reduced my umbrella to a tattered skeleton of bare spokes. No matter. I bought a spotty little number to replace it before heading off along the A377 in the direction of Barnstaple. This year I was happy to deprive myself of Waitrose shopping, cooking and washing up – instead I had chosen to spend a few quiet days over Christmas in a country hotel, a base from whence I could explore the area and visit a few local churches written up by either Simon or John.

The first church en route was St Cyres & St Julitta, Newton St Cyres; it was the only locked door I was to come across on this crawl. Swiftly on to the **Church of the Holy Cross, Crediton** *(EX17 2AQ),* highly rated by Simon though, for me, too large and soulless. Two things did excite me. A wonderfully tactile piece of polished sycamore designed and made by local sculptor Norman Yendell to commemorate the miraculous restoration of Thomas Grey's sight some months after losing it in 1315. And a nativity scene, at once so different and so familiar: tiny figures, crudely carved from balsa wood, exactly matched a set of musicians I watched taking shape under the flying fingers of an African gentleman in Johannesburg. My former husband, with whom I had just had coffee, noticed my delight and made me a gift of them. So used to seeing those balsa wood carvings in my house, it was startling to see the traditional scene, Africa style, arranged in an ancient carved stone recess in a Devonshire church! A modern sculpture and an unusual nativity scene, is all I'll remember of the quite grand Holy Cross. I continued on my way. Not far from Crediton, in the rural middle of central Devon is, **St Mary the Virgin, Stockleigh English** *(EX17 4DE):* C14th chancel; C15th tower, C19th restoration; C20th new roof and a C21st nativity scene in which wise men, shepherds, Mary, Joseph and two pale yellow sheep – all figures were knitted. Unfortunately a somewhat squiffy Mary looked as though she had been celebrating with an excess of mead.

St Mary, Stockleigh English Nativity

St Swithun's, Sandford *(EX17 4ND)* was much more fun. The steps and paths leading to the south porch were laid many years ago with Devon cobbles. Instead of the usual bun shaped uniform squares, these stones are small, narrow, randomly placed with grass tufting in between them. The effect is attractive but also uneven and slippery when wet – no doubt cast iron hand rails steady many a worshipper! Sadly I expect it won't be long before those beautiful cobbles are buried forever under the smooth surface of tarmac in the name of health and safety. Once inside St Swithun's my eyes went straight to the C16th oak pew ends. Such detailed and imaginative carving always intrigues me. I walked up and down each aisle, crouching before a variety of faces. Among them a novel sort of Green Man whose beard, hair *and* tongue were all depicted as oak leaves. There was a gentleman wearing a tall pointy hat with beard to match; a bare breasted African lady; a jolly pipe smoker; a man sporting a wild afro hair do; and two more sombre carvings, the Lamb of God and Dove of Peace.

In 1657 the church benefactors supplied the oak trees from which they built a gallery across the west end especially to accommodate children from the poorhouse. Across the top of a memorial screen, erected between nave and chancel after The Great War, large letters in silhouette spell out *The Great War 1914 to 19* (fighting ended with the Armistice signed on 11th November 1918 but the peace Treaty of Versailles wasn't signed until 28th June 1919). According to the church notes, one day in the early C12th a fight between two men during Mass ended with the death of one, the result of which was closure of the church until 1137. This incident was noted years later by a Tudor sculptor who made a carving on one of the pillars. I went in search and found a very small carving showing two children pulling each other's hair. Another little snippet in the notes caught my eye. In the C10th when monarchs bequeathed land they did so in parcels known as *hides*. As a *hide* was described as "*much land as could be tilled with one plough in a year to support a family*" and land varied in soil quality – the dimensions of a hide could vary between 60 to 80 acres – these anomalies may have been the cause of many a neighbour boundary dispute.

A lengthy drive through some of Devon's famously deep, winding and thickly hedged narrow lanes ended hilltop high, a panoramic view of farmland stretching below. In need of exercise, I parked Ruby on the verge and set off in the direction of a handful of cottages and **St Mary the Virgin, Upton Hellions** *(EX17 4AE)*. After days of ducking the rain, high on the ridge, I revelled in rather than lamented a walk in the gusting wind and rain under a big grey sky. No matter that the church failed to excite me; I only recollect an amusing bench end, a dull memento mori.

The final church I had earmarked for a visit before checking into the country hotel at Eggesford was quite different: had Simon chanced upon **St Matthew's, Coldridge** *(EX17 6AX),* surely it would have been included in his wonderful compilation. I arrived in the aptly named village in driving rain. The church, thatch roofed cottages, period houses and farm buildings, generously spaced, all border a large area, part village square, part village green. I waded, literally, through a large puddle that had formed under the lych gate and followed the cobbled path to the south porch. Just behind it something I had not seen before in a church. A tall chimney rising through the roof above a fireplace in the south aisle; long blocked up, it was once the source of church heating. Although I was chilled through and my feet soaking wet, I was in no hurry to leave the interesting welcoming interior of this ancient church. Worn steps leading up the bell tower, built in 1440, were not closed off but a scruffy notice pleaded with visitors <u>not</u> to venture up. Happily many ancient features survive a major C19th restoration. I'll particularly remember the outstanding wood carving of C15th benches and bench ends; a wondrous unrestored rood screen as wall to wall division of nave from chapel, and the minutely carved oak pulpit. Cheery red hassocks, depicting a variety of emblems, were propped up in colourful rows along bench shelves. Another woolly nativity scene, this one somewhat unsettling; a merry Mary next to a bonny bonneted baby Jesus surrounded by five fleecy lambs and a bright blue donkey but lurking in the shadows five robed men so heavily bearded they looked more like members of Isis than gentle admirers of the Christ child.. Thank goodness I read the notes as otherwise I would not have noticed the *medieval joke* carved into the back of the rood screen in the little side chapel. The screen was the gift of one Sir John Evans. Too busy to oversee the work himself, this task fell to his wife who may have been known as a 'scold', difficult to please. Look carefully above the doorway: discreetly carved next to a *bosse* I found a small triangle inside which one of the craftsman has placed, upside down, the head of a *Tudor Lady of Quality* with her tongue hanging out. Was this his revenge for a tongue lashing?

I was more than ready to check into the warmth and comfort of my hotel where I slept soundly, oblivious to rain and gales. Before continuing my church crawl, I asked one of the local staff how best to avoid flooding and fallen trees. She advised climbing up onto the ridge leading to **High Bickington** *(EX37 9AX)*. The tall tower of St Mary's loomed at the end of a long straight path flanked by tall mature pleached limes, spiky twig topknots silhouetted against a gloomy grey sky. All my interest focused on the richly carved pew ends and unusual choir stall frontals. The seventy-eight oak pew ends from the C15th and C16th (as well as a few even earlier and two or three Victorian) depict a mixture of saints, apostles, musicians and singers and one kneeling figure sporting what could be a luxuriant pigtail or quirky head-dress. I never cease to be amazed by the

St Mary's, High Bickington man kneeling

detail worked by those craftsmen of long ago. The unusual choir stall frontals are, by contrast, modern, carved by Siddie Greenwood Penny in 1904: Noah's animals of Africa are depicted in relief along the north frontal, British birds along the south one.

Further along the ridge the tower of **St Mary's, Atherington** *(EX37 9HU)* loomed over the village. From the teeny weeny village shop and post office I obtained the large and heavy key which opened the ancient oak door to an interior full of more amazing pew ends – these were uniform with elaborate poppyheads – and a spectacular 400 year old rood screen, gallery and loft across the nave. The fan vaulting was so detailed with little cherubs carved in between the spines. Wonderful. Spying the worn stone steps of the spiral staircase leading up to the loft, up I climbed though sensibly decided not to stand on the ancient boards, just peered down into the chancel before descending backwards. An unusual feature of the deep lych gate was a long and narrow ancient stone centred on the path, a coffin rest.

I am grateful to my friendly waitress for encouraging me to visit the next two churches, neither of which was mentioned by Simon or John (*Betjeman's Best British Churches* by Richard Surman). It proved quite a mission to reach **St John's, Warkleigh** *(EX37 9DE)*. I made the mistake of taking the first signed turning along a lane running perilously close to the overflowing river. I drove Ruby – my trusty Red Mini – through a couple of shallow fords then beat a hasty retreat through the third one before Ruby was called upon to swim. A kindly local directed me to Warkleigh by sending me uphill and around. By now the sky was blue and the sun shone so I left Ruby in a layby to walk a couple of miles towards the tower I could see in the distance. I almost burst into song (safe to do so as no one within hearing) it felt so good to be striding out on such a glorious day with undulating Devon fields rolling all around. I approached St Mary's, some way out of the village, past a muddle of farm buildings, noisily guarded by two chained dogs, and through a particularly attractive lych gate into a graveyard falling steeply away from the church. Aside from an extant leper's entrance door, dusty with cobwebs, I remember little of the interior but did note something outside quite bizarre: the four pinnacles on the tower were wrapped around with flapping sheets. Why?

Next stop was **St Paul's, Filleigh** *(EX32 0RU)*. This little church really is a peach. Built in 1730, a larger building to replace a tiny pre-Norman church, it forms part of the Fortesque Estate which dates from 1454 and is owned to this day, without interruption, by the same family. The south door opens onto an interior surely designed as a feast for the eye, splendid with colour and decoration, enough to put a smile on one's face. The organ gallery over the door sits above a bright pink wall and under a pale blue barrel ceiling divided into decorated panels. In the chancel not a surface has been left plain: panels of the apsidal ceiling are a riot of brightly painted medallions, the walls positively Puginesque in that not an inch has been left untouched. According to a church leaflet, this is the work of Lady Susan Fortesque, 1880, a delightful legacy from a creative lady.

On down into the valley to **Chittlehampton** *(EX37 9QL)*. Originally C12th, extended in the C15th, this handsome church faces a large village square. The path leading to the centrally placed south porch is flanked by pleached limes planted six a side to form a delightful arbour. **St Urith's**, known today as **St Hieratha's**, is a unique dedication. While crawling in Cornwall two years prior to this trip I visited Old Kea, site of the C6th Cornish Saint Kea's original church. Hieratha, allegedly St Kea's convert and a devoutly religious maid, lived in Chittlehampton where she became revered for miracles performed. Far from being rewarded with a long and happy life, legend has it her jealous stepmother had her decapitated. Her tomb lies in a corner of the church and her image is carved into one panel of the splendid C16th stone pulpit. Two nativity scenes were displayed, both charming. Inside one three sided box, beautifully emulating a stable, was a somewhat minimalist collection of colourful plaster figures: Mary, Joseph, a cow, a horse and an empty crib. The other scene had the look of a modern domestic interior populated by less than upright knitted figures in colourful robes, faces barely visible under huge wrap around sinister black beards; all of them, including Mary and a leaning ladder, appeared to be a tad worse for wear.

The lime walk must be a picture in the summer.

The Bell pub faces the church on the other side of the square. I went in for a little lunchtime something and to enjoy the festive and cheery atmosphere of a popular village pub before following the road towards **Swimbridge** *(EX32 0PW)*. The village, surrounded by rounded rolling hills, sprawls in a shallow hollow, the tall lead broach tower of **St James'** visible from afar. The lych gate at the start of the tarmac path leading to the south porch was like no other I had come across, its deep whitewashed stone walls an extension of a village house, the entrance to which was reached from under the lych roof by steep steps and a balustrade climbing to the front door! St James' was *the* memorable church of that day. Although far from small, the interior was intimate and the warmth welcoming, as was a recording of carols playing as I wandered around, not knowing what to look at next. The magnificent rood screen – comparable to and as old as the one I had seen in St Mary's, Atherington – stretched the whole width of the church, across the nave and both aisles. Richly carved with fan vaulting above each supporting pillar, it is, according to church notes, forty-four feet long and ten feet high. I liked the plain wooden roof, relatively modern oak pews with ancient bench ends fitted to some of them. Somewhat obscured by seasonal greenery and berries, the intricately carved hexagonal C15th stone pulpit depicts five saints, each holding a scroll on which their names, rubbed off long since, were once painted.

Placed next to the pulpit a curious nativity scene. The interior of a model of a designer stable with arches and two windows, framed with an abundance of greenery and chopped straw thick on the floor a mixed collection of painted plaster figures were arranged around a non-existent crib: Mary, three shepherds, a cow, donkey and a chap wearing a short Roman toga but no Joseph. Maybe he is Joseph. To the back of the south aisle another apparently permanent miniature scene had been set up on a fabric covered plank laid across a settle, the back rest also covered with material. Ranged behind a long narrow table were twelve woolly figures gathered for the last supper. All of them, including the central figure dressed entirely in white, wore serious beards – or neck warmers – and resembled ruffians rather than disciples. The dainty embroidered white tablecloth was littered with woolly blue goblets filled with woolly red wine. I think knitting must be a fashion of the moment. The church notes made little mention of what has to be a most stunning item of craftsmanship, other than to infer it is a mishmash of Italian-French-Tudor design and origin; standing next to a column is a three-tiered carved oak casing comprising five panels attached to an equally richly carved support, topped off with a canopy or tester. Given a little nudge from a nearby lady arranging flowers, I lifted a small catch across two panels of the middle tier. Concealed behind the folding panels was a round lead basin complete with a fine chain caught up on a hook to which was attached a perfect little plug. Delightful, beautiful and practical – only later did I wonder how the water was retrieved.

The window in the Lady Chapel commemorates Reverend John (Jack) Russell who served as curate from 1832 and then vicar from 1866-1880. He was a different sort of clergyman. Born in Dartmouth in 1795, he went to Exeter College, Oxford, and while there he took a fancy to a dog, white with black patches, which he bought from a milkman. A keen huntsman, John Russell bred from "Trump" a type of useful terrier which became known as the Jack Russell. Today Rev. Russell, a founder member of The Kennel Club, is remembered somewhat unfairly more as the Sporting Parson than as a vibrant vicar. When he died in 1883 at least a thousand people came to his funeral. No wonder the village pub is The Jack Russell. It was too early to go from church to pub but I imagine the walls abound with prints and paintings of its namesake. St James' was the last church I visited on this trip. As I left next morning I drove up a cinder track to All Saints, Eggesford. A small, chubby church, it stands quite alone, fields behind, the river below. Although a notice declared it was open every day and it was well after nine o'clock, the door was locked. Time to go home.

More recently I paid a flying visit to Devon to join a day ride on Dartmoor astride one of Tim's magnificent Clydesdale horses, a sort of workout prior to an upcoming holiday involving several days on horseback. I stayed with Jan and Peter, hospitable friends of Tim who not only put me up for two very comfortable nights but shared their suppers with me too! Following directions to their cottage I passed a tiny wayside church with a big fat chimney, a single bell atop the pitched roof, and set into the churchyard wall a narrow red letter box. Irresistible! I read the raised letters on the post-box V & R 1837-1901, installed 1857, then followed a sort-of-path running between church and field, entered through the dark blue south door into a single cell unlike any other I had seen. **St Raphael's, Huccaby** *(PL20 6SB),* the only *Anglican* church in England dedicated to this patron saint of travellers, was built in 1868 to serve two purposes: as school house on weekdays and a place of worship on Sundays. Midway down the north wall a huge stone mantle rests on two chunky piers to frame a wood burning stove, large enough to warm schoolchildren, members of the congregation, perhaps on occasion even wedding guests. Written in chalk on a blackboard propped on an easel cheery words welcome visitors; desks fitted with ink-wells doubled as pews either side of a decorative pink carpet runner leading to altar and lectern; various items of schoolroom memorabilia, surplus to requirements since the school closed in 1924, are mixed with prayer books. The font, small and pretty, is kept in a box when not in use! The room exudes a pleasing sense of recent yesterdays.

St Raphael's, Huccaby, Devon

A very different yesterday permeates the dark dank granite interior of **The Church of St Michael & All Angels, Princetown** *(PL20 6RE)*. I wandered up the main street of this most unprepossessing of high moorland towns, famous only for its proximity to Dartmoor Prison, simply to fill in time until the village shop re-opened for the afternoon. I was unaware of the unique history of this church, the only one in the land built (1812-14) by French prisoners of the Napoleonic Wars (1793-1815) and completed by Americans captured during war with America (1812-15). I wandered around under the high roof, peered through a glass window at the 'green tower' – so called because despite best efforts it continues to ooze mould and slime – trying not to think of those men, toiling in unimaginable conditions. Only simple initials and date of death are carved onto each otherwise anonymous gravestone forming four forlorn rows tucked behind the church.

* * *

Stunning font in St James', Swimbridge, Devon

Kent

One drear November was cheered by Kate's invitation to stay in their weekend cottage in the centre of Sandwich. This was a lovely opportunity to explore some churches of the marshes on my way up the coast and then to see what others I could find over the three days of my sojourn in this ancient former port. I was intrigued by a church bell placed in the branches of a nearby yew tree, came across two 'hudds' and Enid Nesbit's resting place. One major disappointment on this trip was rectified several years later.

Chatting to Peter in Waterstone's, as I often did, when I mentioned I was leaving pre-dawn next day he suggested I made **Winchelsea**, one of the original Cinque Ports, my first stop as he knew just the place for breakfast. I took his advice – the delicatessen deserved the recommendation – before I walked up the path into what remains of **St Thomas the Apostle** after its destruction by the French. For me, the interior is more museum than church, home to some impressive monuments and lit by enormous, not very beautiful stained glass windows. In the churchyard I looked among the headstones for the infamous one with a celtic cross on top and the words

'Love, light, Peace
Terence Alan
(Spike) Milligan, CBE, KBE
1918-2002'

And underneath the infamous inscription in gaelic – the church forbidding it to be in English – "I told you I was ill"! Even at the end Spike couldn't resist a light, zany touch.

I left the coast road long and far enough to find **St Michael's, Playden** *(TN31 7UA)* before I left Sussex for the churches of Romney Marsh, flat coastal terrain between Hythe and Rye. It is a small, tall church with an elegant shingled spire and a rural feel to it despite its urban surroundings. Inside, a very long three hundred year old ladder stretched up along the wall into the tower but no longer in use.

I had wanted to visit **St Augustine, Brookland** *(TN29 9QP)* ever since receiving a postcard from an enthusiastic Vanessa. Quite singular in appearance, next to the double stable doors which open into the porch it has a C13th octagonal belfry with a 'three cone' (or flounce!) roof, the whole built entirely of wood. The interior, furnished with box pews, was light and full of interest. A rare 'hudd' stood to attention at the back, a notice inside describing it as *a C18th hudd or grave shelter used by the parson for burials before the invention of the umbrella to shelter his wig from the marsh rain."* (The Chinese were the first to use umbrellas more than a thousand years ago; the modern umbrella, invented in France around 1700, arrived in England some fifty years later.) Hudd from huddle or huddle from hudd? Possibly a Kentish word as it does not feature in my large Collins dictionary so leaving me to choose which way round! A plain coffin stretcher stands insignificant compared with a stunning late C12th lead font, intricately decorated with two tiers depicting the signs of the zodiac and occupations of the months which delightfully include tilling, pruning, mowing, haymaking, being at table and warming feet.

I drove off the main road some winding way across the marsh to **St Thomas Becket, Fairfield** *(TN29 9SA).* Every now and then I feel instant joy at first sight of something I perceive to be special when I come across it and so it was with this little marsh church standing quite alone on a man made mound, surrounded by fields and water, its bleak yet beautiful isolation somehow emphasised under a grey sky. I parked by the side of the lane and read the notice telling me from which house to obtain the key. Setting off across the marsh I had no difficulty in believing, before the implementation of a modern drainage system, it was only possible to reach the church by horse – there is a mounting block close by – or boat! Originally late C12th, it has been considerably reworked over the years and all the furnishings are C18th. A curious feature is the communion rail: introduced by Archbishop Laud, it has three sides and looks much like a child's playpen, apparently installed to stop dogs fouling the altar! Imagine a candle lit service in this tiny church – heavenly.

Bleak beauty, location of Fairfield

St George, Ivychurch

I found **St George's, Ivychurch** *(TN29 0AL)*, a rather dismal, redundant place. The north aisle was filled with an exhibition of old farm equipment and there was another hudd, this one a little more shapely, having a rounded top. Two coffin stretchers and a note over the entrance proclaiming '*...How dreadful is this place!....*' added to a feeling of gloom. I was more than pleased to arrive at nearby **St Clement's, Old Romney** *(TN29 9QH)* with its merry interior furnished with pink-painted box pews and a small gallery, a little light relief before continuing up the road to **St Mary in the Marsh** *(TN29 0DG)*. There is nothing remarkable about this originally Norman church except it is where Edith Nesbit is buried, her grave marked simply by a piece of inscribed wood between two down posts and this inscription on the porch wall:

This tablet was erected by her
Many friends in memory of
Edith M. Nesbit
1858 – 1924
Who delighted the hearts of
So many children by her books
And who spent the last years of her life in this parish.
I will dwell among my children.

I pressed on to **Hythe** a town on a steep slope, and climbed the steps to **St Leonard's** *(CT21 5DN)*, church. Inside the steps carry on up to the chancel built over a crypt and even further up to the altar. A grand church, yes, but not the reason I made the climb. Drawn to the crypt and its famed ossuary, a rare collection of human bones, I was disappointed to find the crypt is not accessible during the winter months. Bother. In ill humour I stomped down the hill in search of lunch. I struck lucky: a really unprepossessing little café not only served me the most delicious homemade mushroom soup for less than £3 and so restored my good humour, but the chef also took the trouble to explain and draw a route taking me slightly inland thus bypassing Folkstone and Dover. His kindness was appreciated as much as his soup.

I arrived in Sandwich before dark making it easier in this town of one way streets, to find Kate's street, her cottage *and* parking. The following day I had planned to see two churches before meeting up in Ash with Cousin Jane over from Ireland to visit her daughter Cressida and the grandchildren. Of **St Mary the Virgin, Minster-in-Thanet** *(CT12 4HA)*, I only remember, and noted, the misericords. Similarly at **St Nicholas' at Wade** *(CT7 0NT)* it seems I only found the rickety old ladder to the tower of any interest. I was happy to spend the rest of the day with family.

I did enjoy **St Mary's, Wingham** *(CT3 1BB)*. Parking my car outside this rather large church, I made a beeline for the timber framed building opposite, The Dog Inn, where I lingered over a welcome cup of coffee. The interior is as attractive as the exterior and Kate says the food is excellent. I then walked up the approach lined with soldier yews to **St Mary's**, to find misericords and the monument to cap all – or at least many – monuments. Dated 1682, it is an astonishing memorial for the Oxenden family whose surname explains the black horned oxen 'guarding' all four corners of the monument on top of which is a highly decorated obelisk and on top of *that*, an urn. It's quite something and the wonderful vanity, and humour, of it made me chuckle. I was then disappointed on arriving at **St Mary's, Patrixbourne** *(CT4 5BP),* to find it locked. I was only able to stand in awe before its perfect Norman south door.

The furthest point to which I ventured that day was St Mary's Brabourne *(TN25 5LR),*. A heavily buttressed grey stone rather squat building in a field, it didn't look inviting and wasn't. It was locked so I went in search of someone and returned accompanied by an elderly man with a key. He was helpful in pointing out the original C12th glass in a high lancet window and even lifted the cloth covering two very fine brasses in a side chapel for me to admire. I noticed yet another dodgy long ladder to the belfry, very firmly barricaded against all climbers.

Next morning I set off to locate **St Mary's, Stelling** *(CT4 5PT).* I'm not surprised Simon got lost trying to find this rural church. It lies in the middle of farmland and fields, bare of trees, far from a village and with no tall spire to guide one to it. It was locked, a note directing one to a nearby cottage, the owner of which did not answer my repeated knocks. Exasperated, I returned to the church, scrabbled around under a mat and there was the key. I was so pleased the key turned gaining me entry into a delightful Georgian interior. Box pews are painted apple green and laid out in an unusual formation. Across the west end is a gallery and, to one side, a lengthy old ladder, complete with handrail, leading to the belfry. **St Mary's, Elham** *(CT4 6TT)* was not far away. It is the hour glass on the pulpit I particularly remember in this attractive, sympathetically restored church. I'm sure many a congregation feels *every* pulpit should have one.

Unintentionally, I left the best to last that day. I approached **St Nicholas, Barfreston** *(CT15 7JQ)*, by the most twisting of lanes and was almost ready to give up when I came upon it on a bank above me. It doesn't quite compare with Kilpeck but oh so nearly. The carving on the south door is really beautiful and above the windows is a complete table of carvings. The inside is as Norman as the exterior. A little quirk: there is one but bell. It is perched high in the churchyard yew tree although the bell rope is pulled from inside the church.

Before I left Sandwich I did pop my head round the doors of three of the town's churches, two of which are redundant. The only object of interest that caught my eye was a *'rare example of medieval dowelling, that is, stones bonded together with animal bones, in this instance probably a sheeps' bone'.* I departed early as usual, travelling well away from the coast into East Sussex towards Penhurst in countryside alongside a manor house. There was no sign of man or beast. Who worships here? Where do they come from? I didn't linger, driving on to Ashburnham, another church with an exceedingly long and leafy approach. For me there was little to warrant the extra miles driven. I had been charmed, amused, even bowled over, by most of the churches on that crawl but these two did not, as they say, 'do it' for me. I was ready to go home.

One year later Rachael and I set off to visit her sister near Westerham, not too far from **All Saints, Tudeley** the only church in the world to have *all* the windows designed by Chagall. We made several flying visits along the way, the first of which was to the **Blue Idol Quaker Meeting House** *(RH13 8QP)*. Originally a farmhouse built in 1580 as a farmhouse it was bought by the Quaker William Penn (1644-1718) in 1691. A blue plaque on the front of this attractive black and white building proclaimed Penn *'with other friends* *established this place'*. From there, Rachael made a detour to Shipley where a splendid windmill has been restored. Over the door, words on a stone tablet read

Let this be a memorial to
Hilaire Belloc
who garnered a harvest
of wisdom and sympathy
for young and old
MDCCCLXX – MCMLIII

The next morning, Rachel's brother-in-law decided upon a mini church crawl before feasting our eyes on Chagall's windows. I rather liked **St Peter & St Paul, Shoreham** *(TN14 7SA)*. The porch has a fat split oak arch and is approached by an exceptionally long, narrow, and very straight, yew lined path. Inside, I spotted five old leather fire buckets high on a shelf but it is the screen that really deserves mention. It is intricately carved and runs the full width of the church. Rising from the slim screen itself, wooden fan vaulting arches out to support a wide standing platform, accessed by a stair and door in the north wall. I can just imagine a row of 'floating choristers'.

St Mary's, Kemsing *(TN15 6NA)*, is a curious mixed memory. The ancient porch door and shingled broach tower are simple whereas in contrast the interior is dominated by an outsize canopy, golden and decorated, suspended over the chancel and by the screen on top of which two huge golden angels 'guard' Jesus on the cross. All too much! Not so in the churchyard. Rows and rows of plain stone mummies, mottled with lichen, lie between head and foot stones. Maybe this was the Kentish style.

Then on to **All Saints, Tudeley** *(TNll 0NZ*. The single vibrant hectic red Chagall window in Chichester Cathedral was commissioned in 1977 by the then Dean Walter Hussey, possibly to celebrate both his support for the arts and his retirement that year. The Tudeley windows were commissioned as a memorial to twenty-one year old Sarah d'Avigdor-Goldsmid who died in September 1963, drowned off the Sussex coast. From the many reminiscences and tributes paid to her it seems she was exceptionally artistic with an eye for excellence; she bought for her mother the first ever David Hockney to be sold and fell in love with Chagall's windows when visiting Paris in 1961. The d'Avigdor-Goldsmids bought an estate in Tudeley in 1849. Sarah's father was Jewish, her mother Church of England: male children to be brought up as Jews, females as Anglicans, hence All Saints was chosen for a monument to Sarah. Chagall was approached to design a new East window in her memory. The window was unveiled in November 1967. Chagall offered to design windows for the entire church, providing funds were available which they were so his offer was accepted. Seven further windows were completed four years later. However, replacing the existing remaining four windows was *not* plain sailing! One was already a memorial to a former curate, the other three designed by a local artist: parishioners would not countenance their replacements being designed by a non-Anglican foreigner! Sir Hugh Casson eventually came up with the solution: place the Victorian windows on permanent display in the Vestry. By December 1985 the set of twelve windows was completed. They are predominately in hues and tones of greens, blues and yellows, quite different from the strong reds of the Chagall in Chichester Cathedral. If possible try to visit on a day when the colours glow in sunshine. These Chagall windows are quite magical.

St Leonard's, Hythe, skulls

Several years later I returned to **St Leonard's, Hythe** *(CT21 5DN)*, determined to visit the ossuary open to viewing for two hours each day during the summer months. I had recently visited the jumbled, rather spooky bone collection deep below the floor of **Holy Trinity, Rothwell**. Hythe's collection is well displayed and far from spooky. The crypt is more a sort of sub-mezzanine, underneath the raised chancel but only partially below ground level so daylight permeates from both ends of what used to be a thoroughfare. Once through the door the 'keeper of the bones', a steward described in fascinating detail what I saw laid out before us as well as what osteologists have deduced. Two arched bays opposite each other have been fitted with shelves upon which are row upon row of skulls. Along the wall beyond is a dense stack of bleached bones over seven metres long, almost two metres deep and high, remains of possibly some two thousand souls! The earliest bones probably go back to the C13th when the chancel was built. The odd skull peeked out from surrounding bones, a humourous touch! Also displayed are sets of teeth, free of decay though worn down, and some rather nasty clumps of human hair. One almost orange skull stood out among others lining shelves along a wall. Long before a steward was brought in to guard the collection it was pocketed by a gentleman, a heavy smoker, who kept it in his parlour until his death when a friend decided to return it to the collection. Annette pointed out some subtle differences between skulls to indicate gender, age, health, disease and probable cause of death. Osteologists have been able to identify cancers, iron deficiency, Graves' Disease, encephalitis and the difference between attempted trepanning and deliberate violence. Extraordinary. To see this collection was well worth a return visit.

* * *

Oxfordshire

I had been to Oxford once prior to October 2013, invited in the early sixties to a May Ball by a local lad I had met walking in the Hindhead Punch Bowl who was reading theology at Exeter college the time. Theology! Curious, especially as after graduation he joined Johnson Matthey in Hong Kong, leaving behind dreaming spires, paddling punts, sorrowful Sally and no doubt the Good Book, as all part of his student past. Decades later I decided to book a three night stay on a farm outside Fyfield, just north of Abingdon while I spent three days exploring Oxfordshire and its churches, guided, as ever, by Simon and John.

The first three churches on my route are just over the county border, in Berkshire. **St Mary's, Aldworth** *(RG13 9SB)* boasts monuments of seven male members of five generations of the de la Beche family, owners of the manor house in the C14th. Known as the Aldworth Giants, these huge crumbling effigies, as well as two smaller ones of wives, dominate an otherwise plain interior. Some lie dotted about the nave, others are tucked into their own niche – Sir Philip, seven foot tall, appears rather squashed into his! An elderly lady with a duster led me to the millennium tapestry, a colourful illustration of scenes and events, to which every member of the village contributed at least one stitch. Outside the porch, my guide waved her duster in the general direction of Laurence Binyon's grave, close to the beech hedge. I could just make out 1869-1943 but nothing else was legible.

Not a duster-waving lady in sight when I stepped inside **St Swithun's, Wickham** *(RG20 8HD)*, nor, I imagine, had one been seen for sometime. There was something forlorn and neglected about the gothic interior. I paid little attention to the abundance of carved foliage, wood grey with dust, or to the "*three manual Bevington*" organ with weird boxy pipes resembling upright piano keys, as I had come to see the elephants! The roof beams of the nave are adorned with lime wood angels designed by Benjamin Ferrey. It was intended to repeat them in the north aisle but Rev. William Nicholson, made a decidedly quirky decision. When visiting the Paris Exhibition in 1845 he fell for, and bought, four enormous green *papier maché* elephant heads, commissioned four more, and to this day they adorn the roof beams! A truly eccentric vicar!

St Swithun's, Wickham green elephants

Not far from Wickham my eye caught a sign beside a private driveway to indicate a parking bay for *church only*. No church was visible but as churches are meant to be open to all and there was a way marker, I decided to walk up the drive in search of it. I found a gardener in an herbaceous border. He assured me I wasn't trespassing, that some way off to the right in the middle of a field was the church I was looking for. I was instantly smitten by the creamy building ahead and walked through a metal kissing-gate up to the porch. A wooden gate stands in front of the door. No need to pass through it as there is nothing either side. The key, I read, was inside a box by the metal gate! Back I went to retrieve it. Everything about **St Thomas, East Shefford** *(RG17 7EF)*, is just gorgeous. The tiny original Norman church, C13th chancel, C16th chapel, even the red brick porch didn't offend. Whitewashed walls; red brick floor in the nave; a simple stone altar and stunning pattern of mostly faded yellow, apricot and black medieval tiles on the floor of the chancel; and old red wall paintings covering most of the high chancel wall. It is in the care of The Churches Conservation Trust – long may they cherish this little gem in the most peaceful of settings.

All I remember of **Holy Cross** Church, **Sparsholt** *(OX12 9PU)* after entering through a beautiful Norman door with scrolled ironwork hinges, are three worm eaten wooden effigies – Sir Robert Achard (d. 1353) surrounded by wood panelling, his two wives tucked into back lit niches, an obsolete antique clock and a simple font under a dunce cap lid. I pressed on to **St Swithun's, Compton Beauchamp** *(SN6 8NP)* in the grounds of Compton House, a moated manor. Feeling very much as though I was trespassing, I parked Ruby by the stable block not far from the house and walked up a grassy track. The medieval chalk church is built on a mound, its white walls offset by grey roof tiles and quoin stones. The churchyard, dotted with quite a few squiffy headstones, is surrounded by fields in which grazed a number of brood mares and their leggy foals. Later, I stopped to chat to a stable lad who told me the property belonged to a gentleman with a passion for breeding racehorses. The interior of this ancient church was such a visual surprise. A previous owner, Samuel Gurney who lived there 1924-1968, commissioned an artist to rearrange the furnishings, a mix of old and C20th. The chancel walls and deep window recesses are covered with a delightful mural of vine leaves painted in 1900 by a member of the Kyrle Society. Years later in 1967 two artists added little birds, bats and insects between the leaves. A memorable church in the most gorgeous setting.

Last – and least! – before checking into the B & B I had booked for three nights, I paid a very short visit to **St Andrew's, Shrivenham**. The merits of this church passed me by. I recall being transfixed by the humungous Victorian cast iron radiators. That's all. Time to press on to Fyfield, supper in the local gastro pub, hot bath and bed.

After a sound sleep and breakfast, I left my comfortable farmhouse B & B in search of two small churches en route to Burford. **Yelford** *(OX29 7QX)* is a hamlet at the end of a long straight road across marshland reclaimed by the Victorians. Despite driving back and forth, peering left and right, I could see no sign of **St Nicholas & St Swithun**. The gentleman who responded to my knock on his front door wasn't surprised. "Leave your car on the road, walk up the drive of Milton House, and just before the big gate turn left through a little gate and you'll soon come to the church." I did as directed and followed my shadow across the grass to this small essentially C16th church in a dell surrounded by a dense leafy screen. Yellow pumpkins crowded the base of a narrow font and hassocks worked in autumnal colours enhanced a simple interior. A stone cat guards the churchyard bench.

I drove back to and crossed over the main road, following a lane deep into farmland until I could see far away and quite alone in a field, the tiny form of **St Oswold, Widford** *(OX18 4DX)*. What a setting. Another humble place of worship to stay in the memory. It was built in its current form somewhere towards the end of the C12th. Walls of washed apricot are the backdrop to the pale wood of C17th and C18th box pews made by local carpenters working on the estate, the tub font is probably the same age as the church itself. According to church notes there is evidence of once-upon-a-time buildings nearby. Did they disappear after the Black Death (1349) or later for economic reasons? St Oswold was closed after the Dissolution and used as farm buildings until 1859. The church electoral roll in 2012 was 34.

St Oswold, Widford, Oxon

From what is for me sublime though small to the very grand. The lengthy wide high street of **Burford** was teeming with traffic and pedestrians as I inched my way to Church Lane where I just managed to squeeze Ruby into a space. **St John the Baptist** *(OX18 4RY)* couldn't be more different from my preference for small churches but it would have been rude to ignore it. Through a grand porch with vaulted ceiling to a really large interior filled with beech chairs upholstered in royal blue on which are propped jolly red hassocks in a variety of designs: the usual animals and flowers, an aeroplane, even music notes referring to the Burford Singers. A note placed on an old turret clock informs it was made *by Mr Hercules Hastings for which he was paid £10 in 1685 – it used to drive the south and west dials of the tower, its 8'8" pendulum swinging below the floor, until 1967 when an electric clock was installed.* Dominating one corner is a truly ostentatious monument, memorial to an unpopular prominent judge, paid for by his wife. The fact that the church had refused permission was obviously no deterrent to this gentleman's widow. The single item in this church I would gladly take home and place in my garden is a bronze sculpture of a mother playfully tossing her child in the air.

After a good pot of coffee in a nearby tea room, I drove a very long way to see a quite-over-the-top lych-gate-cum-bell-cum-clock tower designed by William White (1825-1900), great nephew of Gilbert White of Selborne, and student of Sir Gilbert Scott. I confess I didn't pay much attention to C13th church itself, **All Saints, Great Bourton** *(OX17 1RW)*, much altered and restored by William. No matter, the singular entrance to the churchyard was well worth the ride.

I had marked several churches to visit along the way back to Fyfield, the first of which was **St Philip's, Little Rollright** *(OX7 5QA)*. The approach to this rural church with a tall square tower is a long single-lane drive through fields home to cows sporting serious horns – English Longhorns? Once again I felt I was driving through private property. Inside all was quiet, just plain worn benches, a stone pulpit and, surprisingly, two grand stone effigies in the chancel. Outside, cud-chewing memorable cows. Not far away, still deep into secret countryside is **All Saints, Shorthampton** *(OX7 3HW),* an unassuming church in very close prximity to the farmhouse. Squeezing past the farmhouse, through a gate in the stonewall surrounding the churchyard, I stepped into the porch of this mellow interior. Still visible above the chancel arch are remnants of a doom painting. The arch is close to the north wall. This indicates the original nave was somewhat smaller until the south wall was rebuilt in the C15th to widen the nave by quite a few feet. An especially wide, deep squint was driven through the wall for the benefit of occupants of benches on the south side of the aisle. A C12th cheddar truckle of a tub font sits directly onto the stone floor. An extraordinary and surely recent feature of this otherwise untouched interior of the past is bench seats and backs as well as the pulpit desk are all fully upholstered in soft green velvet, beautifully finished with brass studs. I wondered whether this work was carried out by a local upholsterer with time, expertise and love to spare, or has a congregation, larger than one would have supposed, contributed for the added comfort for their posteriors and to such aesthetically pleasing effect? The visitors' book reflects the many who have called in while walking, cycling or – like me – church crawling. Someone jotted down these T.S. Eliot lines:

You are not here to verify,
Instruct yourself, or inform curiosity
Or carry report. You are here to kneel
Where prayer has been valid.

Both Simon and John alerted me to the early C13th misericords of **St Mary the Virgin, Kidlington** *(OX5 2AZ),* reputed to be among the oldest in England. The church was locked – after phoning three different numbers on the board, a churchwarden said she would come and open up the church. I had to pretend enthusiasm for her church generally but genuinely did so for the misericords and a couple of once-upon-a-time bench ends, now panels fronting the choir stalls.

Once she learned of my interest in churches my lovely B & B hostess arranged a visit to **St Nicholas, Fyfield** *(OX13 5LR),* usually kept locked. I hadn't the heart to say their village church fell well between my two chosen stools – it was neither small, rustic and quirky nor exceedingly grand. Nevertheless seven o'clock that evening saw me at the church gate in the darkening dusk, waiting for father-in-law John to appear. Such a charming, gentle man. We crept in by the priest's door, switched on what lights there were. It was so not the sort of church I would have usually visited, but I could see John was so happy his church had a rare visitor. There may be various features of interest to the academic though lost on me. Aside from real pleasure in meeting John, one special monument made this little assignation worthwhile; a two tiered *memento mori*, reminder of death, memorial to Sir John Golafre (d.1363). The figure above is depicted wearing his armour, the corpse underneath is wrapped in a winding sheet, the message being no man takes his worldly goods with him, a visual form of the Irish saying 'there are no pockets in a shroud'. Apparently there are few similar two tiered forms still in existence today. I thanked John and went directly to the pub for supper before another sound night's sleep.

St Margaret of Antioch, Binsey *(OX2 0BG)* is the one church I *had* to visit on this trip. During her time in Oxford, Bumble remembers a favourite walk from the city centre to Binsey, a hamlet amounting to no more than a cluster of cottages around The Perch pub, popular then, as it no doubt still is, with the students. The path wound through fields and passed close by a small church, the memory of which Bumble instantly recalled when I mentioned my intended visit to small churches of Oxfordshire. It was a disappointing start to the day's itinerary. Several yew trees cast dark shade over the church. I entered through the Norman south door – great zig-zags! – into a gloomy interior, oppressive under a roof painted strong blue-green in between the trusses. The treacle well in the churchyard *is* interesting. Local folklore has it around 680, a young man, Algar, was blinded by a bolt of lightning. Happily Frideswide, the young maid he loved, prayed to St Margaret of Antioch and her prayers were answered by the appearance close to the church of a 'treacle' well, the water from which cured Algar's blindness. In medieval times the word *treacle* meant *healing fluid.* The graveyard is full of 'Pricketts', many generations of a family that lived in the farmhouse. One member of this family was governess to Dean Liddell's daughter Alice, for whom Lewis Carroll wrote his stories.

On my way out I leant over the stone wall to converse with an inquisitive, glassy eyed goat wearing a cream coat and chocolate brown beard accessory.

Opposite the drive sweeping up to the public school, on the corner of the road and side street, is the churchyard of

St James the Great, Radley *(OX14 2JN),* surrounded by a beech hedge cut most unusually to resemble the serrated edge of a saw. In between headstones are two clumps of neatly cut and shaped yew bushes. I viewed with raised eyebrows the chosen shape of one particularly distinctive yew, an elongated cylinder with rounded tip rising from the centre of a plump mound. What was this creative hedge trimmer thinking? I entered through a door furnished with *two* knockers – why two? – into an interior dominated by four huge, blackened tree trunks placed at intervals dividing the nave from the south and only aisle. It all looked lopsided and top heavy. Trees apart, there was little to catch my eye other than a small note about a recent expensive battle with death watch beetle. The trees are amazing as is the churchyard topiary.

On to another most attractive church with an unexpected Betjeman connection. I pulled up Ruby close to the Georgian façade of **St Katherine's, Chiselhampton** *(OX44 7XF)* beside the B480, the parish church until 1977 when it was put into the care of the Churches Conservation Trust. It wasn't necessary for me to find the key holder; the door on the west façade, under a bell turret above a strong blue clock face, was ajar. Inside Ian, the architect employed by the Churches Conservation Trust, was busy preparing his five yearly report on the fabric of the building. We chatted awhile, both agreed on the best feature: beautiful pews, the ones at the front higher than those behind to deter the l*ower orders* from peeking! Ian suggested I climb the double decker pulpit to read a typed address left on a cushion. The address, one gathered, had been delivered to his extended family gathered from afar, by someone whose five times great grandfather (Charles Peers) built the church c.1762. I read through all eight double-spaced typed pages and particularly noted his mention of 1763 as '*a year as crucial to history as 1919 and 1945, a year in which war ended and the victors divided up the spoils, and redrew the maps not only of Europe but around the world, sometimes even handing conquered territory back'*. We'll never know when this family gathered or the occasion they wished to commemorate. We do know the preservation of this delightful church had the support of John Betjeman as illustrated by a poem he wrote " In aid of public subscription (1952) towards the restoration of the Church of St Katherine, Chiselhampton, Oxon"

Across the wet November night
The church is bright with candlelight
    And waiting Evensong.
A single bell with plaintive strokes
Pleads louder than the stirring oaks
    The leafless lanes along.

How warm the many candles shine
On Samuel Dowbiggin's design
For this interior neat.
These high box pews of Georgian days
    Which screen us from the public gaze
When we make answer meet

From that west gallery no doubt
The viol and serpent tooted out
The Tallis tune to Ken,
And firmly at the end of prayers
The clerk below the pulpit stairs
Would thunder out 'Amen'

On Country mornings sharp and clear
The penitent in faith draw near,
And kneeling here below
Partake the heavenly Banquet spread
Of Sacramental Wine and Bread
    And Jesus presence know.

How gracefully their shadow falls
On bold pilasters down the walls
   And on the pulpit high.
The chandeliers would twinkle gold
   Doctrinal, sound and dry

But every wand'ring thought will cease
Before the noble altarpiece
   With carven swags array'd
or there in letters all may read,
The Lord's Commandments Prayer & Creed
   And decently display'd

And must that plaintive bell in vain
Plead loud along the dripping lane?
   And must the building fall?
Now while we *love* the Church and live
And of our charity will give
   Our much, our more, our all.

The next two churches visited, both over the border into Buckinghamshire, barely warrant a mention. I almost stumbled over an elderly lady scrubbing the medieval floor tiles in **All Saints, Little Kimble** *(HP17 0XN)*, a forlorn little church with rather good wall murals, including an especially clear one of St George standing on his dragon. As my visit to **St Mary's, Haddenham** *(HP17 8AF)*, coincided with a children's service celebrating harvest festival, rather than interrupt, I admired a large duck house among reeds in the well populated village duck pond. I hope it was well used. **St Mary the Virgin, Waterperry** *(OX33 1JZ)*, wasn't easy to locate, tucked behind a garden centre and tea-room and next to what used to be the manor house. Unusually I had company in this church: there were several elderly ladies and walking sticks wandering along the aisles, heads just visible above high sided box pews. In each box, on a high ledge on which to rest prayer books, was a pair of little table lamps with brass stems and matching orange shades. I hadn't come across such lighting before. A three-sided screen forms a backdrop to the altar completely covered with a white cloth on which is emblazoned a peacock in his glory. This church is known for its C13th quality glass, about which I know nothing. A small door tucked behind the pulpit hid spiral steps to a no longer existing rood screen loft. It seemed the only route to the belfry was up a scary *uber* long ladder– maybe the bell-ringers practice their campanology without having to climb it!

So many church treasures were confiscated and lost forever after Edward VI's reign. I enjoyed reading this inventory made by his Commissioners:

2 sutes of Vestments
a cope of sateen
'on chalice parcel gilt
2 awter clothes
a crose of latten
a crose clothe of silke
a banner clothe with a stremer2 candilstike of latten
2 surples
2 little belles in the steple
a broken hande bell
a holy water pote of ledde
a coreris case of velvet
a hearse clothe of blake bokeram

By this time, had it been possible, Tim Tom Tom and I would be having words. After criss-crossing Thame more than once – on one such crossing I whizzed in and out of St Mary's, noting one glamorous husband and wife monument – I decided to make my own way to **St Andrew's, Wheatfield** *(OX9 7EW)*. I did eventually find it in a parkland setting. A large yew and small medieval church, a castellated parapet between roof and walls, sit in the middle of a sloping field surrounded by sturdy weathered fencing. It was locked. Never mind. Overhead, outlined against a big grey sky at least a dozen red kites languidly floated around each other. The church forgotten, I lay down to watch them. They watched me.

After three gastro pub suppers, three comfortable nights and three farmhouse breakfasts, I set off back to Sussex via two towns, two churches. **The Abbey of St Peter & St Paul, Dorchester-on-Thames** definitely falls into the Grand Category. The exterior was not enhanced by the presence of scaffolding, necessary while much needed roof repairs are carried out. Through a beautiful Norman door decorated with cast ironwork scrolls, into a modern glass interior porch opening into a vast empty space. The Abbey Doré in Herefordshire had left me unmoved. This Abbey felt quite different. Simon found the interior to be gloomy. I thought it wonderfully light. Warm wood pews, graced with hassocks worked in autumn colours, faced the chancel furnished with modern beech choir stalls and altar rails, very pleasing. Both Simon and John enthuse, understandably, about a well-known C13th effigy in the south aisle of a knight lying unusually on his side, sword about to be drawn, one leg bent under the other.

By now I was 'all churched out' and should have carried on home instead of paying such a hurried visit to **St Mary's, Ewelme** *(OX10 6HS)* part of a cluster of buildings comprising school and almshouses, homes today for thirteen men and women. I didn't really do this C15 church justice. I do remember the lovely patina of high backed pews with uniformly carved bench ends, and the elaborately carved pulpit on which, according to the church notes, there used

St Mary's Ewelme curious monument

to be an hour glass (the only one I've actually seen is in **St Mary's, Elham, Kent**). Church notes inform that Ewelme belonged to the eldest of Geoffrey Chaucer's four children, Thomas (1367-1434), then passed to Thomas's daughter Alice de la Pole, Duchess of Suffolk (1404-1475). I came across her alabaster monument: the base teems with many figures in alabaster, stone and wood and lying either side of the Duchess' effigy are two little angels with enormous feet, apparently covered in feathers or fish scales! I should have made time to explore further the cloisters and thirteen almshouses and to search for the headstone on the grave of Jerome K. Jerome (Three Men in a Boat), who is buried in the churchyard with his wife and daughter. But I didn't.

* * *

Yorkshire

Dales, rivers and waterfalls, moors, wolds, rugged coast, empty beaches; cities rich and poor; one Minster extraordinare, many plain chapels of ease; green parrots, wooden carved church mice and a 600 year old white rabbit; birthplace of sculptors, cricketers and David Hockney; bi-annual host to Victorian Goths. How could you not love this vast county.

I first visited Yorkshire when Charles and James planned a week of walks on the Dales for the Dawdlers to include the Ingleton waterfalls and spectacular limestone formation just north of Malham. I was thrilled when three years later Charles decided on a return visit to Yorkshire. He arranged for us to stay in self-catering cottages in countryside east of Robin Hood's Bay, this time to walk the moors. He planned various walks including one to and another from Whitby, circular walks on the moors and finally a lengthy one-way leg stretch to finish in Helmsley. Delighted to be returning to such a beautiful county, I made plans to drive up two days before we were all due to meet. After a pre-dawn departure from Chichester and an easy run up the A1 I drove into **Studeley Royal Park** not far from Fountains Abbey and **St Mary's Church** *(HG4 3DY)* a while before opening hour. To fill time before the door opened I walked across fields to nearby **St Lawrence's, Aldfield**. A plain sort of church with an unadorned interior, old box pews set in three bays all facing the no nonsense triple-decker pulpit, leaving a central square space for access. Next to the pulpit there was a simple table model of Christ's burial tomb, a reminder of Easter just past. Outside a blue plaque stated William Frith R.A., born in Aldfield on the 9th January 1819 "*left for London in 1835 'to make my fortune'*". (He certainly achieved fame, if not fortune, as a painter of portraits, scenes showing "the collision of wealth and poverty" and later a series of paintings in the style of William Hogarth). There is a strong sense from this inscription, on the gravestone of a blacksmith who had worked at the nearby Fountains Abbey, that Mister Robinson was more than ready to meet his Maker:

'Here lieth Anthony Robinson late of Fountains
Who died May the first 1756 aged 81
My hammer and stiddy lies declin'd
My bellows too has lost their wind,
My fire extinguished – my forge decayed
And in the dust my vice is laid.
My coals is spent, my iron gone,
My last nail driven, my work is done.'

Several years later, printed on the back page of the order of service for the funeral of a remarkable centenarian, an enthusiastic fisherman all his life, were these words:

God grant that I may live to fish
Until my dying day,
And when it comes to my last cast
I then most humbly pray
When in the Lord's safe landing net
I'm peacefully asleep
That in his mercy I be judged
As good enough to keep.
Blacksmith, Fisherman: heartfelt words for both.

I retraced my steps to **Studeley Royal**. In the 'anything-but-understated' style of High Victorian Gothic, St Mary's was built 1870-78 under the patronage of Lord and Lady Ripon to the design of a Mr Burges, architect. The church is sited on a rise in parkland just off the drive to Fountains Abbey. An obelisk reaches for the sky a short way from the west door while the magnificent east window faces a sweeping broad ride of mature beech trees leading to **Ripon Cathedral** *(HG4 1QS)*. I was already excited by the building so wasn't surprised by the light and fun interior. It is full of colours and touches unexpected. The vast organ dominates the north side, balanced on the south side by a fine marble tomb and an eye catching octagonal font carved from a block of purple pink marble from America depicting the four ages of man: childhood, youth, adult and old age. The chancel is very different: colour everywhere, murals on the walls, cherubs flying high on a golden dome above patterned floor mosaics, marble shafts, modern misericords and – for my added delight – oddities. Behind the choir stalls is a colourful frieze of foliage the architect has playfully interrupted at intervals with painted parrots in a variety of poses: sleeping, scratching, nibbling, cocked head peering. the south side an engineering miscalculation would have left one of the marble columns unsupported, going nowhere, so a substantial stone lion projects just so the column rests on its head. Last but by no means least, the stonemason decided to embellish his otherwise plain corner with two tiny carvings, a mouse and a snail. Go visit.

A thoroughly enjoyable morning spent in two very different churches before lunch in **Ripon** and a tour of the **Cathedral** *(HG4 1QT)* made especially memorable because an enthusiastic steward led me down into the exceptional C7th St Wilfred's crypt, possibly the inspiration for Alice's

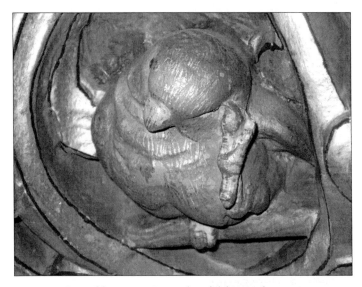

One of four poses in a colourful frieze of parrots,
St Mary's, Studley Royal

wonderland! It isn't surprising the much loved author of *Alice in Wonderland* wrote under the pen name of Lewis Carroll (1832-98): he shared both Christian and surname with his grandfather, a bishop, and his father who was a canon at All Saints, Daresbury, Cheshire at the time of his birth. Reverend. Charles Dodgson went on to become a canon of Ripon Minster as it was then known. Lewis was a regular visitor to The Old Hall, 33 High Street, Agnesgate, a Georgian town house next to the Cathedral. It is quite likely he was familiar with the crypt, descending down worn stone steps into a narrow passage leading to a small room. Leaving this room to ascend steps leading out of the crypt, he would certainly have stooped to peer through a tiny aperture looking back into the room. It is also probable he would have looked at the scenes and characters carved into the misericords and taken particular note of one in which a rabbit has all but disappeared down a hole towards which another rabbit was heading, closely followed by a 'wyvern'. My friendly steward had one other oddity to show me. Above the arch leading into the choir is a small fan balcony on which sat the organist before the huge organ – 3,000 pipes ranging from 12" to 32'. In times past he doubled as the choirmaster. He solved the difficulty of conducting the boys below him with his back to them while playing the organ by manipulating, presumably with a foot, a large wooden hand extending over the edge and visible to those on the ground.

Ripon Cathedral: Griffon and two rabbits

I had almost had enough excitement for one day but turning off the A1 onto the A684 to find my Bed & Breakfast at Askrigg, I couldn't resist two more modest churches when I drove through Bedale and Wensley. Scattered all about

St Gregory's, Bedale (DL8 1AF) for some strange reason which wasn't made clear, were bears! Stuffed bears, dressed up bears, and next to each a card on which was written the bear's name: One-eyed Gregory Bear, *'here to welcome you to St Gregory's and encourage you to look for all the other bear*s'; bell ringer Bob is in charge of *eight big bells and one small one*; Chris in a white christening dress lounging against the font; Fiona, Lucy lighting the way with her candle, a reminder as to who is *the light of the world*. Jenny bear is church warden, not to forget Fiona, Margaret, Peter, each with 'his' or 'her' special task, and Aled Bear seated in the choir because…he sings! (Aled also invites you to hunt for a Thompson mouse). I guess this is an inventive if bizarre way to encourage attendance.

The exterior of **Holy Trinity, Wensley** *(DL8 4HX)* isn't inviting but this interior held a very different surprise: the most extravagant family pew you ever did see (until later on this crawl I visited Croft-on-Tees). Exquisitely carved dark oak, draped with wine coloured curtains, this was originally the C17th opera box in which a member of the Scrope family of Bolton Castle was sitting when he fell madly in love with an opera singer. The acquisition of this box was a precondition to her acceptance of his proposal of marriage.

The Bed & Breakfast I had booked was high on the Dales overlooking Lake Semerwater. Peter and Pat, mine hosts, kindly invited me to join them for supper before falling into bed and a deep sleep. The following day I planned to head north across country, venturing a little way into County Durham before returning in time to walk down to the lake. I left soon after breakfast in the direction of Richmond. **St Michael's, Downholme** *(DL11 6AD),* perched on a rounded mound, has a bird's eye view overlooking deepest countryside. Leaving the car in a lay-by, I climbed a sheep-strewn slope, entered the churchyard through an opening in the dry stonewall encircling this modest little C14th chapel. It was so peaceful, so tempting to go no further, just stay and explore the area on foot. But on I drove through Richmond (littered at that pre-election time with blue boards writ large with William Hague's name) via Darlington on to **St Peter's, Croft-on-Tees** *(DL2 2NR)*. I remember the drive and C12th St Peter's with pleasure. Here is another corner of Yorkshire once home to the young Lewis Carroll while his father was rector of St Peter's, 1843-68. The eldest of eleven children, his ten siblings were a readymade audience for his story telling: on a wall in St Peter's is a memorial plaque depicting a white rabbit on which is written:

> I'd give all the wealth that years have piled
> The slow result of life's decay
> To be once more a little child
> For one bright summer day

Ostentatious family pew, St Peter's, Croft-on-Tees

The opera-box-cum-family-pew in Wensley doesn't quite compare with the Milbanke's family pew in **St Peter's**. This pew is a room. It is furnished, cushioned and curtained in deep red fabric, reached by a staircase with landing and insists on being noticed. The daughter of Sir Ralph Milbanke MP, Anne Isabella, married *the* Lord Byron. Maybe he too on occasion looked down on the 'ordinary' folk seated below. As I left through the south door, my attention was caught and an eyebrow raised, by a crudely carved stone plaque of a medieval gentleman, his pose showing a state – how does one say – of considerable excitement.

Next morning after Pat's excellent breakfast I thanked them for their relaxed hospitality and headed westward along the A170 towards Helmsley. I hadn't intended to stop at **St Mary's, Thirsk** *(YO7 1PR)* – the exterior exudes a heavy darkness, hardly inviting – but an empty parking space just outside was hard to resist. Inside, standing in front of the rather beautiful west window, two old boys deep in conversation, nodded 'good day' then regaled me with all they thought I needed to know about their church. The five hundred year old dark oak door, so large there is a small door within the door, was made, they assured me, from oak already three hundred years old and is still in daily use. They went on to tell me Alf Wight aka James Herriot was married in this church and, best of all, I was introduced to the famous Mouse Man for the first time. Robert Thompson (1876-1955) was born in Kilburn, near York. Although his father wished for him to become an engineer, Robert, inspired by wood carving in Ripon Cathedral, became a skilled craftsman of the medium, and each piece from 1920 was 'signed 'with a small, unobtrusive mouse. From 1930 the mice were carved without front paws as these were too susceptible to damage. Years later Robert wrote in a letter: *'The origin of a mouse as* *my mark was almost in the way of being an accident. I and another carver were carving a huge cornice for a screen and he happened to say something about being as poor as a church mouse. I said I'll carve a mouse here and so it struck me what a lovely trade mark...'* My new friends showed me two wooden wall plaques, each showing a mouse scurrying across the top. From the first mouse carved at Ampleforth College to a mouse hiding in Westminster Abbey, the Mouse Man's tiny mice are to be found on church furniture and secular pieces too. Today mice are still to be found scampering over modern items, carved by Robert's descendants, some displayed in the Robert Thompson visitor centre not far from Thirsk. On later 'crawls' I came across modern Thompson mice carved into restored church furniture in Somerset and Warwickshire; locating them usually meant crawling around under benches, peering behind chair legs.

St Mary's, Thirsk

A year earlier Charles and Angela had sent me a postcard enthusing about **St Mary's, Lastingham** *(YO62 6TN)* and, most especially, the crypt so I continued along the A170 until the village was signed off to the left. St Mary's sits on a hillock directly opposite The Blacksmith's Arms. On the street outside the pub I enjoyed a late lunch in the sun seated at a table I shared with a friendly shire horse waiting, patient and untethered, while his owner downed a pint or two indoors. The path lead to a church much altered over the centuries – nine changes according to the leaflet. What hasn't changed is the Norman crypt assumed to be part of an early stone church on the site. From the centre aisle of the nave steps lead down to the crypt into the most beautiful space with several arches and columns lined up with a tiny lancet window recessed deep behind a simple stone slab altar.

By early evening all Dawdlers had arrived and were comfortably settled: I shared one cottage with Rupert and Kate, the five couples occupying three two bedroomed cottages. Next day, walkers and non-walkers all met up at Magpies, *the* fish restaurant in Pier Road, **Whitby** opposite the fish market. It didn't take long to realise Whitby was celebrating its bi-annual Victorian gothic weekend. What fun. We ate our lunch sitting at pavement tables to watch, wide eyed, as Goths of all ages promenaded to and fro, dressed in many variations of period and modern black dress.

Before going into **St Mary's** *(YO22 4JR)* – on the wall a blue plaque proclaiming William Penn, 1644-1718, as Quaker and Founder of Pennsylvania – I photographed my namesake standing outside and a gentleman with beautiful brown eyes, a gorgeous smile, and his bi-annual hair style: a smooth pate from which he had removed all his dark hair but for two miniscule 'devil' horns to the front and a small diamond shape at the back. Both Goths quaint and quirky. One small regret: had I not been part of a group I would have spent more time in this fascinating sailors' church high above the town and harbour. Worshippers climbed up from the harbour on wooden stairs until the mid C18th when these were replaced with one hundred and ninety-nine stone steps. Not a pretty exterior but once inside I was riveted by….everything. There is no centre aisle, rather an intimidating pulpit looking over box pews which fill the nave, above and around most of which extends a deep raked gallery. Unfortunately an important family pew is positioned in front of the beautiful Norman chancel arch. According to a notice, electricity is used for the organ and bells, candles for light, but no mention of heating. Was one archaic stove coaxed into providing warmth and, if not, what, if any, heating ensures the congregation survives a winter service? Before I ran off to catch up with the Dawdlers I noticed an extraordinary carved wooden chair, several other items of interest and a memorial carved with this epitaph:

'Here lie the bodies of Francis Huntrodds and Mary his wife who were both born on the same day of the week, month and year Septr ye 19th, 1600 marry'd on the day of their birth and after having had 12 children born to them died aged 80 years on the same day of the year they were born Septr ye 19th 1680 the one not above five hours before ye other. Husband and wife that did twelve children bear, Dy'd the same day, alike both aged were, Bout 80 years they liv'd, five hours did part, (Ev'e on the marriage day) each tender heart So fit a match, surely, could never be, Both, in their lives, and in their deaths agree.'

What synchronisity.

We have always enjoyed wonderful weather for our Dawdle weeks: whether following the Parrett coast-to-coast or the Cotswolds Way, climbing in the Red Cuillins of Skye, or yomping across the West Riding of Yorkshire, the sun usually shone and this week in the North Riding was no exception. On one such sunny day three of us decided not to walk but to drive up to Durham. Whether the cathedral is viewed looking up from the river or stepping inside to behold those massive columns, it's not for me to even attempt description of this glorious building. We spent so long in the cathedral before returning to Robin Hood Bay we only had time to admire the sculpture of the Marquess of Londonderry astride his magnificent steed, a focal point in the market place. Erected in 1858 the sculptor was Rafaelle Monti (1818-1881); his most famous piece is the sublime 'Vestal Virgin' commissioned by the Duke of Devonshire which can be seen at Chatsworth House.

The week ended, I said my farewells then set off southwards under a blue sky along the coast road, destination Beverley. Just before Bridlington I made a detour to visit **St Andrew's,** in the small village of **Boynton** *(YO16 4XJ).* Light streamed into a cheerful interior furnished with green painted pews including the Strickland family pew built over the west door entrance reached south of the aisle by a graceful staircase curving upwards. It has a delightful claim to fame. A young Yorkshire lad, William Strickland, sailed to explore America from whence he returned around 1548 bringing with him six turkeys; maybe not the very first turkeys to be imported though around that time a turkey was served for the first time as a Christmas meal. With the proceeds of his trip to America and later the fortune he made from breeding turkeys, William Strickland, by now a member of parliament, was granted a coat of arms in 1550 depicting a turkey cock '*in his pride*'. Boynton Hall is still owned by his descendants and this once exotic bird is much in evidence in St Andrew's. One is depicted in the stained glass trefoil of the east window, another sits atop a rather grand monument and, best of all, the lectern is a plump turkey. Maybe, like Thompson's mouse, there are others hidden about the simple painted interior. Where else, I wonder, has an eagle been usurped by a turkey.

St Andrew's, Boynton

This church crawl ended in the friendly town of **Beverley** visiting two superb churches, one home to a mouse, the other to a rabbit. **The Minster** *(HU17 0DP)* is at the south end of Highgate, the entrance through a porch on the north side. If you haven't already visited this beautiful church I can only say you wouldn't be disappointed. I made a beeline for the choir and the sixty-eight C16th misericords, many of which depict hunter and dogs either in chase or at the kill of fox or hart. More benign are the many carvings of musicians playing different instruments. One carving is of a man having a quick cuddle with, hopefully, his wife. Wandering into a little chapel of the East Yorkshire Regiment I espied a little Thompson mouse scuttling across the base of a table. The chairs in this military chapel commemorate the fallen soldiers of WW2 – a mouse is to be found on each one.

St Mary's, Beverley *(HU17 8 DL)* is north of the square before coming to the city arch, on the corner of the road leading out of town and Hengate. More carvings; grotesques in the Norman porch, an amusing painted carving of five musicians on a pier or ledge round one of the columns, as well as other depictions of musicians dotted about. Beverley must have been big on music. Many of the carvings on St Mary's twenty-eight misericords are quite irreverent and there is an elephant carrying a howdah. On the north wall is a doorway – on the right side of the stone arch is carved an upright rabbit, about six hundred years old, smiling and wearing a satchel. As the Dodgson family lived in Hull for a while it is likely they visited Beverley and Lewis spotted this 'white rabbit'.

Having 'followed' Lewis Carroll and his rabbit from Ripon to Croft-on-Tees to Beverley it remained for me to visit **All Saints, Daresbury** *(WA4 4AE)* Cheshire, the time of his birth (1832) in the parsonage. A memorial window by artist Geoffrey Webb to this Yorkshire lad was gifted to All Saints and dedicated in 1935. Underneath all five large panels is a small one depicting scenes and creatures from *Alice in Wonderland* and Beyond the Looking Glass, surely well worth a diversion.

* * *

Pottering around the countryside the routes taken have tended to be decided by small churches yet included medieval cathedrals and abbeys along the way. It seemed wrong that previous visits, exploring the county so often referred to as God's own, hadn't included the city of York. This called for another church crawl, this time travelling west to east with a day in between exploring the city and minster. Early one morning towards the end of May I drove from Sussex to stay one night near Huddersfield, visiting two churches on the way. Although I was confronted by a locked door – so often the case in these days of organised theft – **All Saints Chapel**, **Steetley** *(S80 3D)* in Derbyshire, not far east of the M1, just to view the beauty of the exterior and the setting made the detour so worth while. There is much to admire even from outside the essentially Anglo-Norman (1066-1350) restored chapel: its easy to see the divisions of nave, chancel and apse and the three arches under a triangular head of the porch leading into the south door are cared with chevrons and zig-zags. Apart from the west wall there is a line of corbels running round the exterior: though somewhat crude and weather worn, I noted a face with puffed out cheeks and a lion's head with gaping jaws. I chatted for a while to the gentleman enjoying a tea break from tending to an already immaculate churchyard before returning to the M1.

By now in South Yorkshire to the west of Sheffield I followed the road into countryside leading to the hamlet of **Midhopestones**. Narrow lanes and no parking bays I could see, reluctantly I parked in a farmyard opposite **St James' Church** *(S36 4GP)*. I could see no one of whom to ask permission other than a friendly black spaniel. This unspoilt chapel was built by the then lord of the manor in 1368, intended as a chapel of ease; these little chapels were built to save people a long walk to their parish churches. According to church notes the porch, bell housing, pews and west gallery were added in 1705. Everything about St James is beguiling. The churchyard slopes uphill, grazing cows next door, a long wide view of hills and trees beyond the chapel. Inside two-foot deep white washed walls, an insignificant small pulpit tucked into a corner, the nave lined with box pews; one is clearly identified as being the seat of Mr Jn Wilson. All the furniture and staircase fitted with a red carpet leading to a solidly built gallery is in dark oak. On a sill a jar of meadow flowers and a china piggy bank.

After a night spent near Huddersfield I drove west to the village of High Bentham just below the Yorkshire Dales and almost in neighbouring Lancashire where I was to spend two comfortable nights in The Coach House. In glorious weather I spent two or three hours walking the nearby Ingleton Waterfall Trail culminating where the Rivers Twiss and Doe conjoin. A leaflet failed to explain the origin of the names given to each successive fall: Pecca Falls, Hollybush Spout, Thornton Force, Beezley Falls, Baxenghyll Gorge and Snow Falls. On impulsive I signed up to an eighty minute walk into White Scar Cave – not for a nanosecond remove the mandatory hard hat if you wish to avoid concussion! The one was heaven, hopefully to be repeated, the other definitely not.

Happy to be above ground again I set off along the high open roads through the bleak beauty of the Dales to **St Leonard's Church, Chapel-le-Dale, Ingleton**, *(LS6 3AR)*. Another chapel-of-ease built for the benefit of the farming families to save them trekking to Low Bentham, the grey walls and roof tiles of St Leonard's sits within the dry stone walls of a graveyard 'meadow' framed by trees. By the south porch a headstone adorned with a stone anchor and chain to the memory of a Tom Kilburn, who one assumes had connections to the sea. Rather more interesting is a stone on which is a plaque which reads: *The Church Community of Chapel-le-Dale erected this plaque to the Memory of the* *many men, women and children resident in this Parish between 1870 and 1877 who died through accident or disease during the construction of the Settle to Carlisle Railway and who were buried in this churchyard.* Inside this little church with several stained glass windows commemorating various parishioners, there is a plaque dedicated to the workmen who died during the building of the Ribblehead Viaduct. They too were laid in unmarked graves. There is also a memorial to Christopher Long who died in 1924 aged twenty-two; a Cambridge undergraduate, he discovered the White Scar Cave. The cover of the information leaflet shows a painting of the church by Turner (1775-1851) dated around 1808 during a sketching tour of Yorkshire. This painting is now part of a collection of Yale University, USA.

I then drove quite literally for miles over hill down dale to visit three more churches of the Dales, each one resulting in disappointment. **St Oswald, Arncliffe** lies on the periphery of a pretty village close by a river which allegedly was the source of inspiration for Charles Kingsley to write The Water Babies: don't we all remember Mrs Do-asYou-Would-be-Done-By! The quite large church was locked. So too was **St Michael & All Angels, Hubberholme** *(BD23 5JE)* where the ashes of author and son of Bradford, JB Priestly, are buried; this was so disappointing as I had hoped to see the rood loft and several Thompson mice. My sole reason for visiting **St Wilfrid's, Burnsall** *(BD23 6BP)* in Upper Wharfdale was to see a rare example of one of John Tapsel's gates outside of East Sussex of which there was no mention in church notes. It was time to retreat to High Bentham.

After a peaceful river walk into the area known as Forest of Bowland I headed east towards Knaresborough. **St Andrew's, Blubberhouses** *(LS21 2NX)* is perched on a hillock next to the main road, built in 1856 by the lady of the local manor. Although not known as a chapel of ease it was built so as to save her ladyship's employees a long walk to the parish church, St Michael's of Fewston. Weathered oak doors to both porch and church, studded and boasting two pairs of huge decorated hinges, open into a charming interior filled with oak pews under a steeply pitched dark wooden roof; in contrast two stone columns divide a narrow north aisle. A sign on the small organ read *Made by John, Organ Builder of Oakworth, registered as made by his 'Positive Organ Company'*. I cannot explain why St Andrew's immediately felt such a friendly place to be.

The evening of my one night stopover in Knaresborough I walked along the riverside to the limestone Chapel of Our Lady of the Crag excavated into the towering rock face as a wayside shrine. John the Mason, a master carver, employed other carvers to assist in quarrying stone for Knaresborough Castle. According to tradition John's son was almost killed by a falling rock around 1408; by way of giving thanks to the Virgin Mary for saving his son John created the Grade I listed shrine that is still here today cared for by Ampleforth Abbey. Too late for entry I stood a while in dappled sunshine. A mullion window with leaded glass and aqua painted door reminded me of something out of Grimm's fairy tales but for a large black on white painted cross and huge carving of a man sporting a fine mustachio and wearing knee high boots.

Although I was to stay just west of York I decided to take a detour slightly south to **Mary's Chapel, Lead, Saxton** *(LS24 9QN)*. A little way out of the village I parked outside The Crooked Billet directly opposite a field on the far side of which sits the smallest of chapels. I walked over spongy long grass and through a tatty wooden gate in an excuse of a fence around the south door. It was locked. Or so I thought. I returned to the pub to enquire where I could find the key holder. The young girl looked surprised. "Just stick your finger in the 'ole, wiggle to find the latch then lift". Feeling rather foolish I hadn't worked that out for myself, I returned to this enchanting little place of worship now I the care of the C.C.T. but once the centre of a community long dispersed. The light filled interior is a delight. No matter some of the irregular stones of the walls are touched with green mould; pale oak pews sit on a floor of stone flags; the font tucked in the corner resembles a cheddar truckle way beyond its best; on the crude stone altar a plain cross and *two* vases of meadow flowers. On the back of the door someone had stencilled and written odd snippets of information in no particular order: ***Re-dedicated by the Bishop of Whitby Nov 6th 1932. This Chappell Repaired in 1784. Restored by Voluntary Labour in Charge of Jack Winterburn 1932 A.D. Built about 1150 A.D.*** Other words and letters were illegible. The gorgeousness of this chapel was so worth the detour.

Mary's Chapel, Lead, Saxton

After a restorative coffee in Pocklington I followed lanes through farmland to **St Etherburga, Great Givendale** *(YO42 1TT)*. It doesn't matter the only memory I have of this church is the ornate 3' tall wooden font lid; the view from benches thoughtfully arraigned along the south wall was beyond description. I ate my picnic lunch looking down the valley far into the distance; in the centre, between sides gently curving into woodland a large lake, no doubt a magnet for vast numbers of grey-lag geese grazing nearby. I fell into interesting conversation with a couple of walkers – genetetists – who came to occupy another bench. I learned St Etherburga is on Wolds Way.

I'm not sure why I included a visit to **St Andrew's, Bugthorpe** *(YO41 1QL)*, a far from small church shaded by a magnificent copper beech. Both nave and chancel are long and well lit by tall, clear glass windows. Three high roofs are painted deep blue, decorative red steelwork within wooden trusses mimicking the red carpet leading through the nave; suspended from the centre roof a highly decorative blue and red canopy divided into squares at the centre of each a golden sun. The hassocks rather than the building engaged my attention. It seemed the good ladies of the parish had decided to cross-stitch each one with the name of a Regiment, a Someone or a Something with merely a handful depicting rural scenes. Here are some I jotted down: *We will remember them; Epiphany; Immaculate conception; Earl of Halifax; Vicar; Sing to the Lord; Royal Fusiliers; Owl; Green Howards; Wiltshire Regiment; Royal Army Service Corps; Christened; West Yorkshire Regiment; R.A.F; West Somerset Yeomanry; Warden; Queen Elizabeth the Queen Mother; Greta's Golden Wedding, 50 years; RAF Red Arrows; Northumberland Fusiliers; York & Lancaster Regiment; Jubilee Queen Regina; 4th/7th Royal Dragoon Guards; Women's Royal Army Corps;*

King's Royal Rifle Corps; and finally *Centenary Birthday 4ᵗʰ Aug 2000 Queen Elizabeth the Queen Mother.* A collection unlike any other I have come across.

Whereas not far away in **All Saints, Kirby Underdale** *(YO41 1QY)* the congregation had to make do with scrappy bits of carpet laid along pews and dull kneelers. However this attractive little church with a large, squat tower dominating the nave roof and rough stone interior walls is most appealing and the hillside countryside location simply gorgeous. A few miles along the ridge **St Mary's, Fridaythorpe** *(YO25 9RT)* could be hardly more unprepossessing. Cottages and farm buildings surround a generous village square at the centre of which is a substantial pond teeming with duck life drifting around a duck house so upmarket in appearance I did not understand why it was named Muck House instead of Duckingham Palace. A marker for St Mary's pointing down a grassy path between two buildings led to a squat, flat-roofed tiny church in a field. It was locked. I wasn't disappointed. I was so puzzled about the location of **St Mary's, Wharram-le-Street** *(YO17 9TN)* I enlisted the help of two policemen but even Dixon-of-not-the Green had to admit defeat. **St Michael, Barton-le-Street** *(YO17 6PN)* was also locked though easy to find. The C12th church was largely replaced in Victorian times but the impressive Norman porch with a splendid triple arch remains intact as do some entertaining exterior corbels, many of them humans faces with popping eyes, twisted mouths, weird expressions. Worth stopping by before going on to admire the single elongated upholstered footstools running the width of each pew in **St Martin's, Bulmer** *(YO60 7DN),* an elegant alternative to hassocks, and then to agree with the words inscribed on a bench by the porch of **St Helen's, Amotherby** *(YO17 6TN)* – locked – in tune with the wildflower meadow that is the churchyard:

The kiss of the sun for pardon
The song of the birds for mirth
One is nearer God's heart in a garden
Than anywhere else on earth

As advised by my landlady I took the scenic high road less travelled running parallel to the main road from York. **St James', Fordon** *(YO2 3HT)* is a pop-in-if-you're-passing picture perfect small church tucked in amongst trees on a hillside above farm buildings; inside a few rows of pews, white washed walls bare but for one painting of the church. My objective that day was a beach walk and visit to **St Leonard's** *(YO14 9TD)* on the periphery of **Speeton**, a coastal village between Filey and Bridlington. St Leonard whose feast day is on the 6th November is the patron saint of prisoners and captives: paintings show him wearing fetters and chains. There has been a church on this spot forever: 1451 made mention of a chaplain; in 1650 the chapel was included in the Parliamentary survey of that year; for twenty years from 1743 the curate was an absent one. In the C19th local farmers maintained the church, It was during this time services were held every six weeks or so; this gave smugglers the opportunity to store their contraband in the chapel furnished in those days with family box pews. These were replaced with pine ones in 1911 until permanent oak ones were made to *'match the altar rails in 1977, the offcuts made into an organ stool, screen and ash trays!'*

In 1940, post the evacuation from Dunkirk soldiers and infantrymen from the Royal Artillery and Royal Berkshires Infantry were billeted in nearby Church Farm granaries while Nissen huts were built to accommodate them. According to church notes *'Bessie Coleman cleared everything out of the front parlour at Church Farm from where she ran a canteen to feed the soldiers, with help from women of the village, until 1944'.*

My final day in Yorkshire was spent in its beautiful medieval city exploring the **Minster** and crypt; walking the scenic stretch of the city wall from Bootham Bar to Monk Bar with a wonderful view and sense of the vast size of the minster; finding Holy Trinity, Goodramsgate, the one city church still furnished with the original box pews. Time to head south pausing only to pop into the graveyard of **St Helen's, Welton** *(HU15 1NH)* curious to find a certain gentleman's headstone before crossing the Humber Bridge. The simple stone stands behind the east wall: *'Here lieth He ould Jeremy who hath eight times maried been but now in his ould Age he lies in his cage under The grass so green which Jeremiah Simpson departed this Life in the 84 yeare of his Age in the year of Our Lord 1719'.* Eight wives did not appear to wear out this Yorkshire lad whereas the very thought of a long drive south made me sigh.

* * *

Old London: Churches and Cemeteries

The most remarkable thing about the City churches is that they are there at all, considering The Great Fire in 1666 and The Blitz in 1940, and considering too the rebuilding and new building in the City. Towers and spires ensure some churches stand out, whilst others are squeezed on both sides by modern buildings or reduced to littleness by the sheer size and height of, say, The Gherkin. In the sprawling C19th cemeteries of London the great, the good and the bizarre lie alongside each other......

One December Vanessa and I took the District Line to the City. Emerging from Monument tube station we headed towards **St Magnus-the-Martyr**, its beautiful steeple soaring high above Lower Thames Street. The medieval building survived until the C17th with minimal change or disruption then after the year the Great Plague of 1665, emanating from a bakehouse in Pudding Lane, came the Great Fire of London. St Magnus was one of the nearest and first buildings to be destroyed. Overseen by Christopher Wren the church was re-built between 1671-84 only to suffer another fire in 1760 started in the south-east corner of the church; it destroyed most of the roof. Since then many alterations though it survived unscarred by the Second World War. The rather gloomy interior, High Church in style, is full of dark finely worked wood, some of it the work of the Anglo-Dutch woodcarver Grinling-Gibbons (1648-1721; the reredos, pulpit and tester are all enormous. What really caught our eyes was an extraordinarily detailed model of the old London Bridge lovingly made, the steward informed us, by a retired policeman. It was teeming with tiny models of people, carts and horses in the midst of which this craftsman had been unable to resist including a modern policeman. The familiar blue helmet blended among the yeomen's brown tunics surprisingly well. Vanessa picked him out first.

We went on to **St Mary-at-Hill**, its square interior empty following a fire in 1988, since when rescued fittings have been held in storage until restoration is possible. We were disappointed to find **St Mary Abchurch** is only open on Tuesdays so we were unable to see the Grinling Gibbons reredos. Of **St Mary Woolnoth** I remember nothing. The fan ceiling in **St Mary Aldermary** is gorgeous, the windows dedicated variously to the Worshipful Company of Tanners, Painters and Stainers, Skinners, Innsmen et al. The church with the wow factor has to be **St Stephen Walbrook;** 1672-79 from foundation stone to completion. We were both bowled over by this sumptuous Wren interior dominated by a huge dome and filled with light from the clerestory windows. Damaged during the War, Lord Palumbo as church warden was the force behind restoration of this beautiful church. This possibly helped him win over dissenting voices when he introduced the controversial rounded modern altar by Henry Moore encircled by rows of pale beech wood seating. To one side, in sharp contrast, is the dark wood of the grand pulpit underneath an ornate oversized tester.

Two years later when Margaret was visiting from Johannesburg we made a similar crawl. I remember we returned to **St Stephen** and **St Magnus** and I took a photograph of **St Margaret Pattens** reflected in the glass frontage of a particularly hideous modern block. We peeked into the gloom of **St Michael Paternoster** where Dick Whittington, four times Mayor of London, is buried and where there is a stained glass window commemorating both him and his cat.

St Stephen Walbrook

Whittington plaque

During our visit to the City churches Vanessa and I settled for a sandwich seated at a counter in an outlet catering more for take away sales than in-house comfort. This mode of eating was not good enough for Margaret. I scuttled after her as she swung into Castle Court and disappeared inside The George & Vulture, into a large and noisy dining room filled with Business Suits where we settled down to a 'proper' meal. Ours were the only skirts in the room!

Long before visiting precious City churches, so dependant for their survival on The Friends of City Churches, one autumnal day I made my way to the original **Highgate Cemetery**. Hopping off the tube from Wimbledon to Archway, a brisk walk up Highgate Road – a route once followed by tumbrils carrying prisoners to the guillotine – led through Waterlow Park to the two cemeteries: the western side opened in 1839, the eastern in 1854. Visitors to the **western Highgate Cemetery** can only do so by joining a guided tour. Entry is through huge iron gates flanked by two mortuary chapels. The groups are small, the guides well informed. I subsequently paid a visit during the height of summer but for me autumn is the perfect time to go: closely planted trees form a dense canopy over dew-damp, tangled rampant undergrowth framing and festooning myriad headstones and monuments, creating an atmosphere Gothic, sombre, not quite spooky. Everywhere are graves adorned with a cross or urn draped in cloth – symbolism so beloved by the Victorians – others eye catching in their difference. A huge lion dozes atop the tomb of G. Wombwell, menagerist attributed with importing the first exotic animal into the country, a boa constrictor. A large sleeping dog guards the tomb of his master Tom Sayers, said to be the last of the bare-fisted fighters. One could be forgiven for thinking George Osbaldeston (1786-866) whose grave is covered with multiple whips, was a devotee of S & M instead of setting the record in 1831 for the fastest journey on horseback over 200 miles. The record held until champion jockey Peter Scudamore just managed to beat the time in 1993. John Betjamin would be pleased his father lies in unkempt undergrowth amongst eccentrics of note; though George Eliot (1819-1880) is buried in the Eastern Cemetery across the road, her partner of many years Mr Lewes (1854-78) and her husband Mr Cross, married in 1880, are both here. An ignominious resting place for *the* most celebrated of scientists, Michael Faraday (1791-1867): devout Christian though he was, is in unconsecrated ground near the boundary wall because he was a member of the Church of Scotland. Rising above all other residents of the cemetery is the magnificent mausoleum of one Julius Beer (1836-80). An immigrant from Germany he was the Richard Branson of his day, business man, newspaper baron who amassed a fortune in London. However, as a Jew, he never achieved the social acceptance he craved during his lifetime. Not to be so put down, he renounced his Jewish faith to become an Anglican. This enabled him to purchase the prime hilltop spot in the cemetery in which is sealed an exquisite marble monument to his little daughter who died aged years old. o in death at last to laud it over all those below him forever more. Love it!

Our guide led us through an imposing gateway into the Egyptian Avenue, flanked on both sides by sort of cupboards, on each door an upside down torch to symbolise the end of life. The avenue opens out into a sunken circle lined with catacombs in the centre of which is an ancient Cedar of Lebanon tree, huge but effectively a bonsai, constrained as the mound is by a retaining wall. In the outer chambers, created after the advent of the first crematorium, rest many, many containers of ashes. Apparently the chamber at the foot of which the most floral tributes are consistently laid is that of Radclyffe Hall, author of the first 'shocking' – at the time – novel about a lesbian love, *The Well of Loneliness*.

It was hard to keep up with the flow of information from both guides: we were taken to a collection of Rossetti graves; one containing Emmeline Pankhurst's children; another a simple headstone for Elizabeth Jackson, the very first person to be laid in Highgate; and, on the second more recent tour, we passed by a simple pink marble new headstone, that of Alexander Litvinenko (1962-2006), the Russian so tragically poisoned allegedly by a former colleague and member of the federal secret service. Also memorable was a tatty old tin lying on a shelf in a catacomb corridor containing the ashes of R. Liston, the first surgeon to perform major operations under ether. Finally I couldn't help smiling at a relatively new headstone of a merry widow: Rosella Burt *"thrice widowed by three loving husbands, a much loved lady who died on 30th May 1995"*. Ninety-six years old, simply of old age, surely not boredom.

A few years later, with several hours to fill waiting for my visa for Mongolia to be processed, I remembered how interesting it was to explore Highgate Cemetery so caught a bus to the gates of **Brompton Cemetery**, created 1840. It was on the verge of a face-lift, of major restoration funded by the Lottery and English Heritage. Vast and hugely over grown, the central avenue in constant use as a thoroughfare, my impression then was of a space in great need of a flock of sheep (an impractical solution as the through-fare is popular with dog walkers). I wandered around a jumble of headstones and huge mausoleums, accompanied by a cacophony of indignant green parakeets perched in the canopies of many trees, disturbing squirrels and blackbirds grubbing around underneath. There are a considerable number of graves of

George Wombwell's grave,
West Highgate Cemetry

Grave of Michael Faraday,
pauper's corner
Highate Cemetry

Emmerline Pankhurst

Polish men and women, most beautifully looked after; I stopped to admire one fenced and kempt area filled with plain white war graves; to pause before a simple headstone marking the very first burial in this cemetery, Emma Shaw (1817-40) who died in childbirth. Emmeline Pankhurst, whose children lie in Highgate, is buried here and one more caught my eye: the two children of one of the Eaton families of Toronto, Canada. It instantly recalled my brief spell as nanny to John Eaton, the then small son of the family, owners of the Eaton department store in Toronto. I wondered why they were laid to rest so far from home.

Time to collect my visa. I promised myself a return visit on completion of the restoration project.

* * *

Mostly East Anglia

I decided to embark on a church crawl, anti-clockwise round London, starting with a visit to sister Liz in Essex, continuing on through Suffolk, Cambridgeshire, Norfolk, then choosing a route traversing Lincolnshire and Derbyshire to spend two days with Penny and Tim in Shropshire before returning home.

I arrived chez Liz and Michael in time for a leisurely breakfast and then set off to find the two Essex churches I had earmarked. The steep pitch of the roof of **St Michael's, Copford** *(CO6 1DG)*, reminded me of St Mary's Hospital in Chichester, the magnificent roof of which sweeps down to just over two metres off the ground. I recall twelve carved animal bench ends – bush baby, hedgehog, rabbit, weasel, rat owl, sheep, falcon, squirrel, duck, fox and pigeon – but to my shame no more of this large church, before driving on to the memorable **St Mary's, Great Warley** *(CM1 33JP)*. The churchyard is more a tidy garden, planted with limes and a favourite of mine, *quercus palustris,* pin oak. Tall and pyramidal, unlike the rounded, spreading form of its English cousin, the familiar leaf shape is much attenuated and when dressed for autumn the vibrant colours are maple red and orange. I wonder why they aren't more commonly grown. The church is kept locked but I was able to track down the caretaker, Sue, who very kindly opened the heavy porch door. A plaque commemorates the laying of the foundation stone at eleven thirty on the morning of July 5th, 1902 by a Mrs Heseltine, wife of stockbroker Evelyn who funded the land and building. What a sensational building if a tad bizarre! The Arts and Crafts interior, surely unmatched in the variety of materials, design, and superb craftsmanship, may well be a little hectic for some sensibilities but other than the font rising from a central marble column on an octagonal plinth flanked by two 'legs' supporting two tall brown angels opposite each other across the basin – hideous! – I admired it all, despite the gloom for lack of natural light, and came out wearing a big smile. Various notable craftsmen were involved but Eric Gill was the only name familiar to me.

From Essex, I followed the A131 to two beautiful Suffolk towns, Long Melford and Lavenham. Once a very rich wool county, this wealth reflected in their extravagant churches. That said, what I particularly remember of the splendid interior of **Holy Trinity, Long Melford** *(CO10 9DL)* is the medieval glass roundel above the north door: a trinity of three hares share three ears yet all appear to have two each! Though slightly damaged, it's a charming depiction of three in one, one in three. While wandering in wonder around the magnificent **St Peter & St Paul's, Lavenham** *(CO10 9QT)*, I came across my first misericords. I have been riveted by these carvings ever since. There were five of them, only the pelican in her piety having any religious meaning; a man crouching; a man playing bagpipes with a pig tucked under one arm; a man's head apparently being attacked by an ibis and a spoonbill; a half-woman, half-dragon playing a viola with a half man, half beast playing bellows. Wonderfully weird! A contemporary feature – and achievement – of this church is the 261 kneelers hand-stitched by eighty-seven volunteers comprising one hundred and fifty designs, all completed by 2000 to celebrate the millennium. Some of the most charming reference Suffolk and the locality: the church bell cast in 1625; Suffolk sheep recorded in the Doomsday book as grazing local pastures in 1086; children at play in the local primary school; the endangered Suffolk Punch heavy horse; the Lavenham herd of Friesian cows introduced in 1920; an extensive range to commemorate local buildings and customs. They received rather more attention from me than did the fabric of the building.

I spent the next two nights with Ailah and Peter, a happy base from which to explore a few more churches before heading for Norfolk and a Bed & Breakfast near Fakenham. After breakfast, I called in at **St Peter & St Paul, Kedington** *(CB9 7NN)* where I remember seeing, propped on a window ledge, an Anglo-Saxon stone cross depicting a crudely carved image of a man with outstretched arms. Driving through Newmarket, past stud farms and centre of flat racing, I fully expected to see horses if not everywhere at least in fields stretching behind miles of beautifully maintained hedging. I didn't even see a pony! On to another once rich town where **St Mary & St Andrew, Mildenhall** *(IP28 7EA)* reflects the wealth of yesteryear, not least in the roof, remarkable for large and small angels with outstretched wings flying between trusses.

Ely Cathedral was my main and final destination that day but, with time in hand, I decided to take a minor road through the Fens. I can only think I pulled off the road in front of **St Andrew's, Isleham** *(CB7 5RX),* awarded one star by Simon, just because it was there and the opportunity to stretch my legs was appealing. I'm embarrassed to admit to not fully appreciating what this church has to offer. I don't recall going into the chancel where I would now make a bee-line for the medieval choir stalls and misericords. Transfixed, I looked no further than the two adjacent family monuments within which Sir Robert (d.1590) and Sir John (d.1616) are side by side with their wives in pious contemplation. They lie on slabs of marble suspended by six shapely white marble 'legs' on stone plinths; above them six tall white columns support marble canopies embellished with ends and frontispieces to include their coats of arms, carved painted and gilded, black red and gold, to grandiose effect; not an inch left unadorned. Even if churches are not your thing – in which case you wouldn't be reading this anyway – should you drive through this village in the Fens, do stop and be amazed by these monuments.

Driving along near empty roads across the Fens, criss-crossed with irrigation canals, I gave thanks I did not, as advised, buy a house near Cambridge upon my return from South Africa to England. I fell hopelessly in love with a little cottage facing the green at Coton, a village perfectly situated just outside the city. Fortunately – though at the time I was hugely disappointed – the survey was dire. No other cottage appealed and so to Sussex and the South Downs, a move never once regretted not least because of the joy of walking the Downs. Meanwhile, ahead lay **Ely Cathedral** (*CB7 4DL*), its vast presence dominating a flat, almost treeless landscape of the fens from whichever direction one approached. I was completely bowled over and awed by this magnificent cathedral, famous for the unique octagonal wooden lantern tower. In no hurry to leave I wandered around, exploring both cathedral and city, for the rest of the afternoon. Over the years since I have visited a number of cathedrals, mostly but not all medieval. Every one of them leaves me awestruck: the many, many years of construction without cranes to lift blocks of stone, without computers to calculate what would and wouldn't stand up; dependent instead on wooden scaffolds, master stone masons, armies of labouring men, skilled craftsmen and inevitably lives lost in the building.

After breakfast next day I took my leave of Ailah and Peter and set off to find Mundford. I expect the vicar is sorry I did find St Leonard's. Having collected the key from him, gained entry, I was unable remove it or even lock the church so returned to the vicarage to make confession. Further into Norfolk three churches more notable than I gave them credit. **St Bartholomew's, Brisley** *(NR20 5AA),* a large church in a small village, with an extensive crypt under the sanctuary, lovely box pews and some fun bench ends. Two other large churches, **St Agnew's, Cawston** *(NR10 4AG)* and **St Peter & St Paul's, Salle** *(NR10 4SE)* dominate flat, isolated landscapes; I didn't venture very far into the vast rather soulless interiors so failed on that excursion to see the misericords and poppyheads.

In complete contrast to those large edifices, and more appealing to me, sitting on a hill outside the village is **St Andrew's, Little Snoring**, a small Norman church with a detached round tower. Apparently this is unusual as is a curious top-knot with what look like bird boxes. A notice directs one to a military tombstone in the graveyard where lies a female officer of the RAF who achieved the rank of Section Officer, WAAF, and died in Singapore. I found my Bed & Breakfast easily in good time for a walk around the fields and lanes before supper and a good night's sleep in a comfortable room. Over breakfast, my hostess told me her husband is a wildlife photographer, sometimes away for several weeks if not months at a time. No doubt hard for her but, judging from the extraordinary camera work which is so much part of David Attenborough's wild life documentaries, much to public benefit. Her life surely compares with that of a naval wife.

I set off to the coast in the morning, to **St Margaret's, Cley-next-the-Sea** *(NR25 7TT).* Large and beautiful though

I found it, I was happy not to go inside, just photograph the ruined south window before following the coast westward to find a church actually on a hill. **St Clement's, Burnham Overy** is a simple little church in which I sat awhile chatting to an elderly lady before driving on to **St Margaret's, Burnham Norton** *(PE31 8JA)*. Also small and simple, the porch and south door are at the extreme westernmost end of the church. A Saxon flint tower is central to the building – unusual, as this isn't the most stable of positions for a tower. I hadn't seen a piscina on the floor before. Admiral Nelson's father, the Revd. Edmund Nelson, was Rector (1755-1766) followed by his brothers, Suckling and William, each serving two or three years. Young Horatio would have walked through the graveyard on his way from the rectory to watch ships at sea.

Walpole St Peter *(PE14 7NS)* was my last port of call that day. It's a shame it's in such dreary urban surroundings because it is such a magnificent church, not far from the Sandringham Estate and apparently a favourite of Prince Charles. There was a flower festival that day so the church was overrun with visitors. Something called a hudd caught my eye. It looks like a sentry box and was used to keep the vicar dry during burial services in the rain. Very few remain; it wasn't until I was 'crawling' in Kent I came across two others. Reached by a flight of steps, the chancel, considerably higher than the nave, is built over a cobbled street passing underneath. Dominating the lawn an enormous copper beech, its canopy almost extending the length of the church: I imagined it in early spring, branches thick with bright pink brown leaves. Glorious!

I'm not quite sure where I stayed overnight after leaving Norfolk though I do remember the Bed & Breakfast was one of those establishments where tissue boxes and loo rolls wore beribboned lace covers, carpets were sensibly patterned and breakfast was mean. The A16 headed north through flat farmland to **St Botolph's, Boston** *(PE21 6NW)* where my sole aim was to climb the famous Stump. A spire was planned for the tower but never built because of fears of overloading the foundations, massive though they were. The tower, at 272 ft, is the tallest in England so no real need for a spire. Overwhelmed by the inordinately and intricately carved grand font standing atop an eight-sided triple stone step complete with mounting-block and angel- topped lid, the whole designed by Pugin – who else? – I failed to take in the full glory of the interior, including the sixty-two misericords in the choir stalls. Instead, I exchanged £5 for a ticket to climb worn stone steps spiralling to the top of one tower from where I was meant to take in a view rolling out for miles over the town and surrounding flat landscape. I can only imagine this view as my silly fear of heights got the better of me. I crouched behind the parapet, scurried across to the other tower and descended in haste, an ignominious retreat.

My last church visit that day was to **St Wulfram's, Grantham** *(NG31 6RR)*. The soaring, slender, decorated spire is beautiful, the huge interior rather daunting. I crept in at the very end of a service and almost immediately I was handed a cup of coffee and offered a biscuit, a friendly case of mistaken identity! By way of conversation I admired the excessively elaborate font cover. A dear old boy noted my interest so folded back a pair of small doors to reveal three highly painted figures. I was told the cover, commissioned to celebrate Queen Victoria's diamond jubilee in 1897, was installed two years later at a cost of £300 and that the figures represent Edward the Confessor and a couple of saints. Carried away with enthusiasm for his church, this friendly man led me to the chancel down worn stone steps leading to the C14 crypt where there is a rare stone altar. Realising I was in danger of receiving a lengthy history lesson, I thanked him sincerely, saying I had to be on my way.

It was just as well I excused myself as the ensuing drive to Ashbourne was something of a nightmare. I had no idea Nottingham is so huge or that Derby is so close and that staying on the right ring road in the correct lane – without the help of Tim Tom Tom I so depend upon these days! – would prove to be so problematic. I lost my way, found my way, lost it again and when, eventually, I really was on the open road there was a road block and diversion due to a bad accident.

St Oswald's, Ashbourne *(DE6 1DR)* is a beautiful church to which, I'm ashamed to say, I paid the most fleeting of visits and left with only one memory. Next to two 'standard' marble tombs – figure lying down, hands clasped in prayer, feet resting on a small dog – is the smaller white marble tomb of little Penelope Boothby who died in 1791, aged five. She lies on her side, hands clasped under her chin, head propped on pillows. The carving is delicate, Penelope enchanting. Leaving Penelope I drove up the B5035 to **St Mary's in Wirksworth** *(DE4 4DQ)* a small town in hills bordering the Peak District National Park. Inside I did, of course, look at the stone for which it is well known. In 1820, a slab within the church was lifted to reveal…. A perfect human skeleton. The underside of this coffin lid, now mounted on a wall within the church, is densely carved, teeming with people illustrating biblical stories. There wasn't time to drive on to Eyam, the Peak District village famous for barricading itself against the Great Plague of 1685 (visited on a later 'crawl'), but time enough to climb into my boots and follow a narrow lane between small stone cottages of some age to stretch my legs awhile climbing though rugged countryside so different from the gentle slopes of the Sussex Downs. En route I paused at a farm gate to commune with a gang of inquisitive rams, possibly out to pasture to rest and recover from an exhausting and busy summer.

As memorable as little Penelope Boothby, though for very different reasons, is the Bed & Breakfast I had booked for one night. My heart sank even as I walked up a path past every kind of garden ornament known to enthusiasts including, of course, a hopeful gnome watching his line dangling into a twinkly little pond. Sprawled on one of those canopied swing seats lay a real live gnome. He raised his can of beer and called across to let me know the missus was indoors. Mrs Double Gnome appeared, complete with welcoming smile, enquiry after my journey and invitation to follow her lurching derriere up the stairs to my room. I think she was genuinely proud of what she offered. More a pine frame than four-poster bed: pushed into a corner it took up most of the floor barely leaving sufficient space for a table large enough for a television, kettle and mug. When I asked where was the promised en suite, Mrs DG pointed to the door next to the head of the bed, suggested a pub for supper, informed me when breakfast would be served, and left. I tentatively opened the door to an en suite the likes of which I had not seen before or indeed, since. It had been, and still was, a cupboard into which a plastic unit had been fitted comprising shower, basin and loo, all compressed into so little space one could have taken care of *everything* at once. After a minimal breakfast comprising white toasted bread, plastic jam and butter, stewed coffee, I was eager to be off to Cheadle.

I walked the short distance from Cheadle's town centre car park surrounded by the usual mix of shops towards the slender, very tall steeple of **St Giles RC, Cheadle** *(ST10 1ED)*. Inside the church railings an old man was hauling an antique lawn mower up and down the grass to no discernable effect. The impressive west double door was but a taster of astonishing treats to come. Nothing I can write could possibly add to what has already been said of the sight to greet one's eyes on entering AWN Pugin's masterpiece, *une eglise extraordinaire:* adorning every single inch of surface in hectic colour there is pattern, design, carving. St Augustine's at Ramsgate, a flint church designed and paid for by Pugin, a superb gift to the country, completed exactly as he had envisaged, is now high on my list to visit. St Giles was a magnificent church with which to end this Crawl. I went on to spend two relaxing, non-driving days with Penny and Tim in Shropshire before facing the long drive home.

* * *

St Peter & St Paul's, Lavenham, 67 box balls

More Norfolk

When friend Rotti moved, somewhat reluctantly, from her known and much loved patch in Sussex to Norfolk, a county unknown to her beyond a distant holiday on The Broads, she urged all her friends to visit as soon as the spare beds were made up. I well remembered the landscape and churches visited when I first explored Norfolk so I didn't need encouraging. It would be fun to catch up with Rotti anyway and even more fun to have her company as we cantered around the county visiting some of the numerous round tower churches for which Norfolk is well known.

It was dark and foggy pre-dawn when I set off from Chichester, hoping to navigate the motorways and the Dartford Tunnel while roads were still relatively clear. I intended to pop in to see the one remaining virgin's bonnet in St Michael's, Theydon Mount *(CM16 7PP),* but of course the church, isolated atop a high mound, was still closed around half-past seven when I eventually parked outside. A little later on, **St Mary's, Burwell** *(CB25 0HB)* compensated for this minor disappointment.

As I approached this large church, it seemed natural to chat to the kind man who directed my car into a tight space. A fortuitous meeting, as he walked me over dew-damp, snowdrop-sprinkled grass to a headstone erected in memory of seventy-eight villagers who perished in a barn fire on 8th September, 1727. According to village records '*a great number of persons were met together to watch a puppet show. In the barn were many loads of straw ....the barn was thatched with straw........the fire flew like lightning in an instant.*' To prevent the rough, unwelcome element entering the barn, the door had been nailed shut. There are conflicting accounts as to how the fire started. Was it the negligence of a servant who set a candle near a heap of straw? Or did someone who, on his death bed, confessed to harbouring a grudge against the puppeteer 'commit that diabolical action' and deliberately start the fire? The outcome, a hideous tragedy, was the same. The interior of this large church is exceptionally light as the edifice has been constructed with almost as much glass as wall. A group of very small children, dressed up as fairies or insects, was gathered in the choir singing a song to thank Him for the sun and rain.

After a quick look at six splendid bench ends, I skidaddled and drove on to **St Mary the Virgin, Lakenheath** *(IP27 9DS),* especially to view the quirky collection of bench ends. After five hundred years of use, some were worn or missing an extremity, but a surprising number are still intact and beautiful. The variety of carved creatures is intriguing: a whale or big fish swallowing another; an otter bent over itself; a bearded man with his harvest; an animal licking itself; a howdah on something that wasn't really an elephant; a big cat looking in a mirror; other creatures, men in various positions and a bizarre carving of two people entwined most intimately! Above, them a host of angels, wings outstretched, gaze down from their lofty position.

Tim TomTom and a "where next?" telephone call combined to direct me up the dirt track to Rotti's house-in-a-field, from where we would go exploring over the two days of my visit. I had come to Norfolk to catch up with my friend, of course, and also to see some of the one hundred and seventy round tower churches for which Norfolk is well known. There are others – in northern Germany, northern Poland, southern Swedan, the Orkney Islands and Suffolk, even three in Sussex – but nowhere else are there so many. I understand most, but not all, these towers are built of rubble or puddlestone, an inferior building material.

No sooner was I fed and watered and several large dogs ensconced in the back of the Volvo, Rotti wasted no time introducing me to a nearby church, part of her own tour for visitors to Norfolk. **St Mary the Virgin, Houghton-on-the-Hill** *(PE37 8FB)* does indeed sit on a mound. The medieval nave sits snug between a tall square tower added in the C15th and a tiny apse chancel rebuilt mid C18th. This out-of-the-way very small, church is special, not least because of the gentleman who made possible its restoration. We arrived to find him, there *in person* to recount its history! Some twenty years before we met bearded Bob Davey, retired Water Board superintendent from West Sussex, together with his wife 'discovered' this church, semi ruined and completely covered with undergrowth, while rambling in the area. Its restoration, much of it funded by him with later support from the Heritage Lottery Fund and others, became a project and a passion to which he has devoted his retirement. Intriguing Romanesque wall paintings dating from the C12th to C14th were revealed, including a rare and significant *mandorla*. The only other complete set from the same centuries is in gorgeous St Mary's, Kempley in Herefordshire. The Italian word for 'almond', *mandorla* is an almond shaped form enclosing Christ and the Virgin Mary. Incidentally the same shape is also known as an *Ichthys*, Greek for fish: it refers to a symbol of two arcs extending at one end to resemble a fish profile. Bob Davey's endeavours and the extraordinary paintings came to the attention of Prince Charles, who visited three times, and Princess Margaret. While Rotti's dogs dozed, sprawled about the aisle, Bob proudly showed us photographs of his royal visitors and one of him receiving his MBE in well deserved recognition of his work. Bob Davey, nonagenarian, died in March 2021, nine years to the month after our visit to his beloved church. His obituary in the broadsheets described in detail the various obstacles – including seeing off Satanists and building a one mile access road – this very determined gentleman had to overcome to restore a treasure that could so easily have been subsumed by nature.

Bob Davey, saviour of St Mary the irgin,Houghton-on-Hill

Next morning we mapped our route for the day over breakfast then piled one rottweiler, one bull mastiff and two shar peis into the back of Rotti's estate car. Armed with Simon's book, our plan was to find the first church south-east of Norwich, follow the coast northwards then head home anti clockwise across county. After several wrong turns we drove along a dirt track towards a small round tower church thatched, no doubt with Norfolk reeds. The setting, beyond a mound it shares with a dilapidated outbuilding and a few bare trees, is lonely and beautiful. I entered through the Norman arch into a simple interior with white-washed walls, neat rows of chairs and a splendid coffin carrier with a brass plaque dated 1908 at which stage realisation dawned – we were in the wrong church! This was not **St Margaret's, Hales** *(NR14 6QL)* but **St Gregory's, Heckingham** *(NR14 6QT)*. A bonus after a wrong turning!

A few fields away we found **St Margaret's**, thatched and very similar to St Gregory's but for the lack of a porch. The substantial round tower is C11th or C12th and thought to be older than the nave. The church notes mentioned a silhouette on the *underside* of the C17th font cover, a strange detail we couldn't resist investigating! Rotti lifted the handsome lid to reveal a silhouette showing in profile an early rector, a gentleman with a fine head of wiry hair and double chin. I was intrigued by a uniform row of graves, all covered with identical coffin shaped slabs of slate inscribed with names of eight family members, all Easters, ranging from Edward and Anne who both died in 1851 until the death of the last of their children in 1909.

We drove due north along country lanes to **St Helen's, Ranworth** *(NR13 6HT)* a short distance west of Norwich and though rural by no means a small church. The misericords were disappointing but for one, carved with a butterfly and dragonfly. However, the medieval rood screen, commissioned in 1419, is an exquisite treasure. The main screen depicts the twelve apostles: on the north side of the aisle Saints Simon, Thomas, Bartholomew, James, Andrew and Peter; on the south side Saints Paul, John, Philip, James the Less, Jude and Matthew. At right angles to the screen are two large panels: on each side the paintings include three saints. It is truly amazing after six centuries the figures and colours are still so clear and vibrant. In each side chapel four panels form a *reredos*, a screen behind the altar – I failed to note who are the various female figures.

St Helen's, Ranworth antiphoner

I spotted an unusual double-sided lectern, also known as a cantor's desk, but almost missed another treasure. Lying open, under glass, in a sturdy locked cabinet (made by inmates of Norwich jail) is an amazing book called an *antiphoner*. It is a service book written by monks five hundred years ago. The 285 pages are sheepskin, there are 19 miniature illustrations (one shows clerks gathered round a lectern similar to the one in St Helen's) and the psalms, hymns, readings prayers and responses are written in medieval Latin. It was bequeathed to the church in 1478 but with the advent of the English prayer book in 1549 it became a banned book! It then vanished to reappear three hundred years later in a private collection. Money was then raised to buy it back and return it to its home in Ranworth in 1912. Scaredy-cat that I am, I failed to navigate eight-nine spiral steps, two ladders *and* a trap door to reach the top of the tower and so missed out on a bird's eye view of surrounding countryside.

By now cold and in need of warming we stopped for a hot drink and directions to **St Mary's, West Somerton** *(NR29 4DP)* just a mile or so off the coast near Great Yarmouth. It was too cold to linger longer than to admire the wine red walls and faint wall paintings. I did seek out the tabletop tomb, sitting on little feet, which contains the remains of Robert Hales (1820-63), known as the 'Norfolk Giant'. He was born in this village to unusually tall parents and grew to 7'8" in height, 32 stone in weight. During his short life he appeared at fairs around the country before becoming licensee of a tavern in London *where his height, generosity and kindly manner* attracted attention and customers.

Keeping to the coast road, we continued north to **All Saints, Horsey** *(NR29 4EF)*. Rotti and I both loved this church. It sat as if on a snowdrop carpet amongst trees, far down a narrow lane. There was something about the interior, wall paintings and a pretty screen we both found most appealing. Maybe it was the feeling of being in a barn created by the exposed thatch of the roof, which no doubt encouraged barn owls to nest and rear their young! A charming photograph of their fledglings hung on the west wall.

We continued north along empty lanes threading through flat fields to the small coastal town of Happisburgh (pronounced *haisbra*). Barely visible under thick ivy stems wrapped around trunks, scrubby wind-tilted trees dotted a landscape enveloped in sea mist. By now we had lost all patience with Tim TomTom and, as I didn't want to be responsible for yet more wrong turns, Rotti became our intuitive map reader. The sea was hidden from view, a lighthouse barely visible through the mist which was a shame as I had envisaged us walking the beach between church and lighthouse, the dogs free to run along the shore. Thoroughly chilled through, our visit to **St Mary's, Happisburgh** was short. The octagonal C15th font made us smile. Jolly angels are depicted holding various musical instruments and a Man, a lion, an ox and an eagle represent Matthew, Mark, Luke and John. More interesting to me than the imposing fabric of this large seaside church are accounts of events connected to it. Such as the tenuous link with William Cowper, poet and hymn-writer, who visited Happisburgh both as a child and during his declining years. Describing one small occasion is this amusing extract from the diary of his cousin, the Revd. Dr. John Johnson:

'"Aug 31st, 1795. Walked to Happisurgh by the edge of the sea all the way. Dined in a Lodging House where I borrowed a room for the purpose, to avoid the noise of the Public House, and after dinner returned to Mundesley. This was the only instance of Mr. Cowper ever eating, as he told me afterwards, with anything like an appetite, in Norfolk; and to be sure he did eat very heartily, though of very ordinary food, for the only things he would touch were Beans and Bacon which were very old, and apple pye, the worst I ever saw. He ate, however, with a most complete relish of them all. I never knew him to enjoy a dinner anything like it after that to the day of his death."'

Over the centuries many ships have been wrecked off this coast resulting in tragic loss of life. Members of the crew of *H.M.S. Peggy*, wrecked in December 1710, are buried in the churchyard as are many other sailors, and German airmen from the Second World War. Under a grassy mound on the north side of the churchyard lie buried 119 crew of the original *H.M.S. Invincible* which ran aground in March, 1801, en route to join Nelson's fleet assembling prior to the Battle of Copenhagen. A memorial stone to those who died on this ship was finally laid in the churchyard on the 24th July 1998 at a ceremony attended by members of the ship's company of the aircraft carrier, *H.M.S. Invincible.*

In the 1800s one Jonathan Balls made a habit, confirmed by subsequent exhumations, of poisoning those he invited to drink with him and very successful he was until he downed a poisoned drink intended for someone else. In 1846 he was buried in this churchyard together with, at his request, a plum cake, a bible, a poker and a pair of tongs. Why? When his exhumed body was re-interred, these items were replaced with him as well!

Rotti's quartet of canines had patiently put up with six church visits and been deprived of a beach run – it was time to take the home after an excellent day crawl.

The following day we drove to the outskirts of Norwich to find **All Saints, Keswick** *(NR4 6TP)*. This involved following a long track in search of Mill Lane Cottage from where we were to collect the church door key. This was handed to me by a very stooped, cheery old lady who said she had lived in the cottage since she and her husband were demobbed from the WAAF and RAF in 1946. We turned back up the lane, parked off the main road, and walked a short distance to a clearing in the woods and a tiny building, half church, half ruin! It is hard to believe this is a parish church, so small that the front pews fold down to 'assist in the movement of coffins'!

At least we found All Saints unaided! **St Margaret's, Morton-on-the-Hill** *(NR9 5JS)*, would be impossible to find without local help which Rotti eventually received after knocking on two front doors. St Margaret's is tucked away on a wooded mound close by a manor house, the home of Lady Ann Prince-Smith who, forewarned of our approach, was busy in the chapel wielding dust-pan and brush, tidying up after an event. I was reminded of Bob Davey in that this little damaged church was obviously cherished by her. On Easter Sunday, 1959, the tower fell down, crashing through the nave. For twenty years it lay derelict until a glass screen was erected in 1980, making usable the east end of the church where today occasional services are held. Beyond the glass, three bells rest forlornly on the grass. The interior is an extraordinary jumble and arrangement of furniture and furnishings. Two pedal organs sit almost side by side, the one playable, if considerable effort is applied, the other irreparably damaged by field mice! A lopsided crystal chandelier dangles to one side and two tired Persian carpets have been thoughtfully laid under rows of chairs facing what purports to be an altar. Lady Ann chattered away to Rotti explaining the church history, giving much credence to the connection – which remains a mystery to me – between the church and Robert Southall, Jesuit Priest (1561-1595) who was hanged, drawn and quartered.

St Faith, Little Witchingham *(NR9 5PA)*, redundant and not on our list but which we were urged not to miss, was something of a disappointment after the idiosyncrasies of St Margaret's church. Set apart from all habitation on the edge of a wood and a field, St Faith's looked forgotten and neglected. Stripped of all furniture, only the wall paintings remained. I could appreciate their age and still vibrant reds and ochres but not in any way read and attach meaning to them. After a short stroll for the dogs' relief we crossed country to **St Peter & St Paul, Salle** *(NR10 4SE)* (pronounced *Saul*). The size of this vast church, built on wool wealth, is astonishing. Population and habitation have long disappeared. It stands alone, bleak and not a little spooky. This was my second visit specially to see the twenty-six misericords. They weren't memorable but, by way of compensation, the bench ends were varied and amusing.

Winding our way through the village of Reepham after a welcome coffee *Chez V's*, I was struck by what appeared to be a double-ended church, that is, a tower at each end. This had to be investigated! I learned that many villages in Norfolk have two, even three churches serving different parishes. They are usually situated in different parts of the village though, in the case of **Reepham**, once upon a time, *three* churches shared the same graveyard (all that is left of the third church, destroyed by a massive fire, is the ruined remains of the porch). This is not unique. There are twelve examples of shared graveyards in Norfolk, four in Suffolk, three in Cambridgeshire and one each in Lincolnshire and Essex. Without going into long-winded detail, it seems this sharing came about due to the reluctant stubborn nature of church and parishioners to countenance an amalgamation of parishes.

We passed by **St George's, Rollesby** *(NR29 5HW)* which boasts the tallest round tower in Norfolk and, by way of contrast, **St Margaret's, Worthing** *(NR20 5HR)* which has the shortest tower in the county. There we found the door locked so were only able to enjoy its quiet isolation in the rural setting before driving on to visit **St James', Castle Acre** *(PE32 2AA)*, the very last church of this visit. It was

St George's, Rollesby highest round tower in Norfolk

memorable for the hexagonal font – the cover of which is not only extraordinarily tall but so slender and surely fragile – and the beautifully illustrated wine-glass pulpit; both circa C15th, both painted dull red and green. From the work of master craftsmen to simple polished wood bench ends; two pert and perky little dogs, surely fashioned for a chuckle.

We drove through this picture postcard village, past The Ostrich pub, and headed for home and more of Rotti's generous hospitality, the end of two days thoroughly enjoyed.

* * *

Three Shires and Misericords

Since Robert and Hannah moved to Bath and while Penny and Tim lived for a while in the glorious countryside of Shropshire below the Long Mynd, I became better acquainted with Worcestershire and Herefordshire on my way to Bath or Wentnor. To ensure I saw as many different churches as possible, I followed a slightly different route each time I made the journey and so came across Norman corbels, a rural calendar recorded on misericords, sin eaters of Shropshire, sat inside a churchyard tree, visited two memorable churches, and played a round of darts with a shaming lack of skill.

My priority on arriving in **Ledbury** was to find a croissant and coffee which I found conveniently at the opposite end of a cobbled lane leading up to **St Michael's**, tucked away from the busy part of town. It's a fine church with wonderful large windows lighting the interior, all the better to see and be amused by some quirky cushions in the choir stalls; stitched on the organist's cushion are choristers and the notes for Elgar's *Ave Verum* motet; the cushion for one Richard Winfield depicts a snazzy Lotus car, and medieval buildings of the town are beautifully worked on others.

St Michael's, Castle Frome *(HR8 1HQ)* is in deep countryside, well north of three churches I planned to visit that day but, curious to see a font apparently unlike any other,

I decided to take the detour. "Oh wow!" was my reaction to the bizarre 'object' just inside the south door. Fashioned from one stone block, the font, a large bowl on a short stem, is an extra ordinary masterpiece of Norman carving dated circa 1170, a little after the church itself was built, around 1125, at the time of the nearby castle. Intricate plaiting encircles the top of the bowl, the stem is decorated with interlacing and carved in between these patterns are interesting symbols: a pair of doves, St Matthew's eagle, St Mark's winged bull, St Luke's winged bull and St John baptising Christ who is shown with fish swimming about his feet. There is more: the stem stands on what were carvings of three great beasts though only one remains intact, its human-animal head resting on hand-paws. A monster beast. The religious and secular combined to weird effect. The interest of this ancient and austere building of unchanged footprint, bare brick and stone interior walls lies in its treasure of a font.

St Michael's, Castle Frome font

From Castle Frome south to **St Bartholomew's, Much Marcle** *(HR8 2ND)*, a simple church inside which are two very different but equally memorable memorials. One is a very beautiful marble effigy of a young girl, the other of a gentleman and landowner. The daughter of the first Earl of March lies under a stone tester displaying the family coats of arms, her arms resting loosely on her body, the folds of her dress, so skilfully formed and draped, spilling over the edge of the bier. Walter de Helyon, gentleman and landowner (d. late C14th), dressed in a red tunic, lies with hands together in prayer, head resting on a green pillow, feet crossed casually at the ankle. The likeness of this gentleman was not carved from marble or stone but, most unusually, from an oak trunk covered with gesso then gilded and painted. Close to the south porch is a magnificent ancient yew tree, dated to be around fifteen hundred years old. The base of the enormous trunk is hollow, tall and broad enough to accommodate three benches. I spent a quiet moment in this 'room' to admire the thick, gnarled branches extending horizontally, resting as if weary on green painted cast iron supports considerately placed by the Victorians.

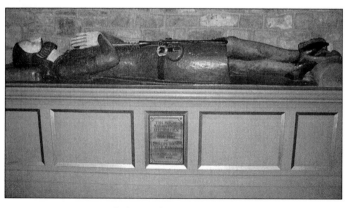

St Bartholomew's, Much Marcle effigy

Much Marcle yew

A few lanes away from Much Marcle in Herefordshire and a mile or so before coming to the sprawling village of **Kempley** in Gloucestershire is the Grade I listed church of **St Mary's** *(GL18 2AT)*. The churchyard, large and under populated, is surrounded by fields, scarcely another building in sight. I stood under the canopy of a large tree to gaze upon the pink washed walls of chancel and nave, weathered south porch and stubby tower of this late C12th church, cherished for its remarkable frescoes. I have no academic knowledge of church murals and frescoes, just a layman's pleasure they survive at all. The paintings in St Mary's dated 1120s are particularly clear and complete. Walk into the chancel and you want to lie down on the floor to feast your gaze on the stunning barrel ceiling painted as heaven with stars and a vision of Christ, Mary and four evangelists. According to the church notes there is a triple *mandorla*, Italian for 'almond', being an almond shaped form enclosing Christ and the Virgin Mary. (Much to my surprise, I remembered I had seen another one on the chancel arch wall discovered during the painstaking restoration of St Mary the Virgin,

Houghton-on-the-Hill, Norfolk). I understood there to be four ages of man but on the north wall of the nave is a '*wheel of life*', each spoke a reference to the *ten* ages of man – how they are squeezed into the three score years and ten we hope for. Hidden to view above the late C17th ceiling of the nave is *the oldest dated roof without tie-beams in the country… timber came from … trees about 50-100 years old, felled after 1125.* Even older, made from three planks in 1114, is the west door, the original entrance before the tower was built a century later. Another ancient item is the parish chest hollowed out of a single cut of solid, 250 year old oak. Long may English Heritage care for this delightful church-in-a-field. In the village centre is the Arts and Crafts style Church of St Edward the Confessor, built in the early C20th, the interior of which doesn't remotely compare with the stunning Arts & Crafts design of All Saints, Brockhampton to which I was en route for a return visit.

Relatively few miles separate two nearby churches. Both are deep in beautiful countryside, both are perfect examples of their very different eras. **All Saints, Brockhampton** *(HR1 4SD)* was built in 1902, commissioned and paid for by a Mrs Foster in memory of her parents. The architect she chose was William Lethaby (1857-1931) whose father was a gilder and carver in Devon. Mrs Foster chose well as her architect was brought up with an appreciation of excellence in craft and design; he was a founder member of the Central School of Arts and Crafts. All Saints was situated on sloping park land known locally as 'Horse Bank' using local stone with Norfolk reeds for the steeply pitched thatched roof. Everything about this church is unique, the design of every single aspect and item so beautiful and quite beyond my descriptive powers: the design is virtual medieval yet timeless. Someone who had visited the church returned one day in 1960 and left inside an altar cloth embroidered with wild flowers which has since been framed to hang on the west wall. The same anonymous, and surely special, person donated seat cushions and some forty or fifty hymn book covers, also hand embroidered with flowers, as a tribute to the variety of wild flowers carved on the choir stalls and for 'leaving this church open to visitors.' All Saints was as memorable, as special on second viewing, with time to spare afterward to follow a public footpath to follow for a welcome hour not sitting behind a wheel.

All Saints, Brockhampton

All Saints, Brockhampton aisle to west

To visit **St Mary & St David**, **Kilpeck** *(HR2 9DN)*, after leaving All Saints', is to step back over nine hundred years into a Norman masterpiece. This small red stone church stands alone on a rise, miraculously ignored by the Roundheads when they destroyed the nearby castle in 1645. I walked past gravestones to the south door but didn't immediately go inside. The C12th carving of the arches and columns framing the heavy oak door is so intricate, such a wonderful example of those Herefordshire masons of long ago. I walked slowly round the church, risking a permanent crick to the neck as I gazed at each of the eighty-five corbels carved in sandstone just under the roof line. The variety is astonishing; aside from a Lamb of God there was nothing religious about monsters, birds, animals, celtic knots, lovers and a famously rather rude woman proudly distending her vulva, a depiction known as a Sheela-na-gig. Beyond the south door, a jewel of Norman decoration, the interior is simple. White washed walls define the stone arches leading from nave to chancel to apse and many more extraordinary corbels made me smile: the boot face of a musician playing a string instrument; dancers glued cheek to cheek; a doleful dog next to his bunny friend.

Outside I waylaid an elderly man coming up the path and asked him to suggest a good country pub not too far away. He suggested The Dog Inn. Ewyas Harold is a tiny hamlet so close to **Abbey Dore** I delayed lunch to make a small detour to visit the imposing Abbey, its red walls rising from a field. I jotted down the following note to myself: '16th Aug 06 Magnificent once, now an empty cavernous interior for which I had little appreciation.' I returned to Ewyas Harold and The Dog Inn, a proper village pub, where the barmaid served my lunch at the bar from where I watched two old timers playing darts. We were the only four in the pub so I should not have been surprised when the men invited bored barmaid and self to form two pairs for a match. My old boy soon realised he had drawn the short straw: we were no match for the barmaid and her partner. Although my long game on the golf course was pretty good, my lack of skill on the green used to let me down – I proved as hopeless at getting my dart anywhere near the bull's eye as I was getting that ball down the hole. No matter, it was good, unexpected fun and made memorable my visit to Abbey Dore.

During a visit to Tim and Penny they introduced me to Ludlow, the town and church, en route to what they really wanted to show me, the surprise that is **St John the Evangelist, Shobdon** *(HR6 9LZ)*. We drove through gorgeous, summer-green countryside to turn up an avenue towards Shobdon Court. We entered through a graceful gothic arch into a church that was built around 1755 and replaced two others on the site. The original wooden church constructed was Saxon then replaced in local stone by the Normans. Demolishing that church was madness and a shame yet you wouldn't wish away the Georgian edifice standing today for surely there isn't any other church interior quite like this one. It is Rococo, it is Gothic, it is painted wedding white throughout with pale blue definition. From bench ends to altar rails, arches to mouldings, columns to gallery, tester to triple pulpit, all is graceful decoration, swirls and whirls. Even Tim, who would probably have preferred visiting an armoury or castle, was bowled over. Horace Walpole and the then owner of Shobdon were friends – it is likely Strawberry Hill influenced the architect who decided Rococo-Gothic was a medieval form made *fun and fit for polite society*. All that remains of the Norman church are carved stone arches erected a short distance away as a sort of feature. None of us was in a hurry to leave so we walked up the hill to see their crumbling remains. Another occasion when I regretted the lack of a digital camera at that time.

The decoration of Shobdon is positively presbyterian compared with the Baroque opulence of **St Michael's, Great Witley** *(WR6 6JT)*, just west of Worcester. I followed the road to it at Penny and Tim's insistence this was a must-see church. And so it is. I walked through the west door into a large space filled with the very best that craftsmen could achieve in glass, wood, marble and painted ceilings. The interior is nothing if not extravagant, a show room for excellence but I had spent more time, had more fun in a junkyard some miles back.

I had not intended to visit the next church, **St Mary's** *(GL20 6HA)* but as I approached a fork in the road my eye was caught by a marker signed **'Ripple'**. I made a snap decision and took the fork which led me to see the only complete calendar set of misericords. Charming. Yet again I regret not having had a digital camera at that time. These C15th misericords are unusual - they depict scenes relating to the rural calendar with clarity and charm:

January, collecting dead wood
February, hedging and ditching
March, sowing;
April, bird scaring
May, blessing crops
June, hawking
July, lammas (a feast or loaf mass)
August, reaping
September, preparing corn for malting
October, feeding acorns to pigs
November, pig killing
December, spinning by the fire.

One May Genny and David, house-sitting for their son, invited me to join them in Herefordshire. On a day off from walking the rounded, rolling beauty of the Malvern Hills, we went into Hereford so I could explore the Cathedral while Genny did some shopping. The difference in scale between a Downland church and a cathedral is self-evidently enormous. Both have been built by the efforts of men: as I have already mentioned, in the case of cathedrals many, many men contributed over many decades until the huge structure was completed. I walk into a simple church or chapel in a field ready to fall in love with its charm, simplicity and peacefulness. I walk into a cathedral and my first reaction is always '*How did they do it*?' As I have already mentioned there was no easily assembled tubular scaffolding, no power tools, no computer programs or architects, indeed no civil engineers to ensure the structure would be sound. Yet they succeeded in creating a stupendous monument embellished with designs and ornamentation fashioned by masons and wood carvers of amazing skill. When I enter a cathedral instead of giving thanks to Him, I thank those men several centuries ago for what *they* so wondrously achieved.

Hereford Cathedral is home to one of three chained libraries in England. It purports to be the largest of the three collections (though according to Wimborne Minster Merton College, Oxford makes the same claim) and is housed in a purpose-built room (funded by Paul Getty) together with the fabulous late C13th *Mappa Mundi*. Apparently, ancient world maps dating from the C7th are two a penny – over a thousand survive – but they are in the form of simple diagrams whereas Hereford's treasure is incredibly detailed. Information absorbed, I emerged into the sunshine to find Genny waiting for me by Jemma Pearson's delightful statue of Edward Elgar wearing plus fours and resting against his bicycle.

En route to visit Penny and Tim then living in Wentnor with wonderful views to The Long Mynd Shropshire I set off in search of two chapels without dedication. It was a lengthy dive and drive along narrow lanes and past isolated farms before I found the hamlet **Heath** *(SY7 9DS)* and still more twists and turns until I came across a plain little chapel sitting in a field. Removing a huge key hanging conspicuously behind a notice board I walked into the twelfth century, or so it seemed. The simple two cell interior is perfect and miraculously unspoilt. Light comes through little lancet windows set deep in lime washed walls onto the worn stone floor, tired pews and crude tub font. It's hard to believe there ever was a settlement as the population served by this chapel probably declined soon after it was built: I counted but six headstones at the far end of the field. Further north, not far from Ruckley, **Langley** *(SY5 7HW)* is another wayside chapel, alone in a landscape of fields but for a farmhouse and the remains of Langley Hall. Built in Tudor times for Puritan worship to serve a population long gone, conserved for its C17th layout and furniture, a museum piece. It lacks the warmth and charm of Heath chapel but the setting is as peaceful and bucolic.

The following morning Tim kindly drove me to see two churches nearby. The painted wagon roof of the village church in Norbury is quite pretty but what did make me stop in my tracks was the yew tree opposite the porch. It is not just large. It is huge. It is not just old. It is ancient. Bemused by my delight in seeing such a tree, Tim hoped **St Margaret's**, **Ratlinghope** might yield something of interest. He set off along those deep, twisting lanes driving, as do those who know their patch well, with speed, optimism and maybe a prayer. Of the church itself I recall nothing. It was in the graveyard we came across the memorial to a sin-eater. According to the church notes, sin-eating possibly originated from the ancient practice of transferring sins to a scapegoat. Since early times in Wales and Shropshire there were sin-eaters until the early C19th. These were poor men on the fringe of society who were paid to attend the funeral of someone who died suddenly before confessing his or her sins. A bowl of ale and some bread would be passed over the coffin to the sin-eater for him to drink and eat before saying; "*I give easement and rest now to thee, dear (the name), that ye walk not down the lanes or in our meadows. And for thy peace I pawn my own soul. Amen.*" For this his payment was usually sixpence. What a sad and burdensome way to earn a crust. The grave in this churchyard is that of Richard Munslow (1833-1906), a local farmer whose personal tragedy, the loss of four children to scarlet fever, may have caused him to revive this custom. He was believed to be the last sin-eater in these parts.

Penny suggested I took the scenic route back to Bath, through the Wye Valley. Another small rural church in the hamlet of **Brinsop** *(HR4 7AU)* then beckoned, just a short distance from the A49. Further and further into the countryside, through a farmyard and beyond **St George's** church perches on a rise overlooking a lake, surrounded by meadows. All so simple, I didn't expect – or understand the need for – so much bling and glitz within. Four golden angels standing atop the rood screen, wings outstretched, each holding a candle, seemed so out of keeping as did a golden canopy suspended above the altar in front of a startlingly blue, gold and marble reredos. At least the well preserved stone relief of St George and the Dragon carved into the semi-circular tympanum over the door was simple and the surrounding countryside delightful.

Onward to **St Catherine's, Hoarwithy** *(HR2 6QH)*. After an al fresco pub lunch I walked past the shabbiest of cottages, home to the Post Office, then climbed the narrow uphill approach to the C19th church. Stepping onto the Romanesque cloister walk, I looked down over fields and grazing horses while swallows, late to fly south, swooped and darted overhead. I did like the carved barrel choir stalls but for me the interior was cold and soulless.

It had been a mixed day on the road ending with a relaxed overnight stay with Robert and Hannah.

* * *

With my discovery of and growing fascination for **misericords** comes regret for those sadly unnoticed by me in churches and cathedrals visited before now. As I record these practical and very often humorous additions to church furniture, it's fun to note the diversity and recurring themes and depictions. Worshippers, congregation and clergy alike, all had to stand as a matter of course during the early church services. This was particularly hard on monks – especially onerous for the elderly ones - a third of every twenty-four hours was spent in church, taken up with Matins, Mass, Vespers and further prayers, all in Latin of course. Eventually the standing only rule was relaxed to allow *reclinatoria*, sort of crutches to take weight off the feet, or to receive support resting on choir-stall arms. The first half of the C13th saw the advent of *misericordia*, Latin for mercy, which greatly improved the lot of monks. Misericords, most of which are dated to the fourteenth century, are in effect tipping ledges positioned at buttock height so as to afford rest to the weary monk whilst appearing still to stand.

The complexity and quality of the carving under each oak ledge is rather wonderful, not least because they are hardly in a position to be generally admired or appreciated. Subjects depicted are hugely varied: some, but by no means all, are biblical – Adam, Eve, Jonah and Samson are popular.

Fantastical, mythical creatures, monsters and serpents abound as do scenes of daily life and events. Men fight dragons, wives beat errant or useless husbands with long handled pans, Green Men grin, foliage entwines.

Despite the passing of centuries and the Reformation when orders were given in 1549 for the removal of 'superstitious images', some 3250 misericords remain in place, if not in use, in England alone. The largest collections are to be found, not surprisingly, in cathedrals, minsters and Oxbridge chapels. Exceptions, with a collective total of eleven, are Canterbury, Chester, Christchurch and Peterborough Cathedrals. The counties of Norfolk, Yorkshire, Durham, Lancashire, Herefordshire, Kent and Warwickshire boast the largest number of misericords scattered throughout the country; Surrey, Derbyshire, Essex and Cornwall the least.

Iris Murdoch in 'The Bell' has Nick remind us '*confession has its charms, since it can allow us some control over the indictment against us, for we invariably take ourselves a little more seriously than we really deserve*'. He goes on, '*What we are really ashamed of, and repress, does not always coincide with what we confess; nor does what we repress always coincide with what we should confess*'. In other words, the secular and somewhat grotesque carvings on the misericords suggest an expression of fun and naughtiness rather than malice and sin; a sort of letting off steam within the Christian behaviour, a wood-carver's free-for-all, an opportunity for satire and subversion – rabbits roasting a hunter as an example. That expression is not the unique work of individual talent as most misericords are copies of designs recorded from illuminated manuscripts and books called 'bestiaries', full of illustrations of real, weird and mythical creatures.

Many carvings are open to more than one interpretation, one of which could well be influenced by the mores of our time:

is he kissing her with affection or is this sexual harassment? We are too far away in time for translations – we can only see what we want to see. There is monastic excess: food and drink, bare bottoms, even, in one carving, three monks *expose their bare bottoms, revealing turds turning into demonic lions.* Medieval carvers seemed to relish depicting all orifices and protuberances of the human form. Some symbolism is obvious or well known. The mermaid, a temptress, a siren to lure sailors onto rocks – watch out, beauty may conceal mal intent! The mythical pelican is symbolic of Christ sacrificing himself and saving mankind with his blood. Supporters, ancillary carvings each side of the main depiction, often – though not always – involve foliage such as oak leaves, roses and grape vine and fruit. In some cases the supporters far from being decorative 'add-ons' are very much part of the depiction and as well executed. In short, I am fascinated by misericords, illustrating scenes and little stories of medieval life and beliefs, tucked out of sight behind the choir stalls, yet well worth hunkering down to 'read'.

* * *

Chichester Cathedral misericord N7 Dancing woman being kissed

More Shires

I came across several quirky kirks in this section en route to a variety of destinations, among them the city of Bath, an inn on the Cotswolds Way, an arboretum, a delightful vestry-cum-schoolroom and a christening.

The road beatween Salisbury and Bath winds through beautiful broad landscape and has become, for me, one of those the-car-knows-the-way routes, linking, as it does mother and son. On one occasion I turned off the A36 to visit Julie, a friend who had recently moved to **Sherrington** from a village on the South Downs. The setting of this tiny hamlet is idyllic, old cottages scattered about, a church, a farmyard and Julie's own cottage overlooks the village pond. Sadly, all but two or three cottages are now second homes, which explained scarce sign of life and, for Julie living there, no feeling of community. **St Cosmas & St Damian's** *(BA12 0SN)* is one of only five churches in England dedicated to these twin saints, patrons of medicine. These twin saints, like Castor and Pollux, are guardian spirits of healing and safe travelling. The original wood boards of the chancel floor eventually rotted as they had been laid directly onto the earth! Beautiful and interesting memorial stones were removed from the graveyard to create an enduring floor. The little church is delightful without being extraordinary. (The other churches with this dedication are: **Challock**, Kent *(TN25 4BS)* in bucolic isolation away from the long relocated village itself; **Blean** *(CT2 9HU)* not far from Canterbury; the Jacobean pulpit with double-tester is a tad grand for the unassuming, dumpy little church-in-a-farmyard that is Stretford, Herefordshire *(HR6 9DG);* and **Keymer** *(BN6 8QL)* in Sussex).

Vanessa sent me a post card of **All Saints', Great Chalfield** *(SN12 8NT),* enthusing about the church and the picaresque setting close by to a moated manor house. She said the church was locked the first time she went yet open the following November so I set off ten months later not knowing whether I would find and open or closed door. The door was open and I do agree with Vanessa this is a church with charisma. Five of the Tropenel coats of arms depicting various images of choughs – members of the *corvidae* avian family – adorn the fine C15th white stone screen separating chapel from nave and although not a fan of stained glass generally, I liked the modern east window and guessed two armchairs are for the comfort of regular churchgoers. I intend to make a short detour on my way to or from Bath so as to explore more thoroughly.

During one visit to Bath during the month of October as it was a crisp, blue-sky day I suggested to Robert, Hannah and flat-mate Robin we visit the Westonbirt Arboretum. Probably to humour me and enticed by the promise of coffee and a bun, they kindly agreed a detour to **Bradford-on-Avon** so Mother could visit *another* – big sighs – church. Happily, even they were charmed by the antiquity and Saxon simplicity of **St Laurence's Chapel** *(BA15 1BP).* It remains as it always was partly because for centuries it was tucked away behind other buildings. Dated early C11th, it was only recognised as a chapel in the late C19th. It proved a happy start to a splendid day amongst beautiful trees brilliant with the brown-reds and orange-yellows of autumnal colour.

The following three churches are to be found within reasonable distance of each other beyond the A36 quite close to the A350. More Georgian meeting house than church **St Mary's, Old Dilton** *(BA13 4DB)*, oozes atmosphere. The road winds into countryside and, despite the church being situated next to a railway line, the feeling is completely rural. A note pinned to the tired oak door advises anyone passing exactly where to find the key. It is not an irresponsible invitation for this delightful church is redundant, furnished only with pale oak box pews and gallery along north wall right up to east window and a little side room boasts an open fireplace and fitted cupboards.

St Mary, Steeple Ashton, Wilts

The contrast between **Old Dilton** and **St Mary, St Catherine & All Saints, Edington** *(BA13 4QR)* could hardly be more marked. The latter is a large, beautifully proportioned building situated at the edge of the village. I hopped through a peculiar non-gate, possibly designed to prevent access by...sheep? Who knows. I found much to enjoy inside from the grey-black-stone patterning of the floors to the finely carved pulpit, from the monuments to funny peculiar figures carved on the corbels in the chancel. On to **St Mary's** in the pretty village of **Steeple Ashton** *(BA14 6EW)* where, on the exterior wall below fancy castellation and pinnacles covered with flower balls, bizarre Gothic heads and creatures leered down at my upturned face.

En route to join the Dawdlers for four days walking sections of the Cotswolds Way, I parked in Malmsbury high street just long enough to admire the stunning Norman porch of the Abbey. I sat in admiration taking in the impressive span with <u>eight</u> arches and walls decorated with wonderful sculptured reliefs and carvings. I regret not exploring the Abbey interior further but the car was parked illegally and I still had a long drive ahead of me. Charles chose The Green Dragon Inn as our very comfortable base. Nearby is **St John's, Elkstone** *(GL53 9PD),* full of Norman arches with zigzags aplenty and some interesting grotesques and gargoyles including two dragons carved into one arch. St John's is probably best known for the rare columbarium under the roof and above the chancel (as is the dovecote with one hundred and thirty nesting boxes in St Michael, Compton St Michael, Somerset). It seems the word columbarium has two quite different meanings. It is a respectful place for public storage of urns containing cremated remains. It is also used to described dovecote or dovecot which may be square, circular or built into the end of a house, barn, church or free standing in a field. Until the end of C18th pigeons and doves were a good source of food, kept for eggs, flesh and guano or, to rephrase, used for meat, manure and feathers.

We stopped for lunch in **Painswick**, a most attractive Cotswolds town with a large though not particularly memorable church, **St Mary's** *(GL6 6QB)*. The churchyard is something else, dotted about with thirty-three table-top tombs and planted with ninety-nine yew trees. According to legend, there will never be a round one hundred trees as, despite many plantings, the hundredth always dies.

Visiting **St Mary's, Tetbury** *(GL8 8DN),* was a prelude to the Saunterers' visit to Prince Charles' cherished garden surrounding his Highgrove House residence. Our coach arrived in Tetbury in good time for us to disperse into various tearooms and cafés for lunch prior to our scheduled tour. With time to spare, several of us went into the church which is quite an odd shape in that it is unusually fat at ground level, very tall and slim above. The spire is the fourth highest in England and, as we were to see for ourselves later, clearly visible down a ride leading away from Highgrove. It was completed in the late C18th. The interior is airy and well lit by very tall windows rising above the galleries surrounding the nave furnished with box pews. A splendid tiered brass candelabrum, suspended over the centre aisle, was being polished and candles checked by an elderly gentleman bravely perched on a very tall ladder. An attentive steward informed us the slender, cream painted columns are made of oak. I found this hard to believe so referred to both Simon (*'cast iron clothed in wood'*) and John (*'Forest of Dean oak sunk 20 feet below ground and encased in plaster moulding'*). Hmmm! Ambulatories are another unusual feature. They are enclosed walkways running the length of the church and through which one has to walk to access some side pews. Various effigies of man and woman, lie close to and along the outer wall. All feet point eastwards.

On one of my routes between Bath and Shropshire I stopped to find a little somewhere to have lunch. I had not intended to visit the **Abbey of St Mary, Tewkesbury** *(GL20 5LZ)* it being neither cathedral nor little chapel. How foolish my prejudice! It is so, so grand. Eight tubby yews, beautifully clipped and shaped, line the approach on the north side. A magnificent copper beech dominates the lawn at the east end of the Abbey. Not far down the road is **St Mary's, Deerhurst** *(GL19 4BX).* The immediate area, teeming with workmen and heavy machinery, was a little tricky to navigate so as to avoid the car becoming bogged down in the churned-up track. How wonderful to find two atmospheric Saxon buildings close together in this patch of riverside country. I followed a low stonewall to St Mary's and entered through the west door, quite unprepared for the simplicity and tremendous height of the nave. The original monastery was built in the C8th; I was standing in what was rebuilt in the C10th. Way above the door arch is a pair of unusual Saxon small triangular windows. The C9th tub font is a rarity but what puzzled me was a memorial window in the north aisle dedicated to the Strickland family and depicting the family crest. More of this Yorkshire family from **Boynton**, its coat of arms and the unusual, definitely unique, feature dotted around the interior of the village church. So unusual it was startling to come across reference to it here.....more of this later.

Almost next door **Odda's Chapel** abuts a medieval farmhouse, a Saxon survivor. Unlike St Laurence's, Bradford-upon-Avon, it felt lonely. A copy of the stone inscription which dates the Chapel reads as follows: *'Earl Odda had the royal hall built and dedicated in honour of the Holy Trinity for the soul of his brother, Aelfric, which left the body in this place. Bishop Ealdred dedicated it this second Ides of April in this the*

fourteenth year of the reign of Edward, King of the English'
that is, 12th April 1056. There is another transcription, this
one of a poem composed in 1919 by Admiral R.A. Hopwood
of Rutland for whom these buildings held something special:

A Little Sanctuary

In the quiet Severn Valley, where it seemed as if at last
Very peace had spread her wings on ev'ry hand,
Stood an old and battered farmhouse, where for generations past
Dwelt the yeomen and the tillers of the land.
Till in time, the hand of progress came to try what could be done,
Both to modernise and renovate with care,
So they chipped away the plaster of the ages dead and gone
And they found – a little Saxon Chapel there.
And I chanced upon the chapel when the world was full of strife,
Entered there, to rest in silence and alone,
And its spirit bare me backward just as far from modern life
As the name of Odda graven on its stone.
For the centuries were speaking thro' the lichen and the moss
Till it seemed that it was blessed but yesterday,
And I thought I saw the Saxons as they knelt before the Cross,
But I'm certain that I heard the Saxons pray.
Their petitions were as humble as the House in which they knelt,
And their faith was just as simple as their prayer,
And I knew the place was crowded, and instinctively I felt
That they always must have found an answer there.
For the truth was in its cradle, so the word was very near;
"What I think" had yet to conquer "What I know."
And they sang a hymn together that the angels stooped to hear
In the quiet Severn Valley long ago.
And I thought of Church and Abbey, half forsaken, nearly all,
Of their splendour, and the learning and the creeds
Of the party of Apollos, or the men who followed Paul,
With their turmoil, and their striving – and their needs.
Then the sunset lit the valley like a beacon from above,
Till I seemed to hear the answer to a prayer:
"An they put away the plaster from the England that they love
They shall find – a little Saxon Chapel there."

Several years later I allowed enough time en route to attend young William's christening in Kemerton, Worcestershire to pop in to a couple of churches. **St Michael's & All Angels, Bishop's Cleve** *(GL52 8BA)* near Cheltenham far exceeds in size my preference for small churches. No matter. There was much I enjoyed and remember about this once Saxon now essentially Norman church, including the approach along the south wall planted as an herbaceous border with hollyhocks, cistus, stipa grass, mallow and other pretties spilling onto the path; perhaps the work of a keen gardener in the congregation or parish? After pausing to admire interesting carvings in the Norman porch I found myself in a large yet inviting interior. Simon describes the architectural features at length. I best remember the west gallery, its blackened wood extravagantly carved, and the beautiful pale oak wood of the C15th staircase leading steeply up to the belfry. Happily even vigilant application of current rules couldn't question the safety of the solid wedges climbing between stonewall and oak balustrade; they form the treads of the oldest wooden stair case still in use in the country. The highlight for me was at the top of a narrow stone spiral staircase leading to two rooms above the south porch: a very small room to house church records and archives and a once-upon-a-time schoolroom. Although this was also probably used as a priest's room and vestry, everything about this small room says 'school'. There are records of various schoolmasters licensed to teach in 1572, 1576 and 1662 as well as a record of the burial in 1746 of Thomas Tomes, schoolmaster of Cleeve. In the centre of the room is a large very old table, on the walls some quite astonishing drawings. There is a battle scene, a biblical scene and a faint Skeleton Fred are all that remain of a Doom painting. His role was to educate the children, a stern warning that *'neither school* *or life was to be taken lightly'.* No less stern are the words *'memento mori'* (remember you must die) and *'Learn or Depart.'* Another section of wall reads *'Rules of the Academy. Mondays & Wednesdays Writing and Arithmetic; Tuesdays & Thursdays, Reading; Fridays & Saturdays, Writing'.* An enormous particularly hirsute lion looking ready to pounce, and an equally large tiger, tail improbably curled between its legs, were painted at a later date, 1818, by an artistic schoolmaster, Mr Sperry. His self-portrait includes an artist's palette, an easel and board and a list of quarterly tuition fees:

> *Reading, 3s 6d; Writing, 6s; Arithmetick, 9s; Grammar, 15s*

I really liked this little room filled with learning tools of yesteryear; I imagined children in their smocks and breeches, quill in hand, seated on forms set around their teacher.

From Bishop's Cleeve I drove on to the churches of **Great** *(GL20 7AR)* **and Little** *(GL20 8NQ)* **Washbourne** , both dedicated to St Mary. Neither church would be on my 'repeat visit' list. The tiny much altered C12th Little one sits all alone in a field, looked after by The Churches Conservation Trust. Great Washbourne was the more interesting of the two. The bell rope, traditionally suspended under the tower, dangles in the chancel divided from the nave by a thick stonewall entered through a simple arch flanked by two stylish squints. Placed central to the arch and altar within the chancel is the substantial stone font. Another unusual and quirky touch.

A little way into Worcestershire and shortly before Kemerton is **St Giles, Bredon** *(GL20 7LE),* with a soaring spire of 160 ft inspired John Masefield who included it in his homage to the area:

St Michael & All Angels, Bishop's Cleeve schoolroom wall painting

> Then hey for covert and woodland,
> And ask and elm and oak,
> Tewkesbury inns and Malvern roofs
> And Worcester chimney smoke,
> The apple trees in the orchard,
> The cattle in the byre,
> And all the land from Ludlow Town
> To Bredon church's spire'

St Giles boasts a really grand monument, brightly painted pulpit, a vertical tomb, medieval and modern stained glass windows and, best of all, beautiful medieval tiled front steps up to the altar. I remember nothing at all of St Nicholas, Kemerton (where young William behaved beautifully throughout the service) other than a row of neatly clipped yew trees along the churchyard boundary.

* * *

Lincolnshire and Back

Nine years to the month after my June church crawl anti-clockwise from Suffolk to Shropshire, I set off again, this time clockwise in the direction of Northamptonshire, through Rutland, Lincolnshire, Norfolk – yet again – and Suffolk. Along the way bench ends galore, a C20th church to treasure, how a family surname became a verb, a gravestone guaranteed to put a smile on your face...

An early C13th church **Holy Trinity, Hinton-in-the-Hedges** *(NN13 5NG)* is in the centre of a small Northants village, the approach path running for some length next to a dry stonewall. Little of interest to me other than an ancient font on a base shaped like a keyhole and a stone effigy of Sir William de Hinton (1284) and his wife, head to foot in the aisle. **Holy Trinity, Rothwell** *(NN14 6BQ)* proved rather more interesting. I had to persuade the rotund vicar to reluctantly open his locked church especially for me. I had come to see the ossuary, one of only two in England. Descending the tight spiral of worn stone steps into the crypt I came face to face, so to speak, with an extraordinary jumbled heap of skulls, some so damaged and fragile I was reminded of discarded eggshells. Legend has it that around 1700, a gravedigger fell into the long forgotten crypt, landing among the remains of about 1500 persons. Osteologists have found two distinct age groups. Analysis of shorter white skulls found evidence of blood group 'O', dating them to be C14th to C15th. Longer skulls, brown with remains of putrified skin, produced traces of the same blood group, 'ABO,' as bones found on the Mary Rose, mid C16th. Far better preserved are two C13th coffin lids lying in the chapel. In 1981 they were discovered lying hidden under lead during roof repairs. Why, and how, were two half-ton lids placed on the roof to lie hidden for some six hundred years? Interesting too are the carvings in the choir. Stone- masons went to town chiseling a row of rather pugilistic dogs (pit bulls?) facing a row of men on the other side of the choir. Was this to acknowledge dog fighting in the community? Surely not. Among the seven late C15th misericords is one of a grinning creature flaunting two excessively long parts of his body – tongue and penis, each as long as a leg! Two mismatched armchairs placed among uniform rows of upright chairs in the nave added a homely touch.

Holy Trinity, Rothwell, lewd misericord, Northants

No wonder Sir Anthony Mildmay (d.1617) is, according to the inscription on his memorial in **St Leonard's, Apethorpe** *(PE8 5DQ)* resting *with certain hope of resurrection*! No doubt his family would have wished he had been able to return to admire the huge marble monument erected in his name, known as the Mildmay Tomb, on which no expense had been spared. He lies, eternally hopeful, on his marble bed under a luxuriously curtained canopy. On the floor nearby is a very small and simple white marble memorial to a year old child. High above, for no apparent reason, two helmets are suspended from the wall and, arranged on the pews, particularly handsome hassocks.

After a reasonable night's sleep and an unsatisfactory mean breakfast, I set off from the B & B to find my first church in Rutland. After navigating road works, a diversion through sprawling farm buildings, and driving some way along a narrow track, I could see the distant tower of **St Luke's, Tixover** *(PE9 3QL)* among trees beyond a huge cultivated field. I tucked Ruby out of the way and set off on foot, passing headstones in the churchyard, just visible through grasses and wildflowers, only to be met with a locked door. Disappointment evaporated with the arrival in a 4 x 4 of three black Labradors and the farmer's wife, a key holder. Cheerful and chatty, she spoke at some length about the spiritual aura of 'her' church, the large number of parishioners who attend and support it, all the while on her knees, trimming grass around the edges of a group of memorial tablets, chatting to those underneath. "Don't look so surprised, m'dear. I knew them all, still pass on all the village news, ask them if my cutters tickle." Medieval key in hand, I left this delightful woman tending, and no doubt talking, to her father's tablet while the dogs roamed at large to pass through a handsome Norman arch into an interior full of interest. There is no electricity so a coal black cast-iron stove remains the only limited source of heat in winter with music provided by a small pedal organ. There are red and black tiles on the aisle floor, uniform *poppyheads* adorn bench ends and on the pews a generous collection of coral red hassocks, designs stitched in yellow and cream. An attractive three-sided square oak lectern is surely unusual, as is the imaginative use of tin-foil cup cake molds positioned as wax catchers under each candle on the two candelabra above the aisle. In the chancel a once splendid, now tired, early C17th monument, all hands and one head removed, probably obeying a Cromwellian order. A short note explains a framed copy of a poem to the church: *"This prayer was spiritually given to Ralph Ticehurst, a visitor to the Church, sitting on the bench below, in the company of a village resident on 19th February 2005. It was given to the current parishioners of the Church from its ancestors and past key carriers from when the first stone was laid."*

I stepped outside. The 4 x 4 had gone leaving me to return the key to its hook in the farmhouse porch,

On to **St Peter's, Brooke** *(LE15 8RE)*. Its recent claim to fame is as a location in the 2005 film of *Pride and Prejudice*. In deep countryside, surrounded by farm and village houses, it had provided a suitably rustic backdrop – no longer, as a large new house in the process of construction will overlook the church. The particular feature of this pretty ironstone building is the Norman door with hinges resembling a pair of fish skeletons.

Only two coffin lids (1320-40), propped up by the west door, interested me in **St Andrew's, Lyddington** *(LE15 9LY)*. According to the church notes, as recently as 1860 seventeen such lids were acting as coping stones on the churchyard wall – some are still in place. Adjacent to the church is a gorgeous building, Bede House, once the wing of a bishop's palace, converted into twelve almshouses for '*poor healthy* (an essential condition!) *beadsmen*'. I regret not making time to go round this house.

So many rural churches are to be reached miles along narrow lanes and **St Andrew's, Stoke Dry** *(LE15 9JG)* was no exception. Happily I judged it well worth the ride. Originally Norman, it is now a bit of everything from C13th to C18th: worn old pews, coffin carrier, dedicated bible, priest's room above the porch. The village was once owned by the Digby family until Sir Everard was hanged for treason in 1606. A grand alabaster monument next to the altar, memorial to his grandparents, shows their eleven children carved in relief as a frieze around the base. Outside, behind the east wall, is a curious sort of patio giving a clue to the possibility of a crypt underneath but if so, it has yet to be discovered let alone uncovered.

I tucked into my picnic lunch parked by a lake, watching a variety of birds on and above the water, then drove to the far north corner of the county and **Holy Trinity, Teigh** *(LE15 7RT)*. Still in use at the time of demolition, the original C13th church, was replaced in 1782 by the Earl of Harborough. He was a fan of the modern gothic style as used by Hugh Walpole to such effect when rebuilding Strawberry Hill, his house in Twickenham. I've always found box pews appealing and these ones are especially so, pale wood against pastel pink walls rising to the pale blue ceiling. Unusually the seats within all face to the centre aisle, ensuring the whole congregation can see the trio of desks and pulpit positioned, uniquely, above the west door. A trompe l'oeil painting behind the elevated pulpit adds to the gaiety of this interior. More sombre is a brass wall plaque listing the eleven men and two women who joined up during The Great War.

They *all* survived so Teigh became known as a *Thankful and Blessed village*, one of only a very few.

Unique pulpit over west door, Holy Trinity, Teigh

With my non-academic approach to churches, the only reason for me to visit **St Peter & St Paul, Exton** *(LE15 8AX)* was to be amazed by its monuments. The church is part of an estate outside the village approached up a private road. I swept up the approach just as a coachload of monument enthusiasts was departing. Once inside the large, light-filled space it's impossible to ignore huge marble or alabaster memorials to a Harington or someone related. I compiled a little list, inadequate though it is without illustration:

- John Harington (d.1524) & wife Alice. White marble
- Their granddaughter, another Alice (d.1627) – beautiful, marble
- Viscount Campden, Baron of Ridlington Lord Lieutenant of Rutland….conjugal affection for four wives and paternal indulgence to nineteen children! Wife No Four had ten, Wife Three six, Wives Two & One the rest! Completed in 1686, a rare marble work of Grinling Gibbons (1648-1721) better known for his wood carving. Cost? £1,000, surely a princely sum for those times.
- Robert Kelroy (d.1681) with son-in-law & daughter. Alabaster. Stunning.
- James Noel (d.1681) son of Viscount Campden, together with baby brothers who died in the same year – Why? How?

- Anne (d.1627) granddaughter of John Harington. Black & white marble
- James Harrington (grandson of John) and wife Lucy (both d.1592) – had eighteen children.

St Peter's, Tickencote, magnificent chancel arches

Before crossing into Lincolnshire, a drive across country to Rutland's own Kilpeck (Herefordshire) or Barfreston (Kent), **St Peter's, Tickencote** *(PE9 4AE).* Simon doesn't rate this stunningly beautiful Norman church as highly as Kilpeck or Barfreston probably because it is no longer purely Norman due to considerable rebuilding in 1792, paid for by a local family member. I disagree with Simon. It is no less wondrous. Exterior walls are decorated with blind arcading, zig-zags follow the arch of each window on the exterior. The mid C12th rounded archway into the chancel is jaw dropping: six arches known as orders are intricately and differently decorated with zig-zags, crenelation and other. Lying in a niche, looking very much the worse for wear – unlike the perky painted local gentleman in St Bartholomew's, Much Marcle (Herefordshire) – is a C14th wooden effigy of a knight, Sir Rolond le Daneys. St Peter's stands alone near a motorway. Is it used? Does it have visitors?

In his poem *A Lincolnshire Tale* John Betjeman paints a rather melancholy picture of water soaked marshes and empty space. Over the border I followed lanes for miles with long views across huge crop growing fields, a countryside with few trees, to a small cluster of buildings, hardly enough to claim even hamlet status. I looked across to **Great Humby Chapel** *(NG33 4HR)*, a tiny little building perched on the far side of a daisy-sprinkled grass rise, with fence and field behind. Idyllic surroundings, the only sounds birdsong and shivering leaves. Known as a *chapel of ease*, it is neither consecrated nor licensed for worship, just dedicated by the Bishop of Lincoln. The simple interior is charming: union jacks draped upon the three window sills added colour to bare brick walls. A painting of a soldier running away from a building clutching a bomb illustrates this story:

'Signalman Kenneth Smith, RC of Signals, was awarded a posthumous George Cross on the Adriatic island of Ist at a time when acts of sabotage were of daily occurrence. On the 10th January 1945 Sg. Smith found a time bomb in a house where members of his attachment were billeted with women and children. From its ticking he realised it might explode at any moment. His one thought was to remove it as soon as possible. He was the only casualty. It blew him to pieces. The King has been graciously pleased to approve the award in recognition of conspicuous gallantry in carrying out hazardous work in a brave manner".

No 2328696 Signalman Kenneth Smith

From the humble and special to the sublime I digressed from my route to **Lincoln Cathedral** *(LN2 1 PX)* in which I wandered for at least an hour, overawed as usual by what magnificence many, many men managed to build some nine hundred years ago. I noted the six construction periods – Norman 1072; Early English 1192; Late Early English 1235; Decorated 1256; Perpendicular 1432 and Modern 1914. I spotted the infamous imp up high and chatted to the Verger about the misericords, the largest single collection in the country, possibly in Europe. I also made a point of looking for, and finding outside on the sward, GF Watts' imposing statue of Tennyson and his dog; a full size plaster replica is to be found in the Watts Gallery, Compton, Surrey.

I lingered in the Service Chapels of Remembrance for soldiers (St George), sailors (St Andrew) and airmen (St Michael), moved almost to tears by a plaque commemorating the loss of 55,000 airmen of Bomber Command. This memorial brought back memories of my father's brother, Uncle Paul (aka Air Marshall Sir Paul Holder) for whom Armistice Day had particular resonance as he never forgot 'his boys' who flew off on sorties, never to return. Standing there it also brought to mind something very special attributed to the South African Sir Percy Fitzpatrick, (1862-1931), best known as author of the story of a dog, *"Jock of the Bushveld"*. On 27th October 1919 a suggestion from Sir Percy, for a moment of silence to be observed annually on 11th November in honour of the dead of World War 1, was forwarded to King George V. On 7th November 1919 the King proclaimed *"that at the hour when the Armistice came into force, the 11th hour of the 11th day of the 11th month, there be for a brief space of two minutes a complete suspension of all our normal activities... so that in perfect stillness the thoughts of everyone may be concentrated on reverent remembrance of the glorious dead".* Lord Stamfordham, the King's Private Secretary, wrote to Sir Percy: *"The King, who learns that you are shortly to leave for South Africa desires me to assure you that he ever gratefully remembers that the idea of the Two minute Pause on Armistice Day was due to your initiation, a suggestion readily adopted and carried out with heartfelt sympathy throughout the Empire".* A simple moment of reflection observed by and for so many ever since.

Mid afternoon, there was still time to find **St Edith's, Coates-by-Stow** *(LN1 2DW).* Miles from anywhere, I approached cautiously along a farm road riddled with deep potholes and lined with soldier-straight poplars. The little church is directly opposite vast farm buildings and an array of bright red farm machinery, hardly a picturesque outlook. Its own surroundings more garden than churchyard, no headstones, just a bench facing across fields. Inside, the only surviving rood loft in the county keeps company with a tub font and worn pews strewn with grubby brown hassocks. Isolated enough to escape Cromwell's heavy hand, little seems to have changed since medieval times including, according to this list, the number of residents: Seventeen adults in 1377, ten in 1428, twenty in 1603, forty-six in 1851 – *"fifteen being church folk and twenty-six primitive Methodists"*! – and fourteen in 2013.

I checked into the next B & B I had booked, a working farm well east of Lincoln. Claire made me most welcome and served her own eggs and conserves for breakfast during which I was treated to the sight of a pair of hares lolloping through the farm gate then casually hopping around the lawn outside! I had arranged to meet up with school friend Sally for a good walk, but judged there was time to drive by **St Margaret's, Bag Enderby** *(PE23 4NP)* where Tennyson's father was rector 1807-31. Gazing up at the greenstone exterior, peering into the crumbling porch, I likened the building to an ugly old man with pockmarked skin and missing teeth. With this in mind I entered somewhat gingerly, prepared for carbuncles maybe, and found instead a goodlooking chancel arch, pretty pale green hassocks and an octagonal font with an unusual carving of mother and child. On the wall, extracts from two of Tennyson's poems written in local vernacular:

> *Doesn't thou 'ear my 'erse's legs, as they canter away?*
> *Proputty, proputty, proputty – that's what I 'ears them say.*
> *Proputty, proputty, proputty – Sam, thou's an ass for thy paains.*
> *Theer's more sense I' one o' 'is legs nor in all thy braaines.*
> *I love the place that I have loved before*
> *I love the rolling cloud the flying rain*
> *The brown sea lapsing back with sullen roar*
> *To travel leagues before he comes again.*

By the time I arrived at **Well** Sally was waiting and rain was pouring from an unbroken grey sky. We mutually decided it was not weather for walking other than across a field to St Margaret's, which was locked. Sally kindly agreed to follow me to **St Peter's, Markby** *(LN13 9QH)*, the only thatched church in the county. As it was still raining hard and we were hungry, we decided He wouldn't object to us eating our picnic inside the church. Afterwards, as it was nearby, we called in to **St Andrew's, Hannah** *(LN13 9QL)*. A funny little roadside chapel, it proved more interesting than St Peter's. We walked through the south door into a porch over the west door, a sort of dogleg entrance. Different too is a well rounded altar rail gate and mini windows set within full size lead paned windows. After Sally headed home there was still time to see two churches recommended by landlady Claire and local to her farm.

Once there was grand Kirkstead Abbey. Now *"so apart from the crag, all that is left .... is the tiny church of St Leonard which was once its humble neighbour."*

Not at all humble. **St Leonard's, Kirkstead** *(LN10 6UH)* west façade is beautiful, the interior quietly pleasing, whereas stepping into nearby **St Margaret, Waddingworth** *(LN10 5EG)* is rather like entering a jumbled junk shop. Originally C14th this redundant little church was sympathetically restored in 1808: the exterior, a rosy muddle of iron and greenstone and pink bricks, is gorgeous and in keeping with a farmyard setting and a rope ladder leading to a tree house nestled in a nearby beech adds a homely touch.

St Margaret's, Waddingworth Lincs

Despite repeating my lack of interest in big churches, even as I was leaving mine hostess continued to urge me to call in to **St Mary Magdalene, Gedney** *(PE12 0BJ)*. Who was I to disobey? I'm pleased I did. This church is worth visiting if only to feast your eyes on the outstanding medieval door.

I was also intrigued by the roof which has the look of an apprentice carpenter nailing together in any old way many broken up pallets to quite pleasing effect! Best of all is the garden for that is what this churchyard is. Surrounding the entire church are flowerbeds filled with lavender and hydrangea, lilies, roses, box, cat mint and more. It has all been created, tended and stocked by a retired gentleman, John, who I came across weeding the long bed separating gravestones from lawn. All for the love of this church garden. I do hope when age overtakes his body someone else will pick up spade and fork, care for the garden as much as John.

Before checking into the next B & B – another farm – I called in to **St Lawrence's, Harpley** *(PE31 6TL)* drawn by the promise of interesting C15th bench ends. I liked much about this church: an attractive door within a door; C14th rood screen with painted panels restored in 1877 for £82.10.0d; a variety of creatures carved on the bench ends, some smart, others weird or amusing. After supper in a jolly pub nearby, a good night's sleep and plenty to eat for breakfast in the kitchen with mine host and hostess, I was ready for a return visit to Norfolk and its churches. Again, I thank my farmer host for flagging up three churches. The first, **St Peter's, Melton Constable** *(NR24 2LE),* was near to Edgefield where I was based. I parked on the grass off the drive leading to the Big House then walked up the path and through the Norman arch of the west door. Inside Mrs Barnes was busy setting up for tea after the Sunday morning service and happy to chat while she did so. I learned the church, though much altered since, was essentially nine hundred and twenty years old, nine hundred years older than her grandson "*who was christened in this very church twenty years ago!*" She chattered on: her father worked for Lord Hastings of the Astley family – "*kind man he was*" – on the estate of which the church is part and Mr Barnes – "*Russell was 'is name*" – died in 2007 and she still misses him. Unfortunately there were no church notes and Mrs Barnes knew nothing about the church other than its age. I could only wonder about the unusual chancel arch and beyond it a tiny window with a possibly original pull up shutter acting as a sort of squint. It is a really pretty church in a beautiful park setting.

On to **St Andrew's, Thurning** *(NR20 5QY)*, situated not far off the road though no houses nearby, just a pig farm across the road. I liked the feel of this interior as soon as I entered. A sermon delivered from the triple pulpit would ensure nobody in the box pews escaped the parson's eye. Each box, all of a size other than the larger one allocated to The Rectory, displayed the name of the householder owner: Farms Craymere, Church, Manor, Rookery, Hall and Lime Tree. There are three boxes across the west wall: a small one just for the rectory coachman, two larger ones for rectory and hall Servants. Anyone else below the salt was seated on basic benches: until 1920, boys sat on the right under a row of twenty-four hat pegs, the girls on the left. Outside, ponies sheltered in a small stable while their owners were at prayer. Everyone, but everyone, knew his place!

The roof is *the* impressive feature of **St Peter & St Paul's, Knapton** *(NR28 0SB)*. Constructed at the beginning of the C16th of Irish oak it is over seventy feet long, thirty feet wide and only slightly more than a hundred degrees at the apex. Even without any cross ties the high yet not deep walls are apparently as true today as when erected in 1503, an achievement to impress even engineers of today. Thank goodness signs of deathwatch beetle were detected early and treated. According to church notes, a mix of some one hundred and sixty Prophets, Apostles and Angels adorn spandrels and beams. A puzzle: I counted seventy-two!

Under this roof is another decorative font cover above a medieval octagonal font inscribed with the words *wash thou my sins, not my face only* which would, if written in Greek, be a palindrome. Hmm! One hassock is stitched with Nelson's famous line – that *England expects every man to do his Duty* – not *Kiss me, Hardy*!

All Saints', Morston *(NR25 7AA)* was memorable only for the most muddly collection of cushions/runners/carpet ever to grace a set of pews so on to **St Botolph's, Trunch** *(NR28 0PU)* especially to see the C14th font canopy which stands high over the font on six legs, the whole structure exquisitely painted and carved with foliage and figures – there is even a pig wearing a bishop's mitre.

The second church mine host suggested I include a visit was to **All Saints', Bawdeswell** *(NR20 4UX)*. Somewhat reluctantly I made the detour to this 'modern' church, the only one in Norfolk built after the war. It sits on a grassy knoll in complete contrast to C15th Chaucer House facing it across the lane. Built of flint and shingle, the chancel apsidal, a neo-classical portico over the south door, it's a touch New England in appearance if not intention. Oh me of little faith. Even before I stepped inside I knew I was going to be delighted. Once upon a time there stood a C14th medieval church until replaced in the C18th. The Victorian third church was destroyed in 1944 when a Mosquito bomber crashed returning from a mission in Germany. A tragedy for the two airmen killed but not for the church as a combination of war damage compensation and donation enabled **All Saints'** to rise from the ashes in September 1955 as designed by architect James Fletcher Watson with input from the villagers. Pale blue ceiling above tall, clear-glassed windows, white walls and aisle tiles, wood flooring under pews and a modern triple decker pulpit fashioned from limed oak, have created an interior of simplicity and light. The organ is positioned above the vestry on the white painted gallery, underneath and centred is the plain tub font with pale wood lid, Gorgeous.

Another detour, this time to **Norwich** to explore the medieval **Cathedral** *(NR1 4DH)*. Look to historians and academics for a tour around this magnificent building. Apart from smiling at the funky light cast from highly coloured modern stained glass into the ambulatory, I remember a sheep tethered on a grassy quadrangle within the cloisters, waiting for his walk on part in a Shakespeare play about to be performed; the polished copper font, previously used in chocolate making; and two misericords, one a C14th depiction of a schoolboy receiving a caning upended on his teacher's knee; the other a C21st commemoration of Norwich City FC; the latter showed football fans on the left supporter with cheering faces, those on the right the picture

Norwich Cathedral, misericord schoolboy beating m.cord

of despondency! I paid a brief visit to **St Peter Mancroft** off the market square to see the C15th font canopy, even more grandiose than that at Trunch though not as attractive, before exploring the lanes and alleys of the city centre.

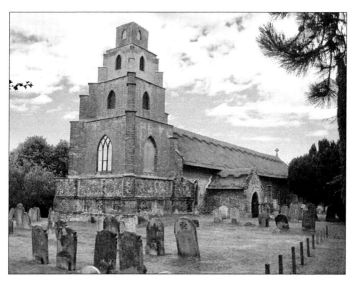

St Mary the Virgin, Burgh St Peter

The third excellent recommendation from my B & B host required perseverance and direction from a wayside gardener. Eventually, way beyond the village, I came upon a church with a tower unlike any other. The walls of **St Mary the Virgin, Burgh St Peter** *(NR34 0BT)* are part brick, part puddingstone, part flint, the roof is thatched and the tower telescopes as it rises – described variously as pagoda, pyramid, monstrosity, folly, hideous, there is no other like it in all the land. All that remains of the original C16th tower is a flint layer; it was enclosed to become the tomb for five generations of the Boycott family. Once inside I recall only the early C19th pulpit, the sides of which shine bright with polished copper plaques – I counted twenty-three – commemorating a whole string of Boycotts, five of whom were rectors of the church over a period of almost two hundred years (1764-1899). Since then the family continues to serve as patron to the parish. I saw no claim that those Boycotts might be related to Charles Boycott (1832-97), who after time serving in the Army moved to Ireland where he was employed as estate manager for the Earl of Eme. In 1880 though tenants were still suffering in the aftermath of the potato famine, he refused to reduce rents. Not only did tenants refuse to work, organize 'moral coventry' against Charles Boycott so soldiers had to be brought in to bring in the harvest, Boycott's family was so persecuted and intimidated they had no choice but to flee back to England resulting in the family surname becoming a verb.

I headed south towards the coast from a church with a singular telescopic tower to a church within a church. driving some way down a lane to where, opposite cottages and farm buildings, I parked by the churchyard gate. **St Andrews, Covehithe** *(NR34 7JJ)* is not itself imposing but the majesty of the scene is. All that remains of the very much larger C15th church, which almost certainly replaced an earlier place of worship, are tall fragments of walls and windows and the tower. When it became apparent that such an edifice was too costly for the congregation of a small village to maintain, permission was granted to remove the roof, allow dereliction in 1672 and create the space in which to build the small C17th thatched church of today. A landmark for boats at sea the tower, against which 'mini' St Andrews was built, is still intact and both church and ruins are today in the care of the Churches Conservation Trust. There is nothing of much interest inside the church other than the original font and a couple of notes on the wall dated 1672 to the memory of Girling and Gilbert, two churchwardens involved in the building of St Andrew's. In the porch a cheery plaque advising *"The church is still in use for regular worship"* adding *"The tower and ruins are maintained by the Redundant Churches Fund, St. Andrew –by-the-Wardrobe, Queen Victoria Street, with money provided by Parliament by the Church of England and by the gifts of the public."*

I spent sometime walking through and around the ruins, looking for and finding war graves in the unkempt grass, taking in the atmosphere of this rather wonderful ruin which in years to come will be claimed by the sea. I would have liked to walk down to the beech but the path is no more and time didn't allow.

Covehithe south side

My home for the last two nights of my small adventure was in the rural heart of Suffolk, not far from Aldeburgh. The accommodation could not have been more comfortable, my hostess more welcoming, the location more idyllic. The pièce de résistance of **St Mary's, Ufford** *(IP13 6DS)* is yet another extraordinary font cover. Pier upon pier telescopes to rise eighteen feet above the font, crowned by a pelican in her usual piety, pecking blood from her breast. The whole wooden edifice teems with embellishments, an impressive display of mid C15th craftsmanship and engineering, evident too in some of the bench ends and a kneeler table. However, these are as nothing compared with two beautiful screens either side of the chancel and the astonishing carvings of C15th bench ends, armrests and panels in nearby **St Mary's, Dennington** *(IP13 8AA)*. Various real and invented creatures include a mermaid, a two-headed eagle and the only known carving in England of a sciapod. This is a mythical human sort of desert creature with one humungous foot: as legend has it, this equips him with shade under which to rest! It was worth visiting St Mary's just to see him.

Talking of bench ends, ecclesiastical wood carving spanning some nine hundred years is a magnificent inheritance bequeathed to us by numerous pairs of mostly unsung hands. Cathedral quire stalls, bishop's chairs, rood screens, misericords, pulpits, bench ends, poppyheads and panels: again and again I stand before them in admiration, amazed and, quite often, amused. How, if ever, are these intricate carvings adorning churches and cathedrals throughout the land dusted, cleaned, preserved? Is there such a sight as a cherry picker carrying a cleaning person to lofty pinnacles armed with duster, or, even better, solvents to delicately remove decades of grime? I think not.

The variety of carvings on medieval bench ends is endless, from the plain honey pine panels of St Mary's, Honeychurch, Devon to fronds, foliage and green men exquisitely carved into dark oak in St George's, Dunster, Somerset and St Matthew's, Coldridge, Devon. Lambs of God, doves of peace, pelicans in their piety, cherubs, saints and clerics there are aplenty but it is the amusing, jolly and unexpected carvings I particularly recall with a smile or raised eyebrows. A bow legged jester and a bewhiskered musician playing the bagpipes next to a stacked pile of sheep in **St Nonna's, Alternun, Cornwall**; a man, hands clasped in prayer, sporting a decidedly Chinese pigtail in **St Mary's, High Bickington, Devon**. Most memorable of all those I've seen is the collection of bench ends and poppyheads in **St Mary's, Lakenheath, Suffolk** – walking up and down the aisles is an entertainment in itself. Carved into the top section of four panels are profiles of heads ranging from elderly man with attenuated neck to austere academic; in others an obviously male horse being whipped uphill by a rather camp chap with bulging upper arms, a flautist rocking on a log and – my favourite – a baby snail and mummy snail smiling at each other. **St Mary's, Dennington, Suffolk** boasts a particularly splendid bench end topped with an outsize poppyhead above sloping armrests, one of which is 'guarded by a maned lion, and on the panel itself a unique carving of the mythical sciapod lying at rest in the shade of his one outsize foot.

Bizarre. Not all bench ends are squared or rounded at the top, some are decorated with elaborate finials, also known as poppyheads (from the latin word *puppis* mean poop /figurehead of shop). Some are extraordinary creatures copied from the medieval Bestiary (*liber de naturis bestiarum,* literally "book of natural beasts"), a collection of all sorts of animals, real and imaginary: wyverns, winged creatures with dragon head; scitalis, slow moving hot to touch serpent; griffin griffon gryphon, lion body tail and back legs, eagle head, wings and front legs, talons; and not to forget the unicorn unicorn. An eclectic collection of finials adorns the bench ends of St Mary the Virgin, Lakenheath:

St Mary's, Dennington sciapod

reclining dragon, cringing calf, dog with hooves carrying a howdah, hunched man, a copulating couple, fish eating fish, a tigress admiring herself in a mirror, a dog licking itself. Not only does St Mary's, Dennington lay claim to the only known sciapod carving, it also has fine poppyheads as well as a miscellany of freestanding creatures and a mermaid on sloping arm rests. I remember three elephants carrying howdahs adorning arm rests in the quoir stalls of Beverley Minster, Chester Cathedral and Ripon Cathedral. Ripon also has a despondent organ grinder's monkey. The variety of creatures carved on elaborate arm rests in the qu oir stalls of Salisbury Cathedral are truly magnificent. In St Lawrence's, Harpley, Norfolk weird dogs and dismal clerics; in St Mary & All Saints, Checkley, a double sided Red Indian with feathered head dress and somewhere a miserable looking member of the crow family hunched into itself. So many more.

(In Wales I came across bench ends like no others I have seen. The ancient black oak benches of **St Gwyddelan's, Dolwyddelan** *(LL25 0SJ)* with slatted back rests are linked with curious scalloped borders to resemble a sleigh without runners. These ones are quite plain whereas in **Rug Chapel, Denbeighshire** *(LL21 9BT)* the same scallops are carved with a variety of animals and a frieze of foliage along the bottom edge.)

I have digressed. Again.

Running down the lane approaching **St Andrew's, Bramfield** *(IP19 9AB)* is an unusual brick wall, built in sweeping curves instead of the usual straight line, a brick extravagant way to avoid the necessity of piers – well worth a non-church photograph! The church, with its detached round flint bell tower, the only one in Suffolk, is so attractive. The long thatched roof has added detail not only on the ridge but midway along the pitched sides above cream painted walls. Inside, a fine screen, a poignant monument to Elizabeth Coke who died in childbirth (1627) depicting her with child in arms, and – best of all – the memorial stone in the nave to Bridgett Applewhaite. Here's the memorable – and unintentionally hilarious -inscription:

Between the remains of her Brother Edward and of her late Husband
Arthur,
Here lies the body of Bridgett Applewhait once Bridgett Nelson.
After the Fatigues of a married life, Born by her with Incredible Patience
For four years and three quarters, barring three Weeks;
And after the Enjoiment of the Glorious Freedom of an Easy and
Unblemished Widowhood,
For Four Years and Upwards,
She Resolved to run the risk of a second Marriage-Bed, but
DEATH forbad the Banns.
And having with an Apoplectick Dart (the same Instrument with which
He had formerly Dispatched her Mother)

Touch't the most Vital part of her Brain.
She must have fallen directly to the Ground (as one Thunder strook)
If she had not been Catch't and Supported by her Intended Husband.
Of which Invisible Bruise, after a Struggle for above Sixty Hours, with
that Grand Enemy to Life (But the Certain and Merciful Friend to
Helpless Old Age)
In Terrible Convulsions Plaintive Groans, or Stupefying Sleep
Without Recovery of her Speech, or Senses,
She died on the 12 th day of Sept in the Year of our Lord 1737 and of her
own Age 44
Behold Death came as a Thief.
But O Thou Source of Pious Cares
Strict Judge without Regard
Grant tho' we go hence unawares
We go not Unprepared. Amen.

Poor woman – her mother died when she was sixteen; her brother died aged twenty-seven of a "wasting disease", Aunt Bridgett who cared for her, died of the dropsy. Bridgett didn't marry until she was thirty-five, and apparently her husband Arthur left *"no Legacy but a Chancery-Suit with his Eldest Brother ….."*

Someone had told me of a small church above a field overlooking the water across from Snape. Mid afternoon, I parked Ruby at The Maltings then set off under a clear sun warmed sky towards **St Botolph's, Iken** *(IP12 2ES)*, just visible on a distant promontory. The path crossed a field, continued on boardwalk through reeds then hugged the shore until it came out on a lane. A short walk before the stubby tower and thatched roof of St Botolph's came into view beyond a low gate set in a tall yew hedge encircling the churchyard. A path led to the south porch next to which grew two large fennel plants! I entered into and was enchanted by the minimally furnished flint-rubble Norman interior. Behind a dozen or so simple benches a Saxon cross and C15th font; on the benches cushions on which all kinds of animals have been appliquéd. It was a special church with which to end the day and this crawl, before I retraced my steps. I had intended to treat myself to a proper birthday meal but decided what could be better than a peaceful picnic supper among the reeds while shadows lengthened and birds sang before bedtime.

* * *

View across reed beds to St Botolph's church, Iken, Suffolk

Pottering up to Cumbria

Ten years on from my first visit to the Peak District, the Dawdlers spent a dawdling week around Arnside. While there I visited a ruined chapel, spent a day in the company of Monty the Clydesdale, then on the way home popped into three very different churches and walked a path along The Roaches to find a church-not-a-church.

I parked in the square of old **Heysham** village, happy to pause on the long drive north to Arnside where team leader of the Dorset Dawdlers had booked us for one week in self-catering accommodation from where we would set off each day, booted up, picnics on our backs. A way marker to **St Patrick's Chapel** *(LA3 2RN)* pointed along a narrow cobbled street flanked by C17th stone cottages. Passing St Peter's, the parish church disfigured by scaffolding and blue plastic sheeting, I followed an uneven, tree shaded sandy path uphill. I hadn't expected to emerge onto the headland to such a spectacular panoramic view over Morecambe Bay. Little remains of the ruin of this Anglo-Saxon chapel rising above rocks tickled with grass but two walls, an arch, and a massive lintel, yet the silhouette is somehow impressive. This Christian monument dates from the C8th, the eight nearby graves cut into solid rock, carved crosses still clearly evident, probably C10th or C11th. Excavations during 1977-78 revealed many burials, including a woman with a Viking age comb next to her. I imagine the view over the water has changed little since villagers climbed to worship in the chapel.

St Parick's Chapel, Heysham estury view and stone graves

The area around Arnside is where my eccentric Aunt Veronica grew up and to where she returned in older age. **St Anthony's, Cartmell Fell** *(LA11 6NH)* was especially dear to her so, finding myself in the area, I felt almost bound to visit it on her behalf. High in the fells, C16th St Anthony stretches long and low in a daffodil strewn churchyard, a field within woodland. Inside, a wide aisle leads past benches to a collection of family box pews, one of which has a centre table because it was used as a schoolroom. Until 1727, when flagstones were laid at a cost of £9.3s.4d.the aisle floor was earthen, strewn annually with rushes. My aunt, who spent so many years devotedly tending her son so stricken with multiple sclerosis, surely found peace in so beautiful and remote a corner of Cumbria. So beautiful that one day, rather than participate in the designated walk, I decided I would cover more ground, see further over the moors to the coastal landscape, from the back of a large horse. High in the hills above Millom winding lanes took me to Cumbrian Heavy Horse stables, where I was introduced to my steed for the day, a strawberry roan Clydesdale. Monty was huge but such a gentleman! The comfortable ride aback this gentle giant was memorable, affording a lofty vantage point from where to absorb those vistas.

At the end of a wonderful week of walking with friends as they headed south I drove north along the M6 to find **St Ninian's, Brougham** *(CA10 2AD)*. I would not have found it without directions from a gentleman on high. East of Penrith I was parked in a farmyard apparently having 'reached my destination' according to Tim Tom Tom even though, so far as I could see, the surrounding fields were devoid of all other buildings. Fortunately a bright green monster farm machine grumbled into the yard with a smiley face behind the steering wheel. Somehow, despite the considerable distance between us and after a hollered exchange, I was directed to a cleared space concealed behind a hedge opposite, from where a marker indicated the way to St Ninian's. Smiley Face pointed to his boots so I took the hint, donned mine and set off. To one side of the track, far below flowed a winding river; to the other, a flock of grazing Brent geese. Such beautiful countryside stretched ahead of me, a panorama of lush grass and trees on the turn to autumn colours, away from the thrum of road traffic. After quite some way I saw St Ninian's, just visible through trees and an open gate within the stone wall of an oval churchyard in the middle of a very large field. Two ancient doors opened into a simple interior: white washed walls, dark oak box pews, a few hatchments, the church bible, a battered prayer box, wall plaques dedicated to various Broughams. I particularly liked the inscription to *Elenora Brougham, widow of... "the able mother of an Abler Son"*. St Ninian's, with no family or house to serve, is in the care of Church Preservation Trust. I wonder if Aunt Veronica visited this tranquil location.

I had arranged to stay that night in a B & B outside Leek well positioned for an adventure the following day. The C13th church of **St Mary's, Whalley** *(BB7 9SY)* wasn't too much of a diversion. I stood awhile before three Saxon crosses standing in the churchyard – the tallest is well over two metres – before entering the south porch. Unfortunately the rotund vicar was locking up, about to leave to officiate at a wedding in another church in his parish. When I mentioned my particular interest in seeing the fine C15th misericords, this jolly, helpful man cleric kindly took the trouble, and time, to make a note of my address, promising he would take photographs, put them on a CD and forward them to me. He was as good as his word. The variety of subjects include several angels and a couple of plants; foliage spilling out the mouth of a green man; a couple of dragons, one with St George another carrying a child; a man shoeing a goose, a fox stealing a goose; pigs under an oak tree; two eagles eating; a chap being beaten by his wife with a frying pan. Secular themes and 'stories' rather outnumber the religious ones.

After a leisurely breakfast following a comfortable night I followed the A53 north towards Buxton. Over the years I've spent seeking churches and chapels mostly medieval and small I have wound my way along roads, lanes, streets, tracks, even paths, but none as magical as the route I followed on foot that afternoon to **Lud's Church** *(ST13 8UA)*. After a few miles I turned onto a quiet road running beneath and parallel to a rocky escarpment strewn with boulders known as The Roaches. Leaving Ruby in a layby I set off under a brilliant blue sky lit with sunshine, dependent on a few scribbled directions to reach the 'church'. I saw a cottage built into the rocks way above me just as two walkers appeared. Before indicating the path I should take, they told me something of the history of Rockhall Cottage. In the C17th it was no more than a cavern, home to eccentric Bess Bowyer, well known for hiding smugglers and deserters from the authorities, until in 1862 it was adapted into a primitive gamekeeper's dwelling and used as such until the Peak District National Park came into being. Today a memorial to local rock climber Don Whillans (1933-85) it is used as accommodation for climbers. No rock climbing for me. I scrambled up what passed for a path until I reached the top of the ridge. I felt as though I was on top of the world! All around me, ahead and below to both sides, the magnificent countryside rose and rolled, a kaleidoscope of rusts and greens. Without encountering a single other person I walked on through heather, round a pond, under huge overhanging boulders until eventually the path led down, down, down into woods and **Lud's Church**. In the late C14th a group of church reformers and dissenters led by John Wycliffe (1351-84) broke away from the church to become known as The Lollards, dissenters whose forbidden preference was to worship in English rather than Latin. One group, led by Walter de Ludwark, held meetings on the floor of an extraordinary narrow canyon deep between sheer green rock walls dripping with moss, hence the name by which this singular ravine is known. A 'church-but-not-a-church'. I emerged into the soft dying light of early dusk and followed the low road back to where Ruby was parked.

The following morning after an unhurried drive through stunning Staffordshire scenery I arrived at **St Peter's,**

Alstonefield *(DE6 2FX).* It's on a slight rise looking to far hills beyond a spread of many fields enclosed and linked by dry stonewalls. Although St Peter's two-decker-once-triple pulpit is deemed the main attraction, a family pew, painted a fetching avocado green with pelmet board tassle trim picked out in gold, is hardly less eye catching. I spent more time in the churchyard with a view where, guided by church notes, I found two little headstones: one resembles an upended round millstone with lettering running round the edge for Anne Green, died 3rd April 1518 – surely one of the oldest still in existence – and a more recent one dated 1731 to commemorate Margaret Barclay, died aged one hundred and seven!

My route south of Ashbourne lay across country to **St Mary & All Saints, Checkley** (ST10 4NJ). I was disappointed to find it locked until a kind gentleman tending graves telephoned a verger who appeared within minutes, only too happy to share his enthusiasm for 'his' church. I interrupted the verger as he launched into a serious history lesson I didn't want by pointing to a life size toy orangutan, orange and hairy, slumped in a heavily carved dark oak chair: "What on earth…?" "Oh, he's the quiet bishop. The children love him". Of course they would! More oddities: a crude depiction of a donkey carved along one side of the Saxon font and in the chancel a bulbous stone bowl on top of a matching plinth, memorial to 'Charlotte Dix who grew flowers for the sanctuary', and an unusual bench end finial showing two Red Indian heads complete with feather headdress. The east window is C14th and very fine but so too are the C17th Dutch roundels set high up in the south window of the chancel, each one framing a rural scene, a pictorial farm calendar of which only the months February (pool netting!), March (pruning), May (flower gathering),

July (mowing), September (reaping), October (harvesting fruit) and November (tree planting), remain. The paintings are quite charming, small yet full of detail. I was pleased to capture them with the excellent zoom feature of my 'new' camera.

Roundel in St Mary & All Saints, Checkley, acorn harvest Oct

I was even more pleased to drive only so far as Bath to spend time and the night with Robert and Hannah before heading for home.

* * *

Northumberland and Back

I have visited many churches in the south of England, few in the north. Northumberland doesn't appear to have many small, quirky churches; nevertheless one October I decided to include beach, castle, wild cattle, Saxon perfection and a bell cage on my itinerary to lure me along the wearisome drive up from Sussex.

At the foot of the Cheviot Hills in Northumberland's National Park on the very outskirts of **Alnham**, all but hidden among trees – unusual among churchyards, not one of them a yew – is **St Michael & All Angels** *(NE65 7BE)*. According to church notes there is a burial chamber *above* the chancel. The scenery was so beautiful I decided, despite the grey damp day, to follow the path onto the hills to the Shepherds' Cairn. The story of this memorial is told on a board by the lych gate. On Saturday 17th November 1962 after leaving the market, shepherds Jock Scott and Willie Middlemas dropped off Willie Bulloch at Castle Hill Farm before driving their tractor across the moor in a blizzard. They never arrived. Their bodies were discovered three days later, half a mile from Jock's home. Exactly one hundred years before their demise, walking home from work in the same hills, Nellie Herron never arrived: she froze to death resting on a stone. Following written directions borrowed from the church, I climbed up and up into the hills. After some distance a mist descended, startled sheep appeared from the gloom, a stone wall wasn't where it should have been – I realised I had somehow taken a wrong turning and common sense prevailed. Down the path I went, probably startling the same sheep.

The owner of the Bed & Breakfast where I was staying, told of my interest in small churches, said there was an interesting chapel in the tiny village of **Biddlestone**, not far from Alnham. Nearby the village is Harden Quarry, source of the red rock used in the grounds of Buckingham Palace and to surface The Mall. I parked Ruby and read two rather alarming notices tied on a deer fence before walking up a grassy track to find the chapel. One was a directive regarding deer management that *"internal organs must be buried at least One Metre deep after they have been examined for signs of disease"* and the other ungrammatical and puzzling advice for visitors to the Chapel Woods *"asking dog walkers should be you, or more likely your dog, may come across un-buried deer entrails away from the track so best keep dogs on lead."* I walked on, glad on this occasion to be dog free. Extraordinarily tall and narrow, the C19th Roman Catholic chapel is perched above the C14th undercroft, or 'pele' tower, all that remains of Biddlestone Hall, and is now in the care of the Historic Chapels Trust. Far away from any other building, it felt weirdly 'wrong' to find it on the edge of pine woods. I had intended to visit St Aiden's, Throckington, another small isolated church where Lord Beveridge is buried, but decided against the long drive further into the Park to find it.

Had my kindly hostess not directed me to **Holy Trinity, Old Bewick** *(NE66 4DZ)* I would have missed out on another isolated church, small and Norman. Surrounded by a large churchyard liberally planted with a variety of trees, it's a shorter, fatter version of St Michael's & All Angels, Alnham with a much more atmospheric interior. A perfect Norman arch led from nave to chancel with two bell ropes suspended above a door in the south wall leading to the wee bell tower, through another arch to a fat little apsidal east end and altar under a soft blue ceiling. Holy Trinity was restored in the C14th and, after falling into ruin, again in the C19th. I'm glad it was rescued not least because there are snowdrops peculiar to the church – they are yellow. Legend has it they came with the Vikings. The other oddity close to the churchyard gate is what appears to be a potting shed, furnished with a carpet offcut and floor cushions. An elderly lady fussing about on hands and knees with dustpan and brush informed me it is in fact a *poustinia* from the Russian meaning 'hermitage'. It is a local tradition to provide a haven in which a person may rest and contemplate.

These were the only *small* churches I visited while in Northumberland. At this time of year a boat trip to the Farne Islands was just that, a trip to, but not onto, the Islands. I thoroughly enjoyed watching large colonies of grey seals milling around in the sea between boat and land, looking remarkably like wet Labradors. A handful of brand new white pups lay about on shore while mothers fished. Had I come during the summer months I would have watched myriad sea birds, landed on Inner Farne Island and been able to go inside the tiny wood lined stone St Cuthbert's Chapel instead of peering at it from the sea.

A short drive along the narrow and blissfully empty Northumbrian lanes brought me to the **Chillingham Estate**. The medieval castle is a popular attraction for visitors but my one and only objective was to see from close quarters the unique herd of wild white cattle. Ruby bumped and climbed a rough track through still leafy deciduous trees to a small clearing in the woods, an excuse of a car park. After parking

Ruby by two other cars I walked my boots through a tray of disinfectant then set off through several large fields, dipping into two more trays along the way. To be in such an isolated and peaceful landscape I was already in heaven, even before sight of the herd, sunlit on a distant slope. Nestled in a glade is a narrow three sided rough stone edifice. It houses a motley collection of skulls, hides, horns as well as the sad little form of a preserved new born calf. Posters on the long wall detail the history of these cattle. Next door a shepherd's hut serves as the visitor centre and warden's 'office'. Ellie the warden was waiting to take two couples and myself onto cattle territory, cautioning us to stay close to her, speak softly.

It is hard to describe how exciting and frightening it was to be in such close proximity to these cattle: young calves beside protective mothers, bulls bellowing and pawing the ground, heads lowered, clashing horns. The Grey family took possession of, and enclosed, the Estate in 1250 though there is no written record of the cattle before 1645-46 when one of Lord Grey's servants wrote to him (Grey's principal seat was Uppark House, near Chichester) to warn *"this continuing Storme if it lye but one Month more there will bee neither Beast nor Sheepe left in the County. Your Honour's Deere and wild Cattle I fear will all dye, doe what we can as the lik of this storme hath not beene knowne by any living in the Country ...."* since when to this day the *only* interaction between man and beast is the provision of hay during winter months. Should a calf be born less than perfect it is left to die – Ellie told us a calf born without a tail was abandoned by its mother – hence a herd in which only the fittest have survived down the centuries. According to the Chillingham Wild Cattle Association (CWCA) *"in most experiments of prolonged inbreeding, populations die out because of this accumulation of harmful genes. But in a very few, maybe 5%*

*of cases and especially if inbreeding is very gradual, by sheer chance harmful genes can be purged from the population because in any one generation of young only a few individuals are affected. It looks as though this is what has happened at Chillingha*m." Following the last devastating outbreak of foot and mouth disease in 2001 ensure the continued line of this very rare bovine breed a small number of the herd were relocated to a secret location somewhere in Scotland. My visit to the Chillingham herd was a memorable – and educational – interlude.

I was rather pleased the rain poured down the day I visited **St Mary the Virgin, Holy Island** *(TD5 2RX)* as only a handful of raincoats wandered the lanes. Saints Aidan, Bede, Cuthbert, Columba, Oswald *and* Wilfrid are all linked to this large, dour church. Before leaving I admired an impressive elm sculpture in the north aisle. 'The Journey' by Fenwick Lawson is a carving of six more than life size monks, St Cuthbert's body carried on their shoulders, heading for the door to take him from the island. Chatting to the owner of a small gallery I learned there are around one hundred and fifty residents on Holy Island. The school had four pupils when I was there – two of them the teacher's children! They join classes at Lowick's school when tides allow and, from the age of eleven, they board at school in Berwick, fees paid by the government. My chatty 'new friend' said although the island has a fire engine it isn't in service as the island no longer has a resident fireman. He went on to say before he became a resident, a fire which started in the roof of a cottage during high tide when the causeway was submerged, had to be extinguished by the islanders forming a chain of buckets. Since then they've asked if a fireman could come over to give them some tips as to how best to deal with a high tide emergency but the answer was an emphatic no! Health and safety or job protection?

Before driving south I completed my sojourn in this wild and empty county with a long bracing walk at low tide along an empty stretch of beach to the magnificent ruins of **Dunstanburgh Castle** – long may it escape restoration. Before gates closed I made a hasty visit to **Woodhorn Museum, Ashington** *(NE63 9YF),* once a C19th colliery, to see the Weeping Window, part of the iconic 2015 Tower of London poppy installation touring the country: standing as a lone spectator before the cascade of flowers tumbling down the derrick above the disused shaft I found far more moving than the slow shuffle of huge crowds moving along the moat in London. From wild cattle to castle to a waterfall of poppies I progressed to the town of Alnwick. For me there was no contest choosing between Alnwick castle and the wonderfully eccentric 'station' bookshop. Wandering round **Barter Books** *(NE66 2NP),* the secondhand bookshop in what was Alnwick Railway Station was huge fun. Model trains trundle along tracks overhead, sofas encourage browsing at leisure, rows and rows of bookshelves fill what was the concourse, original posters cover the walls of waiting rooms left much as they once were– brilliant.

Before leaving this gorgeous county which boasts a National Park encompassing the Cheviot Hills and stunning beaches as I drove south I decided to divert from the A1 near Cramlington so as to explore the extraordinary landform, designed by landscape architect Charles Jencks, that is **Northumberlandia**. Well, the giant form of the Angel of the North a few miles south is spectacularly vertical whereas the vast form of Lady of the North is a horizontal spectacle. I emerged from a wood to just stand for a while, taking in the length, form and huge size of her before setting off to walk all over her. From the high point of her forehead I looked down her nose, up her nose; I followed paths spiraling up her breasts, over a knee and a hip and down to a sundial placed near her feet. Such fun! Far in the background the Shotton open cast mine was a huge scar on the landscape but not for much longer as a notice informed that in 2018 coal mining was to finish and "the site will be restored by 2019 and include 88,000 trees being planted and 9km of new paths." A wonderful new public space created from humungous amounts of slag and entirely funded by private money – amazing. I was bowled over and really hope to return in a few years to see the changes to the Lady and her surroundings. Even though she is known locally as the Slag, nevertheless she is quality.

Northumberlandia

From an adventure on the land I continued south to find the miraculously preserved late C7th **Saxon Church, Escomb** *(DL14 7SY),* County Durham. I had been warned it is in the middle of a council estate and it is, within an oval churchyard, sparingly planted with deciduous trees, not a single yew. On the iron gate set into the surrounding stone wall a notice directs visitors to the church keys which are to be found for all to see hanging on the front wall of house No 28! This small but really tall church is perfect in every way: it looks stunning, unspoiled and almost unchanged despite the passing centuries – the C13th porch with sundial and Celtic cross, is a 'recent' addition. The centuries had taken their toll on the fabric of the building when a cleric, realizing the significance of this Anglo-Saxon church, ensured its late C19th restoration – for once without the heavy hand of Victorian interference. The only change made was to create a decent sized west end window below the tiny Saxon one high under the roof, bringing welcome light into the cell. Rounded Saxon windows, deep sills splaying widely from the back set in the south wall whereas those in the north wall are rectangular. Beyond lay the chancel, as tall though slightly more narrow. I looked about me, enjoying the age and atmosphere of this ancient interior. I was not completely

Saxon church, Escombe

alone: according to church notes rare minute whiskered bats have made their home in the rafters. This little church was by far the queen bee of churches visited on this 'crawl'.

None of the churches I saw in Essex came close to Escomb in any way. The countryside en route to the coastal village of **Wrabness** isn't Essex at its postcard prettiest. Neither is the oldest building in the village. Small, dating from around 1100 **All Saints** *(CO11 2TG)* squats in the middle of a relatively empty and treeless churchyard. I had come to see its unusual feature. To the left of the approach path is a square construction, weathered oak beams crisscrossing to form walls under a pitched red tiled roof. When the bell tower collapsed in the C17th a 'temporary' cage was constructed to house the church bell. It remains home to the bell to this day. Low to the ground is the exterior housing for the one remaining bell of **St Michael the Archangel, Quarley** in Hampshire and a quaint thatched roof covers a bell and frame outside **St Nicholas, Woodrising** *(IP25 7SG)* in Norfolk but surely **St Mary the Virgin, East Bergholt** *(CO7 6TA)* in Suffolk boasts the most impressive bell cage erected in 1531, home to a unique set of five enormous C16th bells.

A recent addition to the village is an extraordinary house built on the outskirts of the village, not far from the waters edge. This had to be seen! The house is every bit as unusual as its owner, the wonderful artist and communicator, eccentric and colourful Grayson Perry. The route to it is a narrow path towards the water. Photographs had not prepared me for this bizarre building when it came into sight, end on to the water. Behind a double storey, key-hole shaped porch four pitched roofs descend each lower than the other, each section flanked on either side by a pair of arched dormer windows, reducing in size as the pitch lowers in height. The roofs and dormer frames are mustard yellow, the geometric tiles, real or faux, form patterns of forest green and white and everywhere the eye is caught by startling embellishments; a metal lollipop with a double headed snail without a shell and a small metal figure of a naked pregnant girl balancing on a roof ridge being two of them. No garden, just an unkempt grassed and fenced surround. Empty, maybe just for then. Interesting.

The triangular tower and hexagonal spire is, I believe, a unique feature of **All Saints in Maldon** *(CH9 4QE)* where I paused briefly for a coffee and nibble before following the coast road to find allegedly the oldest rural church in England. Built by St Cedd in 654 AD, **St Peter-on-the-Wall, Bradwell-on-Sea** *(CM0 7PN)* stands alone by the salt marshes at the end of a lengthy cinder track. There was something majestic about its simple form despite, at the time of my visit, being covered with scaffolding and blue plastic sheeting, closed for structural repairs. A walk along the coast under a vast sky above a gorgeous view did much to assuage my disappointment. On to the very last church I had marked for this crawl. Another lesser disappointment: **St Margaret's Margaretting** *(CM4 0ED)* was locked. Medieval and wooden, I would have liked to read its history begun long before the railway line passed yards – and I mean yards – from the entrance. I parked Ruby just out of reach of the barrier; it came down three times in the short time I was there.

* * *

Midlands Meander

This clockwise crawl was peppered with much to interest and amuse: from dovecotes to converted gasworks; frizzy sheep to church owl; exquisite sculpture to shrunken effigies; pub quiz to a testing walk; a handful of churches, a windmill ....

I planned the route and booked Bed and Breakfast stays at appropriate intervals early in the year, in the hope that, by the last week in March, the weather would be more clement, more spring than winter. I was in luck: apart from a handful of raindrops in the Peak District, it was sunshine and relative warmth for the whole week I was on the road.

After an overnight stay in Hungerford and long overdue catch up with Penny and Tim, curious to see the **Holy Austin rock houses** *(DY7 6DL),* I took a cross country route to Kinver Edge, south-west of Birmingham. The 'houses', halfway up the side of the ridge, excavated into sandstone, are quite extraordinary and the only such dwellings in the country. According to the 1861 census eleven families lived in the rock. Their water was supplied by a deep well and without any form of lavatory, 'everything' was dug into the gardens so the soil was well fertilized. If more space was required for a growing family, another room was chipped out of the rock. The families were completely self-sufficient, growing vegetables and raising animals for their own needs. Local iron works, agriculture and trades provided employment for the men, children went to school in the village and some went on to university. The Housing Act of 1960 compelled every dwelling to have basic facilities these homes rather lacked. The last occupants left in 1963, the National Trust

Holy Austin rock cottages of Kinver Edge au naturel …

Cottage living room, dressed

acquired the site the following year. I wandered through two cottages the Trust has 'dressed' as well as those left in their raw state. It was strange to realise some members of those families are surely still around with tales to tell of their childhood. I would have been so interested to reminisce with one or some of them.

I headed west towards the farm I had chosen on the outskirts of Stratford-on-Avon for Bed & Breakfast. En route I decided to make a small detour along wonderfully empty country lanes, past a collection of farm buildings and a dejected looking church to see the medieval **Kinwarton Dovecote** *(B49 6HB)*. I found a huge C14th circular stone 'tub' of a building alone in a field, the only remaining evidence of a moated house. Doves would have entered through three louvered openings in the roof: I crawled through a double door tunnel-like entrance into a vast cylindrical interior lined with row upon row of nest boxes. The original sloping rotating ladder attached to the arm of a central wooden column or pivot enabled access to these boxes. I've seen other ancient *columbaria* in a sorry state so I was happy to see this dovecote maintained by the National Trust.

The following morning after an excellent farm breakfast I strolled over to admire a mixed flock of frizzy fleeced Grey Faced Dartmoor and black faced Suffolk Clun ewes. Their brand new lambs skittered through the straw on wobbly legs playing a game of catch-me-if-you-can in between pausing to suckle on bended legs, tails a-whizzing. Leaving this charming bucolic scene I set off to find my first church. On the periphery of a working farmyard, framed by huge horse chestnuts and limes (not a yew to be seen) the tall and narrow west façade of **All Saints, Billesley** *(B49 6NF)* is almost Georgian in style. Essentially C13th it's apparent there have been many and various later additions: wooden gallery over the west door, box pews, a C17th fireplace. In the south transept a dusty organ made by Sterling Company of Derby, Conn. USA obscures the name of a thirteen years old child on a flagstone dated June 18th 1826. I peered at words, mysterious to non-musical me, beautifully inscribed on the stops: *dulcet, hautboy, principal, bass coupler, vox humana, treble coupler, flute, violin, dulciana, echo.* By 1361 following the Black Death (1346-53) the village of Billesley was no more and no registers survive before 1816 yet it is alleged this is the church in which William Shakespeare (1564–1616) married Anne Hathaway (1556–1623) and where later his grand-daughter Elizabeth married her John. I liked the following story: "*The Billesley rector, Rev. Fortescue Knottesford (d.1852), would drive by coach with his family the six miles from their home, Alveston Manor, for eleven o'clock matins. The curate took the service, the rector preached. After the service the family had dinner in one of the pews which had a fire grate after which, while the children played in the churchyard, the Reverend snoozed in the pew until 3 o'clock evensong.*"

East of Stratford I found **St Giles, Chesterton** *(CV33 9LG)* on a mound, squat, grey, isolated, locked. No need to search for a key holder as this proved to be the dog owner walking past. While waiting for the kind lady to return with the key I observed a very recent grave, that of a twenty-seven year old son, husband and dad was covered with flowers, some of which spelled out Daddy. Also poignant and just inside the south door is a C16th alabaster memorial with faint traces of sepia hand painting. Humphrey and Anna Peyto lie side by side, a growling fanged dog under his feet, a miniature dog curled up on her left leg, and behind the parents a frieze with effigies of their ten children: three sons, two in doublets, one wearing armour; seven daughters, six wearing dresses, one wrapped in a shroud. I retraced my way past empty fields to park Ruby near a path I followed uphill to a striking local landmark on high, the **Chesterton Windmill**. Commissioned by the Peyto family, designed by Inigo Jones and built of local limestone in 1632, it is one of a kind. The tower rises fifteen feet above six semi-circular arches with a cap rotating on fifteen huge cast iron rollers and a hand operated winch turns the sails, spanning sixty feet into the wind. It's a magnificent sight from afar, even more so standing next to it.

I spent the afternoon exploring the town of Stratford and its famous theatre, descriptions of which are all too well known to include here, before returning to amuse myself watching the early evening playtime antics of sooty frizzy lambs having mad moments before bed time.

After another substantial breakfast and taking leave of the farmer's wife – and the lambs – I headed north to **St John's, Berkswell** *(CB7 7BJ),* a substantial village church within a large stone walled churchyard. On the boundary a *magnolia stellata* was in full flower near a pair of small yew trees. Above the C16th porch is a priest's room accessed by an external staircase. A rather bright yellow plaster and oak arcading contrasts with the mellow red brick of early C13th body of the church much altered over the centuries. Inside I was surprised to see that the musicians' gallery runs above the south aisle, seats facing east. The main 'feature' of St John's is the extensive Norman crypt, its vaulted roof underneath the chancel and part of the nave. Narrow, blocked staircases descend from pulpit and lectern. I confess to spending most of my visit hunting the Mice of Berkswell to be found on chair and table legs, the pulpit, altar and font as well – my tally was eight of the nine! Robert Thompson's descendant, also Robert, had included the family trade mark on furniture either recently repaired or made for St John's.

Onwards north to **Lichfield Cathedral**. This cathedral will be memorable for one single monument tucked away in a corner. I waylaid a church person in a gown who was only too happy to expand on the story behind it. In 1812 tuberculosis caused the death of Rev. William Robinson, prebendary of the Cathedral, whilst still a young man in his thirties. His wife Ellen-Jane was left to bring up their daughters, the elder also named Ellen-Jane and Marianne. In 1813 daughter Ellen-Jane died from burns suffered when her nightdress caught fire. In 1814 Marianne sickened and died. The grief stricken widow commissioned sculptor Frances Chantrey to create a memorial for the sisters. The monument to little Penelope Boothby in St Oswald's, Ashbourne is delightful but this is *the* most exquisite white marble sculpture of two little girls. They lie asleep in each other's arms as often observed by their mother. In Marianne's hand a posy of snowdrops. The detail of the mattress and cushion, tiny fingers and toes, folds of the nightdresses is extraordinarily beautiful. It's

Beautiful memorial to two sisters, Lichfield Cathedral

alleged when someone commented to the sculptor his work was perfection he made sure it wasn't, insisting nothing is absolutely perfect so he left the sole of one child's foot rough, unfinished. In 1826 a poet was inspired by the sculpture to write a lengthy poem. These are the closing lines:

> Age after age shall pass away,
> Nor shall their beauty fade, their forms decay.
> For here is no corruption; the cold worm
> Can never prey upon that beauteous form.
> This smile of death that fades not, shall engage
> The deep affections of each distant age.
> Mothers, till ruin the round world hath rent,
> Shall gaze with tears upon the monument
> And fathers sigh, with half-suspended breath;
> How sweetly sleep the innocent in death.

On to **St. Nicholas, Mavesyn Ridware** *(DE13 7HP)*, another large church in a rural setting, with an ancient stone tower and chapel onto which has been added a C19th red brick extension under the canopy of a huge cedar. The absence of yew trees in this part of the country was interesting; wasn't it *de rigeur* for a yew to be planted in churchyards? A helpful homeowner nearby showed me where the key was kept. I rather liked the dark oak pews, shapely and open backed, each row sitting on an oak platform. A toy red squirrel wearing a white surplice was perched on one bench end. A shiny brass plaque screwed into the bulbous stone font inscribed with several lines of Latin seemed a pretentious way of telling us an erstwhile Rector was resting in peace. But the fun is in Trinity Chapel. Two families are integral to the history of this church: the Charwicks and Mavesyns, the latter name being a variation of the French *mal voisin, its* meaning 'dangerous neighbour'. The raised west end is brightened by a dozen or more seriously purple surplices with plain white cowl collars hanging from a clothes rack such as you find in any dress shop, vivid against scarlet carpet. I stepped down onto the sunken tiled floor to examine walls faced with vertical slabs. Outlined on the marble are effigies of two ladies with earnest expressions and various armour clad knights. Tablets on the west wall tell tales of the murder of a member of the Berwicke family while hunting and of the death of Sir William Handsacre by the hand of Sir Robert Mavesyn:

The bugle sounds! Tis Berwicke's Lord
O'er Wrekin drives the deer.
That Hunting-Match, that fatal feud
Drew many a Widow's tear!
With deep mouthed haste be to rouse the game
With His generous bosom warms
Till furious foemen check the chase
And dare the din of Arms.
Then fell the high-born Mavesyn
His limbs besmirched with gore –
No more his trusty bow shall twang
His bugle blow no more!
Whilst Ridware mourns her last brave son
In arms untimely slain!
With kindred grief she here records
The last of Berwicke's train!
He rushed from yonder moat-girt walls
With lace and bill and bow
"Down, down (he cried) with Bolingbroke!
"Dares Mavesyn! Say no!"
Sir Robert spurring said "Rash Knight,
King Henry bids thee die!"
Like lightning came Sir William on
And "Percy!" was the cry.

Soon Mavesyn his prowess proved,
Pierced with his spear the foe
Both steed and baffled Knight o'er threw

And laid his Honours low.
Yet not till valour's brightest need
Bold handshake had won
This earth which bore the rival dead
Bore not alive a braver son.
By yon old gateway Rideware's Knight
Vaults on his barded roan-
How graceful did his bearer sit
How bright his armour shone.
Triumphant waved his plume.

At Shrewsbury with the King I'll stand
To hasten Hotspur's doom.
Say Royal Henry whose stout arm
Could launch the vengeful dart.
Did Douglas damp the hero's fire
And Percy pierce his heart.
Though Percy once for Henry fought
(How bravely none deny)
Bled he at Shrewsbury for his King
Did he for Henry die.

Good rousing stuff!

I returned the heavy iron key to a hook on the wall of the archway central to a building nearby known as the Gatehouse. Particularly beautiful on the south side, I was curious to see inside and was brazen enough to ask most politely of the slightly haughty gentleman owner if I could see inside his beautiful timber framed building. He was a tad taken aback but generously granted my request. I'm glad he did so. We climbed stairs to the upper level into a sort of ante room before walking through a narrow doorway into a vast space dominated by oak beams and planks of an age and girth such as I had never seen before. I was speechless. Mine host, warmed by my enthusiasm, led me to the far end, through another gap between oak posts, into a rather shabby columbarium. Wonderful. I was told this magnificent barn was built in 1391-92 by Sir Robert Mavesyn, the last of his family. I thanked the barn owner most prettily. What a treat with which to end the day.

Except the day was far from over. I drove through Buxton, directed by Tim Tom Tom to where I was to spend one night. That evening and the next day empty roads climbed and curled, dipped and dived through the glorious heights and valleys of the Peak District. Everywhere dry stone walls, complete or crumbling, formed myriad squares and rectangles, a reminder of the Enclosures. How many man hours went into the making? Sadly few of them contained any livestock: a small flock of sheep here, the odd Belted Galloway cow there. Eventually I arrived in Bradwell and located the Bed and Breakfast where I was greeted with a cuppa and introduced by hosts Helen and Richard to their visiting friend Alison. So warm was their welcome it really wasn't that surprising I found myself later that evening accompanying Richard and Alison down the hill to Ye Olde Bowling Green to participate in the pub quiz! With the help of Tall Paul, Train Paul, Bungalow Sue, Blot Richard and Yorkshire Alison – and Blind Sally* – we came second! Several rounds later, we trudged up the hill after a very unexpected, different and hugely enjoyable evening! *(*I better explain. In my working life I make soft furnishings – this includes Roman Blinds)*

So far I had seen as many interesting secular buildings as I had churches. My very last 'church crawl' was bereft of the small, characterful churches I had come to love. It seemed the Midlands specialized in rather dismal little chapels or large austere churches. The following morning, after breakfast in the family kitchen, I continued to **Eyam** *(SS2 5QH)*. The church of **St Lawrence** is large and unremarkable.

The village is full of reminders of the plague of 1666 when the villagers decided to cut themselves off from the outside world to avoid spreading disease which was carried to them, innocently, by a travelling tailor's contaminated cloth. (*The Year of Wonders*, a novel by Geraldine Brooks, envisages so well this little bit of history) Boards outside all the plague cottages identify the names and ages of family members, the many who died, the few survivors. The cottage immediately next to the church is particularly eye catching in that the front garden is a veritable wonderland filled not with gnomes but many, many small painted creatures – bunnies, ducks, frogs, mice – peeking out from a colourful abundance of plants and flower pots. Uncomfortable with the touristy aspect of Eyam, I was on the verge of driving on until a chance chat with a young schoolteacher sent me off on the walk of the week. I followed a path through fields to the boundary stone: it's about two foot wide, large and bun shaped, into the surface of which six rounded coin sized depressions had been gouged which were filled with vinegar to sterilize coins left in exchange for food left by the villagers of Stoney Middleton in the valley for the inhabitants of Eyam during the plague year, much of it donated by the Duke of Devonshire. It was good to stretch my legs after so much driving so I dropped down into the valley to the village then climbed up onto a ridge to sweep round in a broad circle through wide empty countryside back to Eyam and Ruby.

Helen and Richard encouraged me to visit an award winning building conversion at **Hathersage** *(S32 1BA)*. What was a huge defunct gas works is now a strikingly stylish cutlery factory, its unsupported cone roof reminiscent of a Chinese coolie hat. Next door is The **David Mellor Design Centre**: inside are examples of the designer's product designs (which included a working traffic light, for which he is best known,), a kitchen shop and a café. Far, far away from any major town! My last visit of the day was to wonder at the gargantuan girth of the **ancient yew tree** of **Darley Dale**, estimated to be around two thousand years old.

D/Mellor Cutlery factory, Derbyshire

For the next two nights my base in Nottinghamshire was a Bed & Breakfast comfortable if a tad depressing and oppressive as my pleasant landlady's favourite colour was dark brown. Everything in my room, including bed linen, was this dreary colour. However, it was well placed for the next four churches I intended to visit. A short drive away near Newark Chapel Lane led to a five bar gate and standing next to it, watching my approach, a bay horse. After a few words with the inquisitive equine I walked across the field to **Elston Chapel** *(NG23 5NY)*. At last, a small church to delight me! Mentioned in the Domesday Book, this humble little church, once a place of village worship now tired and crumbly, is in the care of the Churches Conservation Trust. Despite being devoid of life today with no prayer books in the box pews, hat pegs for gentlemen broken by vandals, traces of wall paintings barely discernable, it still exuded warmth and atmosphere. I risked the stairs up to the dusty gallery just for the pleasure of looking down onto the whole of it.

I was attracted to **All Saints, Hough-on-the-Hill** *(NG32 2AZ)* by the unusual Anglo-Saxon 'extruded stair-tower' which has been built on to the even older tower. Tall and rounded, it's one of only four in the country – the other three are St Mary's, Broughton, also in Lincolnshire, and St Andrew's, Brigstock and All Saints, Brixworth, both in Northamptonshire. Reason enough to visit this substantial church is the woodwork of Mr John Lord, local farmer, church warden and skilled craftsman. He designed and made the vicar's chair and desk; the pulpit, completed in 2006 in his wife's memory, teems with creatures, birds and scenes from the countryside; the sturdy church board by the lych gate – which he also made in 2011 – depicts shire horses at work, a windmill and the church itself. I've not before described a pulpit as charming. This one is.

The following day I had arranged to meet up with schoolfriend, another Sally, for lunch halfway between where I was staying and her home not far from Grimsby. I left in good time to visit **All Saints, West Markham** *(NG22 0GW)* on the way to Gainsborough, or so I thought. Rounding a bend on the lane to this rural hamlet I think I squeaked with pleasure. As soon as I saw before me the plain, worn body of All Saints crowned with an excuse of a little wooden tower I determined to see inside. Primroses, celandines, violas, speedwell sparkled pink, yellow, deep purple and blue like Smarties strewn over the graveyard grass, nature's floral carpet. A note on the ancient door asked visitors to treat it carefully. It was locked. Where to find the key holder? Some time later after enquiring of a man in a Landrover, a young man in a nearby garden, a walker and a substantial lady on a cob, I traced the huge key to a nearby farm. Perseverance paid. Dated around C13th the nave and chancel, divided only by the most minimalist of screens, was bathed in light streaming in through the south windows, one of which had an unusual vertical stone carving on either side of the deep angled reveals of the south window – a vine on the left, serpent on the right. Little remains of the Saxon origins. After years of being passed from pillar to post for income, by the mid C17th All Saints was in a parlous state. Two local farmers did their best to patch things up to deflect intentions to demolish the crumbling building until the parish decided to support this brave church on a mound. High above, four crudely crafted bosses centred on original beams look down onto a pattern of bricks laid simply onto bare earth. Of more interest to me than the Norman font and C12th crumbling stone effigy were six wonderful oak benches. History has it they were paid for in 1584 by monies owed by a landowner so as to avoid sentence for his part in the death of someone during a fight after a game of football. Sadly the benches, plonked to the back of the nave, have been replaced with rows of chairs *trés ordinaire* – surely some of the (probably unused) back rows could be removed and replaced with these chunky benches so much more in keeping with the feel of this delightful church.

After a rather longer than intended lunch with Sally by the River Trent, a long drive ahead of me to Sandy, Bedfordshire, I almost decided against making a detour to **St Giles, Holme by Newark** *(NG23 7RY)*. Had I done so I would have missed out on another delightful church. That it exists at all is almost entirely due to Mr Nevil Truman who was responsible for the restoration in 1932 of their church in a state of near collapse. Do not be off put by the unfortunate red tile roof. You'll step into a light interior with high rough stone walls, white washed and dazzling. Mr Truman ensured everything that could be saved and restored was, hence the ancient, worn oak stalls with a fun variety of poppyheads; odd pieces of medieval glass in the east window; old oak pews and stone altar; a rather splendid family tomb 'floating' above a boney corpse, a reminder of things to come! With memories of lunch in the good company of Sally and two delightful churches to sustain me I continued south, deliberately taking a longer cross country route to avoid braving heavy Friday afternoon traffic on the A1. A far cry from the splendor of the Peaks and Downs, the countryside of Northamptonshire and Bedfordshire is a tad dull, but country roads, flanked by mile upon mile of uniform blade cut mixed hedge, were blissfully quiet. I arrived at my Bed & Breakfast near Sandy with one full day left before the long drive home.

Setting off next day in the direction of **St Mary's, Clifton Reynes** *(MK 46 5DT)* I spotted a brown sign indicating "Willingdon Dovecote and Stables". This church crawl, already light on churches, was once again interrupted by a detour to other interesting buildings. Just beyond the church, on either side of the lane, these two magnificent Tudor buildings preside over a wide grassed area. Both the stables (1539), and the dovecote (1543) are rectangular, high stone walls of creamy grey stone, each end of the pitched roofs framed with stepped stone work. The shape and style of Willingdon dovecote could not be more different from the Kinwarton tub. It towers over the stables with 1500 nesting boxes. I longed to step inside (without a rotating adder how were these nests accessed?) but sadly both buildings, owned by the National Trust, were locked. I drove on to **St Mary's** which proved to be yet another large church, home to rare C14th oak effigies of two rather wizened and scrawny Reynes family couples, both wives lying as if in prayer, both husbands lying with bent legs casually crossed at the ankle.

I was reminded of the jolly painted wooden gentleman in St Bartholomew's, Much Marcle, Herefordshire and the forlorn knight in the magnificent St Peter's, Tickencote, Rutland. I was startled to look up to see an owl staring down from its perch on the rood screen. For a moment I was taken in: it was very real but also very stuffed!

No more churches. Instead, following my landlady's recommendation, an excellent lunch at The Horse & Jockey, Ravensden to round off a week of warm weather, a handful of churches, and several splendid buildings. Time to go home.

There is of course no end to delightful corners of countryside and rural churches to explore: quaint and curious, odd and obscure, treasured and neglected, in the heart of a village or alone at the end of a track, each with a story to tell or a little treasure to admire or amuse, but my feeling is I have been nourished enough by their delights for now. I hope most if not all the churches I have visited will continue to be cared for, by trusts and other bodies if not by ever diminishing congregations. They have all made such an enormous contribution to the history of communities, past and present, and so deserve to be cherished. Other less significant churches where religious attendance has all but ceased could be rescued from neglect and find new purpose in a different guise. Hopefully. With or without a church to find hidden in its folds the countryside continues to beckon: woods, moors, rivers and coasts, vistas, follies, not to forget characters to meet along the way.

* * *

Autumn Amble in Anglia

(Covid Canter)

2020, a year like no other for everyone. Tending the garden throughout the restrictions of that year helped maintain good spirits but by September I was more than ready for the opportunity to stay with my sister in Essex, school friend Sally in Lincolnshire and B & B Sue in Suffolk. I didn't anticipate counting sixty-seven box balls in a churchyard or learning of the legend of an evil Suffolk dragon.

Following my first visit to Northumberland, *the* county of huge skies, I was lured to the bleak beauty of the Essex coast by a desire to see the oldest rural church in England. It was so disappointing to follow the coast path only to find it under blue plastic while the structure was being repaired. Several years passed before a return visit to Essex. I resolved to leave home very early to drive straight to **St Peter-on-the Wall, Bradwell-by-Sea** *(CMO 7PN)* before heading inland. I parked Dusty (my new-to-me Mini bought this year to replace no-longer-trusty Ruby) by the barrier to walk five hundred yards along a cinder track lined with straggly, trees buffeted by gusting winds, towards the tall, narrow structure standing quite alone in the distance. To then find this ancient chapel open was thrilling; already happy to be there, to walk inside without blue plastic crackling overhead, was an unexpected bonus. Light streamed in through two small windows set high midway into the north and south walls; horizontal huge oak beams span the width below the steeply pitched roof; under a surprisingly colourful depiction of Christ on the cross hung on the east wall a simple modern stone altar on what is a modern and slightly raised stone slab floor. To think this chapel, built in 654 on the remains of a Roman fort, was the inspiration of St Cedd who had sailed from Lindesfarne where he had been educated by the monks only to die of the plague in 665. The church we see today is pretty much as it was built some 1300 years ago. Only yards away is the cockle spit built up over millennia comprising mostly cockle and oyster shells. The salt marsh, reduced by erosion, is a rich feeding ground for terns plovers, oyster catchers, hen harrier, merlin, peregrine, even owls. Before closing the door behind me I copied down this poem by Ian Yearsley:

> How many men have sought such solitude
> As I seek now in this same sacred spot?
> Such stillness, silence, timelessness cannot
> Leave pilgrims unaffected, unimbued
> With healing feelings in this special space,
> So spiritual, so calm, so awe-inspiring,
> As kneeling and appealing and desiring
> They seek salvation in their Saviour's place
> Outside, the sea and sky merge into one,
> The chapel looms up lonely from the la,
> Like Roman sentries stood here centuries back,
> A silhouette against the setting sun.
> In busy, modern lives we build a home,
> But peaceful isolation's our true friend.
> My search for solitude is at its end:
> I've finally found a place to be alone.

Approach to Chapel of St Lawrence, Bradwell-on-Sea, Essex

After two relaxing days before leaving Essex to head north through the fens of Cambridgeshire I made a slight detour hoping to find **St Andrew's, Greensted-juxta-Ongar** *(CM5 9LD)* open. It was disappointing though not surprising to find this very beautiful old church closed. I stood in front of this intriguing Saxon building with an oak shingled spire – allegedly the oldest wooden church in the world – itching to step inside and explore. It's a building of three parts, ages, design and restoration. I could only stand and admire the exterior walls of the middle section faced with fifty-one wide thick oak trunks, split down the middle, rounded part outside, almost black with age, dated 1060. There wasn't even the smallest of windows for me to peer through! In the churchyard I noted an ancient battered wooden headstone with one arm of the cross missing and a fenced off gravestone believed to be of an archer who had been on a C12th crusade. I will definitely be returning to this explore this attractive little church, witness to Saxon, Norman, Tudor and Victorian work and worship.

En route to stay with an old friend just south of Grimsby east of Lincoln I turned off route shortly before Market Rasen to follow a winding rural lane to find the redundant church of **St Peter's, Kingerby** *(LN8 9PB)* – another beneficiary of the Churches Conservation Trust – surrounded by trees in a graveyard among fields, the village it once served long gone. It was larger than I expected though smaller than originally built as the north aisle hasn't survived: plain and chunky, the tower is C12th, the body of the church mainly C13th and C14th. The door wasn't locked – I could enter. I stood for a while under the C17th wooden roof, taking in the quiet simplicity of unadorned white-washed walls, light streaming in through plain lead panes onto an ancient floor laid with honey coloured stone slabs, large and small, square and rectangular. Gorgeous. Along the wall of the south aisle lie two effigies one behind the other, both somewhat worn and disfigured, thought to be of father and son, early ancestors of Walt Disney. Sir William Disney, depicted in his chain mail suit, fought alongside Edward, known as The Black Prince; he died in 1316. The Black Death of 1349 killed his son, also Sir William; he is wearing plate armour. I wonder if Walt ever paid these forbears a visit.

After two days spent enjoying good company and long walks over a pre-dominately flat, gently undulating landscape, it was time to follow the A16 south to finally take up a booking in a Suffolk B & B not far from Lavenham, twice delayed: in March when flooding put paid to exploring the city of York and surrounding countryside; in June when restrictions imposed on behaviour and movement applied. With the day still young I decided to visit two churches sort of en route. **Guyhirn Chapel, Wisbech** *(PE13 4ED)* in the care of the C C T was open. A squat little church with an excuse of a bell tower perched on its red shingle tiled roof, it was built around 1660 for Puritan worship; though restoration work has been necessary it remains almost unchanged. I wandered around the churchyard so well cared for; a row of young rose bushes, each one in memory of a named person, appeared to be recently tended and weeded. I was struck by the names on two headstones: George Liquorice 1894 and Joseph Liquorice 1898. Brothers maybe? The interior was bare but for an altar table, original plain pulpit, a lectern, and truly beautiful pale wooden original pews, tiny slivers of paint revealing there had once been layers of paint. I was surprised how close behind each other they had been placed then remembered Puritans did not encourage kneeling. On one of the pews lay a laminated copy of this apposite and heartfelt poem, distributed by The Churches Conservation Trust to all the churches in its care:

Defeated?
A Sonnet to Empty Churches
Anon, June 2020
Come on. You lot have survived worse things:
Black Death, Plague and two World wars,
The Reformation (Cromwell clipped the wings
Of angels on the roof); and there are scars
On ancient faces, marble noses cropped
And poppyheads beheaded like the King;
And modern vandals too. But you have not stopped
Your ageless plain ability to sing
Of something quite indifferent to the now;
Built with a trusting love and potent faith
You stand there still in testament to how
Beauty is not a wafted fleeing wraith,
A ghost which chance can whimsically destroy;
You can be filled, if not by faith, with joy.

From Cambridgeshire into Norfolk to find **St Mary's, Barton Bendish** *(PE33 9DN)* just east of Downham Market. Though sorry to find this tiny C14th church closed I did not regret the detour. Honey cream walls beneath old thatch, windows a tad too high for a glimpse inside, churchyard grass lush and unkempt, the setting idyllic and peaceful. I could only stand and admire the fine Norman west door and hope, should I pass this way again, to pass through to see the pews for which it is known.

In the middle of farmland I turned Dusty down a long drive, past farm buildings to park outside a C18th farmhouse, my B & B accommodation for the next two nights. Mallard ducks and white geese cackled and squabbled on a wide moat that encircled the house, lawns and herbaceous beds. A perfect and peaceful location to bookend a one-day saunter through Suffolk.

After my favourite choice of holiday breakfast (scrambled eggs and very crispy bacon) I set off to follow a route my helpful hostess had devised for me to various churches and a riverside pub. First stop C14th **All Saints, Ixworth** *(IP31 1QH)*. This gorgeous little church, still serving what's left of the village, stands in a quiet rural location. A large Tudor brick porch extends into the thatched roof, topped with an ornamented and scalloped ridge, slopes down to the rendered Norman walls of the medieval nave and chancel; a weather boarded bell turret sits firmly on its C16th brick base. My fussy eye would have liked the colour of the turret to be rusty red instead of the rudely contrasting black that it is. It didn't matter it was locked as the delightful exterior was so interesting and I was able to peer through the clear glass to admire C15th bench ends: although a little blurry I could make out a lady with her lapdog, a unicorn, hare, a mermaid with mirror and possibly an owl. In different times

I would like to borrow the key from a nearby farmhouse so as to better explore inside.

Nearby another redundant church, **St Andrew's, Sapiston** *(IP31 1SA)*. A little way out of the village I followed a long drive past fields and hedges then parked Dusty on a verge before a closed gate. Shanks' pony led me passed fields of ponies, donkeys and a goat or two on my left, to my right a rather grand farmhouse and immaculate outbuildings. A wonderful bucolic setting for this mostly C13th and C14th once thatched church in a churchyard dotted with many tilted or collapsed headstones. No resistance from the door latch; this church was open! I stepped through a magnificent Norman arch into a light filled interior, spectacular in a low-key sort of way: high above the narrow nave braces and beams support the original scissor-beam framework of the roof; ten rows of age dark benches flank the south wall and on the north wall, before the chancel, an especially slim door opened to reveal within the deep wall a stone and brick staircase which once led up to the non-existent rood screen. I looked down upon two black memorial slabs set within the brick floor of the nave. There is little to read on the older one but the other is a work of art in it's own right; letters and numerals, beautifully inscribed in Latin, surrounded by six depictions of the Croftes' family coat of arms carved in fine detail. Tucked into the corner of the tower floor a splendid old coffin carrier. St Andrew's may be redundant but if feels far from sad or neglected – how could it be in such a setting, so rural, so peaceful yet within yards of life on the nearby farm.

I slipped just over the border into Norfolk to find the next church on my land-lady's list. Another little redundant church **St Andrew's, Frenze** *(IP21 4EZ)* is all but in a farmyard. Short and tubby, a muddle of brick, stone and rubble and heavily buttressed it looked so appealing sitting in a grassy field with the odd headstone, I was surprised and disappointed to find it closed. All I could do was peer in through windows on both sides, just able to make out a family pew and the pulpit, both in pale blond wood. Something about a notice pinned up inside the porch about the sister church – not on the list – piqued my curiosity. I set off to find it.

I followed a twisty lane between dense hedgerows for some distance off the main road into nowhere, well away from any village, before parking on grass facing the unusual timber framed Tudor north porch of delightful medieval **St George, Shimpling** *(IP21 4UF)* part C12th, C13th and C15th. (The church of Shimpling, Suffolk *(IP29 4HF)* is also dedicated to St George so note the postcodes carefully.) What a find. And it was open! Norfolk is famed for its round tower churches and here was one, like a sharpened pencil rising above farmland stretching in every direction. The interior is beautiful; light streamed onto whitewashed walls above dark oak pews, the bench ends adorned with candle holding poppyheads; plain stone memorial floor slabs set in between original black and white tiles; an old pedal harmonium and an ancient crude wooden chest, lid padlocked on with steel straps, completed the furnishings. I was charmed by the figures depicted on four side of the rather crumbly C15th font: a winged horse, various plump women, or angels, with huge wings and two birds, one with spread wings holding a branch in its beak, another with a snake. Pinned to a board I read a short biography of the sculptor Ivor Robert Jones (1913-1996), born in Oswestry, Shropshire, possibly the only person of note buried here. Best known for his portrait heads – such as Somerset Maugham, Yehudi Menuhin, the Duke of Edinburgh – and the life size bronze of Winston

Churchill in Parliament Square. **St George** was well worth the unintended diversion. No doubt Roger Last, author of this poem, agreed.

This is a simple place, never in favour,
No benefactor sought to immortalise is name
By raising monuments or more than a village
Peopled by the poor could forge and labour to put up.
The tread of History passed us by –
And it is all that we do to keep the water from the wood.
And crumbling lime pointed back again.
The bareness of our Church here
Does not denote a lack of care, or pride or love –
For we love it dearly.
It is the symbol of our future and our past
Of the erupt and petering away of Life.
These earthern baked tiles
Worn and hollowed like the tread to the pews
Are our riches.
The pitted rails wobbly by the altar
The rusted band of trefoils encircling the bent handle to te door.
The lone buttress leaning on the South wall –
All unnoticed except by us,
As in the settling dust of evening
Hovering in the latticed beams of a weary sun,
Or the winter pain of the wind among the sunk stones in the yard.
Here is nothing loud to fasten to the senses –
No guide book pilgrimage to force a response
But within the bare walls a glory of long and ender use,
A pouring out of the continuity of these stones
In each new grave, and splash of water from the font,
And the black unbolted door.

I slipped back into Suffolk towards **All Saints, Saxted** *(IP13 9QP)*, sort of en route to the Ramsholt Arms where I intended to lunch. A plain little grey stone church All Saints sits in a lush shaded by many trees with the exception of the usual yew. Inside the C15th porch is what had lured me there – a whipping post and set of stocks proclaiming one should 'Fear God and Honour the King', medieval tools of shame which once had a prominent place in the village. I entered through the original studded oak door into the restored though still essentially C13th and C14th body of the church. On the wall to the left a pretty illustrated copy of the Lord's Prayer; opposite a jolly organ painted an eye catching Wedgewood blue and white. Also on the wall a series of photographs recording the restoration work carried out in 1986 by a local builder. Of more interest to me was the graveyard churchyard densely dotted with headstones, upright or leaning over, many in small family clusters, three under an almost horizontal bough of an ancient cherry tree. The scene was a reminder of Thomas Gray's observation *"Beneath those rugged elms, that yew-tree's shade, Where heaves the turf in many a mould'ring heap, Each in his narrow cell for ever laid, the rude forefathers of the hamlet sleep"*. With hindsight I wish I had made time to visit the Post Mill in the centre of the village. The current mill was built in 1796 but there has been one on the site since the C13th. There to grind corn the whole body revolves on its base, sails activated by winds blowing unimpeded across he flat landscape

Before visiting the church of Ramsholt I was hungry for lunch. **The Ramsholt Arms** *(IP12 3AB)* deserves its reputation. Seated by a picture window I enjoyed a welcome lager and delicious meal looking out upon the estuary of the River Deben flowing past a narrow apron of grass and beach, a jetty lined with a higgledy-piggeldy collection of dinghies and a couple of wooden sail boats. I knew **All Saint's, Ramsholt** *(IP12 3AE)* was on high ground inland and right of the Arms so set off along the beach before crossing a style leading through marsh reeds into a field beyond which the church tower above was outlined against the sky. I noted peacefully grazing cows, far to one side a lone man with two gun dogs at his side and to the other side a row of Landies and 4 x 4s. All was quiet so, deciding the shoot was enjoying lunch, I set off confidently towards the ridge. Suddenly the peace was shattered. No longer confident, imagining the indignity of buttocks sprayed with shot, I turned and ran in the style of Richard Hannay racing over the moors. Not to be deterred from visiting a church in such a wondrous location, I drove Dusty along a track bordering several fields, giving way to a stream of departing vehicles, the day of sport over.

It was hard to understand why this isolated old church, with no long ago settlement nearby, was closed while other far less rural redundant churches had remained open to infrequent visitors. No matter. The beautiful exterior and of course the location made the drive down to the foot of this mini peninsular so worthwhile. All Saints is one of the thirty-eight round tower churches in Suffolk (there are one hundred and twenty-four in neighbouring Norfolk); stumpy, built with honey coloured stone, it appears protective of the worn out little building at its base. All I could make out through narrow windows were pale wooden box pews. A notice board told us of commonwealth war graves and two stories of 'miracles' concerning Ramsholt. At the end of the C12th the Saxon Edric was priest of Ramsholt. The story is about a small rather than serious miracle: Edric's daughter suffered a large pustule in her left cheek which suddenly burst so pus flowed and hardened on her face which was soon covered by many other pustules. Salves and medicines proved ineffective, the girl's parents were in despair. Time to light candles around her head and pray to honour St Thomas, hoping the Lord would help. Ten o'clock one summer evening the pus crumbled, pustules disappeared to reveal clear, healthy skin but for one tiny spot. The other small miracle achieved a happy result. The wife of one of the villagers gave a cheese to her small daughter Beatrice who put it to one side and resumed playing with her brother. She then couldn't remember where she had left it and despite brother and sister searching everywhere they could not find the cheese. Reluctant to ask the original owner where it might be they decided to ask St Thomas for his help so, at bedtime, they both prayed. That night the handsome saint came to both Beatrice and her brother in their sleep and asked what was bothering them. They confessed the loss to be told by St Thomas the cheese was in the old churning pot.

All Saints, Ramsholt vista

(Eight months later I returned with a friend to both **The Ramsholt Arms** and **All Saints** church. After another excellent lunch under the sun beside the River Deben where a troop of small boys were having the best time crab hunting in squelchy low-tide mud, we followed a path leading past reed beds, through meadows up to the ridge confident on this occasion shooting was out of season; no need to fear being peppered with shot. A garden gate framed with still flowering blackthorn opened into the churchyard, headstones only just visible among tall grasses freckled with poppies. This time the door opened into a tall, narrow brick paved nave with white washed walls. Box pews flanked each side, benches placed so everyone could look to the raised pulpit halfway down the south wall. On the west wall written descriptions and detailed drawings informed how round towers were constructed; several notices commemorate the lives of local lads who fought and died in The Great War before descending through the meadow. A cuckoo called intermittently.)

After the romance of Ramsholt **St Mary's, Bawdsey** *(IP12 3AH)* warranted no more than a cursory glance at its closed door and brief stroll around the churchyard with little to note other than one pretentious monument to a family of Quilters surrounded on three sides by close planted 'soldier' trees. Reluctant to return too early to the moated farmhouse I decided to drive across country to the coastal town of Orford. **The Castle** (1165-1173) completed during the reign of Henry II, has long gone; only the massive three sided keep remains, lording it over town from above a grassy mound. Owned by English Heritage, due to covid it was of course closed to visitors.

Since the mid C19th the number of thatched churches remaining in Norfolk has dwindled from almost three hundred to fifty-one and one thatched bell housing, twenty-five in Suffolk, and no more than one or two in fifteen other counties. The risk of fire was always a problem – original fire hooks still hang on the wall of no-longer-thatched St John the Baptist in Bere Regis – and the craft of thatching is no longer widely practised. Water reed is used primarily in East Anglia, wheat reed and long straw in other parts of the country although today a general shortage of reed required for re-thatching, repairs and its high cost has led to reed being imported from Europe and South Africa. So far on this covid canter I had seen two thatched churches; before heading south and home to Sussex I was to see one more.

The following morning I took my leave of noisy Mallards, waddling geese, friendly Labrador and welcoming landlady to make a return visit to the gorgeous medieval wool town of Lavenham. It was a joy to walk around streets lined with nothing but wonderful old buildings, almost all houses and shops painted Sudbury yellow or a shade of Suffolk pink. Surely Suffolk is *the* county best qualified to boast of the prettiest villages, least affected by either the eyesores of '60s architecture or sadly squalid tenements. In the churchyard of magnificent **St Peter & St Paul's** I counted sixty-seven balls of box – huge spheres measuring five to six feet – and wondered how long it took to trim them to round perfection twice a year.

The drive to **St Mary the Virgin, East Bergholt** *(CO7 6TA)* threaded along lanes, crossing woods and farmlands, through the picturesque village of Hadleigh – surely one of the longest High Streets in the county, lined with pink or yellow painted buildings seemingly untouched by passing centuries – to the village where John Constable (1776-1837) was born and lived in East Bergholt House. I was there not to see the large church – a reminder of the county's once considerable wealth – rather the unique bell cage. Building the church tower was delayed due to empty coffers so to house the five huge bell destined for the tower a 'temporary' cage was constructed in 1531. There is nothing temporary about the massive oak frame and horizontal planks beneath a red tiled pitched roof. There are other less impressive bell cages; what is unique about these bells, the "heaviest five-bell peal in the country" is they hang upside down which necessitates a quite different method of ringing. Ear defenders are surely mandatory for the campanologists and sensible wear for anyone passing nearby during a peal.

St Mary the Virgin, East Berghold, bell cage

Another twisty county drive led to **St Stephen, Bures** *(C08 5LD)*, the pièce de résistance of this church canter. A dirt track led alongside farm buildings to skirt several fields and pass through a copse before petering out in front of a long, low thatched building with oat-cream walls, a thatched roof and a pitched roof over a short transept. No wonder this unpretentious church is known locally as the Chapel Barn. It can boast several guises since it was dedicated to St Stephen in 1218 one hundred and five years after King Edmund's body was taken for reburial at Bury: as a hospital during the plague of 1739, as cottages, as a barn until it was restored to its original purpose in the 1930s to be reconsecrated in 1940.

I entered via the transept cum vestry; it has the informality and furnishings of a parlour. Under stairs leading to a small gallery an ancient cupboard door and through deep walls a narrow arch leads into a nave filled with light from five arched windows along south and north walls. A plain stone slab altar, a crude stone font; in the centre of the aisle and at the west end three striking effigies of Robert, Thomas and Richard de Vere, the 5th, 8th and 11th Earls of Oxford, the latter with his wife by his side, dominate the space leaving the congregation to sit in rows of two either side.

Legend has it that St Stephen is the site where Edmund, probably born in 841, was anointed King of the East Anglia. Unfortunately his reign – and life – was short, his body moved from Suffolk to London before it was returned to East Anglia: to this day no one is sure where he was finally interred. The following notice on a board behind the church picks up the story after the Vikings took him to the village of Hoxne where he was tied to a tree: *In Loyal Rembrance of Edmund, King & Martyr who tradition has it was crowned here on Christmas Day 855 AD. A good king he was martyred in 869 AD by the 'Great Heathen Army' of the Danes for refusing to renounce his faith. Captured, they shot arrows into him 'until he bristled like a hedgehog'.* Legend has it that after Edmund was decapitated – the Danes believed this would prevent any form of ennoblement – *'a wolf protected his head until his friends could recover it.'* (In the chancel of the thatched round tower church of **St Edmund's, Fritton** *(NR31 9EZ)* Norfolk a faint C12th wall painting above the altar shows St Edmund with his crown being shot through with arrows from the Danes on either side. Also visible is the wolf alleged to have protected Edmund's head. St Edmund, decapitated and guarded by a dog is to be seen carved on a roof beam in St Andrews, Greensted-juxta-Ongar). A similar depiction of Edmund's crown, pierced by two arrows, is etched into a huge boulder to the edge of the copse. Pinned to a tree another notice, another legend:

The Old Bures Dragon.

In these days there appeared lately an evil dragon of excessive length with a huge body, crested head, saw like teeth & elongated tail in the land around the village of Bures near Sudbury, which destroyed & killed a herd of sheep. The servants of Sir Richard Waldegrave who owns the land haunted by the dragon came forth to shoot it with bows but its body resisted the arrows which sprang forth from its ribs as if they were metal or hard stone & from the spines of its back with a jangling as if they were hitting bronze plates, and flew far away because its skin was impenetrable. Almost the whole county was summoned to slaughter it, but when it saw that it was to be shot at again, it fled into the marsh, hid in the reeds & was seen no more.

The notice goes on to say the re-creation of the Old Bures Dragon – *ninety metres long, seventy metres high* – was the work of Sir Richard Waldegrave's distant kinsman to celebrate Queen Elizabeth's Diamond Jubilee in 2012. Only then did I look across the fields rolling away to a distant hillside and the chalk white outline of a fork tailed, fire breathing ... dragon!! Had I made time to visit St Mary the Virgin, Wissington (*CO6 4QY*) I would have seen a rather older depiction of the Bures dragon, a mural dated around 1280. Nevertheless, as a last image to take home from Suffolk that of a chalk dragon was memorable!

Chalk Dragon, Burres, Suffolk

I'll end the sum of these scribblings with a poem I came across, a simple homage to the land on which these churches stand.

The Unkempt Churchyard,
And all the Wonders it holds
From the Weeds of the fields
To the cultivated Rose,
The Kestrel hovers above,
Searching for a meal,
While the Mouse hides below,
Hoping to live until tomorrow,
The Swallows catching Insects,
The Bats asleep in the belfry,
All God's own Creations
In God's own Garden.

* * *

Wandering in Wales

My first visit to Wales was also my first 'crawl' in Ruby, my Mini. Over the course of several years and further visits we've followed coastal roads, country lanes bright with wayside flowers, climbed through the Black Mountains, walked at low tide to a chapel in the sea off Anglesea; pursued puffins on the isle of Skomer a family holiday; followed coastal paths with the Dorset Dawdlers; revelled in the tranquil surroundings of tiny remote churches.

My plan was to 'crawl' up the right hand side of Wales via several churches to Bettys-y-Coed, staying in one B & B en route. Simon directed me to my first Welsh church, **St Aeddan's, Bettws Newydd**, (Welsh for a *new place of worship*). The approach is flanked by three ancient yews; one, positively peppered with peep holes through the bulging gnarled trunk, would be a hit with small children. The circumference is 30 ft and its age has been authenticated as having been there since *"the star to shine out over Bethlehem also shone on this noble tree; it stood here still when Norman knights claimed their victory; as King Charles lost his royal head, this tree made growth anew; thanks be to God that we still have our mighty Bettws Yew"*. So says the inscription decoratively carved into a piece of yew in the porch, almost the width of the west wall and under a double belfry. The central aisle, covered with a rather ghastly mustard coloured carpet – surely only there for warmth – leads to the stunning C15th rood screen, dense foliage beautifully carved in dark oak. Unusually, the tympanium reaches to and follows the curve of the barrel ceiling. I imagined choristers, from their position on the wide loft above the screen, looking down through tracery into the chancel. Beyond this pleasing little church on the outskirts of the village lie fields dotted with, of course, sheep and a view of distant hills of Herefordshire.

I spied **St Mary's, Llanfair Kilgeddin** *(NP7 9PG)* from far off, a lone edifice deep in open countryside. I collected the key as directed from a nearby farmhouse, then followed a sloping single track down past a farmhouse which was either neglected or in the process of being rebuilt, surrounded by a large muddle of machines, rubble and rubbish which didn't help set the scene. Nevertheless I drove up to the gate into the churchyard and crossed unkempt grass towards what is a quite large, originally medieval church re-built in the late C19th, now in the care of The Friends of Friendless Churches. The River Usk runs nearby and a newly laid hedge along the south boundary of the churchyard showed someone cared.

The forlorn appearance was misleading. I entered and stood, momentarily shocked into stillness. The interior is spacious and simple, designed by John Sedding (1838-91), architect of the restoration, and responsible for the marble and alabaster altar, floor tiles and hanging oil lamps. He may be long forgotten but Heywood Summer (1853-1940) should be remembered for the really stunning sixteen sgraffiti panels dominating all four walls of the interior. His background is an interesting one. Grandfather Charles was Bishop of Llandaff; great-uncle an Archbishop of Canterbury; father Bishop of Guildford; mother founder of the Mothers' Union. Heywood trained as a lawyer only to exchange Lincoln's Inn for life as an artist. This led to him, together with some others, organizing the first Arts & Crafts exhibition in Crane Street, London. His special area of expertise was sgraffiti, known to Romans in ancient times and in Renaissance Italy, a technique described in a 1986 catalogue as follows:

"In the studio, prepare a full-size cartoon and prick small holes along the outlines. On the site, strip the wall back to brick or stone and cover it with a coat of coarse plaster, fix up the cartoon with register nails and mark the pricked design onto the plaster. Cover with a second coat of plaster in up to five distemper colours butting up against each other. Then lay a third, thin coat of light coloured plaster to cover as much of the wall as can be worked in a day, replace the cartoon on the register nails and mark out the design again. Later the same day, when the plaster is firm enough, cut the design out of the thin layer to reveal the ground of colours below. An assistant would prepare the walls, lay on the plaster, remove it at the end and clean up; whilst Summer would prepare the cartoon, mark it out on the plaster and execute the final cutting. The process was one to delight any member of the Arts & Crafts Movement, it was so earthy, so simple, so resistant to refinements of detail; and so much depended on that last quick and all but irreversible cut."

And, I would add, zeal, patience and a nearby bed and breakfast. The panels in Llanfair are charming simple depictions in praise of Creation: I spotted two fat walruses in the panel '*O ye Whales and All that Move in the Waters*' and there is a little boy rolling a hoop in '*O Ye Children of Men*'. I'm so pleased I didn't hesitate and so miss seeing such beautiful and unusual artwork. Perhaps one day I'll visit other sgraffiti panels by Summer in St Agatha's, Landport

Portsmouth *(PO1 4RL),* and/or St Mary's, Sunbury-on-Thames *(TW16 6RG).* May The Friends long continue to care and preserve this special rural church and its art.

Another hesitation. Did I really want to drive out of my way to see a preserved C15th cope? The day was still young so, decision made, I set off from Abergavenny through a scenic far corner of Monmouthshire towards the Herefordshire border. The crumbled red ruin of a castle lies to the left of the road and next to it **St Bridget's, Skenfrith** *(NP7 8UG),* large, stout and red with a rather squat tower. Inside a variety of interesting if uncomfortable pews of different woods and ages and a modern lectern forsaking an eagle for an image of the head and shoulders of St Bridget (St Brigid), Irish saint to whom the church is dedicated. Rather dutifully, I admired the cope that has survived so many centuries and read about its history and composition. Laid out to form a fan, it is encased in a large glass wall case since its restoration in the 1980s. Designed to be worn for special outdoor processions and ceremonies, it is made from velvet and linen in three parts: semi-circular cape, embroidered band called an orphrey, and rounded hood or shield which joins all together – this one has lost its 'morse', the fastening across the front. Sewn in pre-Reformation times, various motifs, using rolled gold metallic thread, are embroidered on the deep red (madder) velvet of the cape and figures (saints?) on the yellow (weld) linen orphrey. Feeling just a mite more cultured I retraced my route, listening on the radio to news of the death of Margaret Thatcher. "Remember where you were when you heard of her death?" Easy. Wales.

Pondering on this sombre news received while driving reminded me of two very different moments, laugh-out-loud ones, when listening to the radio while driving. Towards the end of an episode of *Quote Unquote* the presenter turned to ask each member of the panel for a favourite 'home grown' quote that became part of the family lexicon. I still chuckle when I think of the dotty pronouncement of Esther Ranzen's grandmother: *"It's a good thing we're all different else there would be no assorted biscuits!"* On another occasion, rather dispirited how few answers I knew to questions already put to the panel on a testing radio quiz on classic and best selling books, I was taken by surprise when the presenter suddenly asked in all seriousness "What was the reason for the only disagreement between Noddy and Big Ears?" At that precise moment I met the eyes of a motorist passing in the opposite direction – we were both grinning, surely tuned in to the same station. I have always remembered both grandma's biscuits and this one word answer: curtains.

> *"There was a crooked man, and he walked a crooked mile*
> *He found a crooked sixpence against a crooked stile.*
> *He bought a crooked cat, which caught a crooked mouse,*
> *And they all lived together in a little crooked house."*

A few years before this 'crawl' I recollected this rhyme from childhood visiting a squiffy church in Shropshire. I was reminded of it again as I set off to the famously crooked church of **St Martin's, Cwmyoy** *(NP7 7NS)*. As with so many rural churches and chapels, it is not easy to find. A single-track lane winds for miles through the Black Mountains leading towards Capel-y-ffin. An easy-to-miss marker leads off to the right, from where the narrow track plunges to the valley floor, over a little stone bridge, then on and on, to climb the hillside above the River Honddhu. I arrived at a cluster of houses to find tracks in all directions blocked by various vehicles belonging to a utility company. With the patient help of amiable drivers, I navigated Ruby through the mélange as they manoeuvred their trucks and vans in a sequence of road dance moves. After several more bends of the track I parked off road opposite a lych gate. Into every sixth stone of a path of flagstones leading to the south porch was chiseled a single word informing visitors *This was laid in memory of Mark Gibbons 05.05.1965.* Perhaps in life Mr Gibbons enjoyed hopscotch.

I left the path to climb up through the churchyard so as to look down upon the extreme irregularity of this C13th hillside church. Walls and windows and most noticeably the tower itself lean and tilt to an alarming degree: there can be no other church such as this one in the land, held up as it is with huge buttresses – hardly features of beauty in themselves! – to counter the shifting subsoil and geology of the underlying rock. The tower, leaning well out of perpendicular, is home to six bells, a surprising number for such a small rural church. Church notes point out they are never rung, sometimes 'clappered', presumably on special occasions. Inside, I gazed up the aisle through the slightly leaning chancel arch to the really wonky east window. Memorial slabs and plaques on the walls are particularly decorative, framed with motifs of cherubs and flowers in baskets. Apparently many such memorials in this area were similarly inscribed and decorated in the C17th and C18th by members of a locally famous family of stonemasons, the Brutes. One quirky memorial tablet, the lines as irregular as the building itself, reads:

> *Thomas Price he*
> *Takes his nap mo*
> *Ther lap waiting*
> *To heare the bri*
> *Degroome say a*
> *Wake my dear –*

Despite there being few parishoners to attend these days, I noticed services continue to be held every Sunday in this singular little church which should be well known to walkers down the ages. It is on the ancient pilgrim route to St David's in Pembrokeshire and, cutting into Hatterrall Hill, is on the popular Offa's Dyke Path. It is also on the Cistercian Way, a six hundred and fifty miles long circular walk circumnavigating Wales, following ancient ways and passing many historical sites. I walked outside and climbed again through the churchyard and stood, looking down into Cwmyoy and the Valley of the Yoke. Behind me ancient woods framed sloping fields divided by dry stonewalls, in one of which a man and his collie walked towards still unsuspecting sheep. A scene surely as tranquil and unchanged as when, some seven hundred years ago, men laboured to build this little church, in ignorance then of the slowly shifting ground.

As a bird flies, the little church of **St Issui** is only a valley away from Cwmyoy. However, I drove for miles, following twists and turns of narrow lanes sunk deep between dense, cropped hedges, still leaf bare, climbing and dipping on the slopes of the Cader range above the Grwyne Fawr valley, through a landscape almost devoid of dwellings. I wondered at the remote location, empty of buildings but for one roadside cottage, in front of which an elderly woman tended her flowerpots. One can only imagine the distances travelled by farmers and farmhands of days long gone in order to worship on the Sabbath. Immediately the hillside church of **St Issui, Patricio** *(NP7 7LU)* – some say **Patrishow** – became visible through the generous arch under a wide stone lych gate, I felt I was somewhere most special. To the right of a path of stone slabs, before the hillside fell away steeply, bright clumps of daffodils swayed amid a scattering of neglected headstones. Beyond still dormant trees of the valley, snow sprinkled far hills. Not one sheep bleat to spoil the quiet! The church lies long, facing the view. Set into very fat walls before the south porch, a door opens into a tiny white washed chapel with no access to the main body of the church other than to peer through a grille set into the wall behind a simple stone altar. Tucked into a corner above steps on which lay spent candles is a niche, home to a modern statuette representing St Issui. Leaving this simple, bare cell I went next door, into a Norman interior with so much of interest. Greeting the visitor from the west wall is the first of several Doom paintings of standing skeletons I was to come across during this chapel 'crawl' in Wales. (When visiting All Saints, Llangar in Denbighshire two days later, Geraint, volunteer guide par excellence, said the splendid sepia skeleton depicted on the wall is known locally as Fred so now, to me, all wall paintings of skeletons, *memento mori*, are Freds). Fred Patrisio, upright on the west wall, quite clearly holds a spade to symbolize growing food, a bow to illustrate hunting, and an hourglass as crude reminder of Man's short life. Beneath St Issui's vaulted barrel ceiling are wall paintings and decorated memorials; an ancient font is inscribed with Latin dated to be mid C11th and, beyond the intricately carved oak screen and loft, another stone altar.

The churches of Cwmyoy and Patrishow are little jewels of the hillside and how fortunate both were rescued from disrepair, even collapse. I was tempted to walk through the garden gate beyond St Issui's churchyard and explore but regret time didn't allow. I'm sorry too I could only imagine, not hear, musicians and singers atop that beautiful screen.

Returning to the valley floor I continued through beautiful, gentle countryside along the Vale of Ewyas towards **St Mary's, Capel-y-Ffin** *(NP7 7NP)*, the last church to visit that day. I was becoming used to narrow roads and infrequent passing bays to accommodate the occasional vehicle as we inched past each other. I eventually reached the hamlet and pulled up next to the lych gate to be greeted by a most friendly collie dog, apparently delirious with joy to see A Person. The reason Welsh churchyards often boast two or three yew trees, so Geraint later informed me, was the refusal of farmers of medieval times to allow in their fields trees bearing poisonous berries, for fear of harming their livestock. Yew and hazel woods were essential to make bows and arrows, firearms of the day, hence the planting of two or three yew trees within an enclosure free of grazing sheep and cattle. We'll never know whether a yeoman of yesteryear was over zealous or merely concerned about sapling survival when planting eight young yews to form a protective semi circle around the church of St Mary. Complete circles of ancient yews are peculiar to Wales. I understand there are around twenty-five such circles in Welsh church *llans* comprising anything from twelve to twenty trees, their huge girths and interlocking branches embracing to form a canopy over the graves beneath them. There is a Welsh saying "*gorwedd dan yr Ywen*" which translates as "sleeping under the yew".

Despite the top-knot of a small wooden bell cote, the appearance of this small, square whitewashed building with a porch centred under two windows appears more house than place of worship. The interior too has a homely feel. Stairs to the left of the door climb to a gallery running along the west and north walls, looking down on a simple altar and small organ. Facing the pulpit dated 1780, a few years after the church was rebuilt, are four handsome settles, the front one of which was occupied by a family of four teddy bears seated in descending size and importance: dad, mum, child, baby. Where was Goldilocks?

I walked outside in time to watch a stream of loose ponies skittering along the lane behind a running lad, all of them ignoring the collie dog quite beside himself with excitement. Leaving Ruby in first gear, I followed the ponies as they pursued the lad, apparently confident there would be no oncoming traffic to interrupt the changeover of pasture. I drove on towards Hay Bluff and over the Black Mountains where snow still lay, patchy and occasionally quite deep. Reluctant to continue as far as Hay-on-Wye, I put myself at the mercy of Tim Tom-Tom to send me down the hills, criss-crossing a patchwork of fields before cleverly returning me to a main road heading for Builth Wells.

The Bed and Breakfast I had chosen to spend my first night in Wales was a rambling farmhouse at the end of a long drive through fields of sheep. A note by the front door invited me to find the farmer's wife in one of the sheep-sheds where ewes were giving birth on straw litter under the watchful eyes of the farmer and his family. Inside the shed all was noise and movement: cud chewing ewes, tiny newborn lambs sleeping, older ones feeding or playfully pronking about the pens. Mrs Farmer's Wife, all smiles and warmth, showed me to my room, and reminded me as she would be in the lambing shed breakfast would be served by her daughter-in-law. I was given directions to The Red Lion for my evening meal. Allegedly the oldest pub in Powys, the actual bar room dates back to 1189 though the rest of the building is a century or two younger. I imagine the old boys dotted about the public bar gather most evenings. Curious as to my appearance among them, I mentioned my interest in churches. Well! They couldn't wait to tell me about the somewhat forbidding church opposite the pub, **St Afan's, Llanafau**r **Fawr** *(LD2 3PN)*. Not only does it boast a mighty yew, authenticated to be two thousand years old, there is a headstone with a grim tale to tell!

It is said on April 23rd 1826 John Price was murdered on the Darren Hill in this parish by R. Lewis. In 1789 Lewis Lewis murdered Thomas Price, then, with his brother Thomas, tried to dispose of the body, first throwing it into water then by burning. Thomas ratted on his brother who fled the district on his *'wonderfully developed legs'*!! The family feud was ongoing between Lewis and Price families of this neighbourhood for years, though hopefully the current members of these families are not considering carrying out the same crimes. The publican showed me a copy of an extract from The Cambrian dated 29th April 1826 which reads: *"On the evening of Sunday last the 23rd April a most atrocious murder was committed on the body of John Price of Parishlow in Llanafar Breaks on the Darren Hill. The deceased was found that night, his neck was twisted til the blood ran out of his ears, so that his death must have been occasioned by a dislocation of his vertebrae. A neighbour by the name of Rees Lewis, who has absconded, is suspected of his murder."* Rees Lewis was a nephew of Lewis Lewis who murdered Thomas Price those 36 years before. Rees was caught, tried, convicted, hanged at Brecon Gaol. A gruesome tale to add considerable interest to my supper in this pub!

As interesting to me was meeting next morning the charming and lovely looking farmer's daughter-in-law, Nathalia. She is the daughter of a Russian mother and Indian father who went quite different ways when they eventually divorced; father returned to India, mother married a Norwegian where Nathalia grew up to speak four languages fluently. The surprise outcome of a holiday, back-packing in Australia, was meeting and subsequently marrying a Welsh sheep farmer. Some years and a small daughter later, she does not speak Welsh but English with a strong Welsh accent! Breakfast was served to me, the only lodger, in solitary splendour until Nathalia reappeared with her sleepy and utterly enchanting baby girl. Wide eyed and smiley, this little Russian doll cum bush baby soon discovered I could blow raspberries just as well as she; this we did until her father and grandparents joined us in the kitchen for their breakfasts. Mr Farmer proved a fount of sheep information. Did you know, as I now do, should two rams head butt with serious mal intent the larger of the two is more likely to come off worse, even incur a fatal injury? (Though a sheep's head is extremely well protected, the neck is weak: for a large ram to counter the butt of a smaller ram, he has to bend his head so risk breaking his neck). I found this as interesting as he found amusing I use udder cream for dairy cattle as face cream.

Nathalia's scrambled eggs were rather better than her coffee so I returned to Builth Wells in search of a strong dose of caffeine where, while chatting to the owner of a tea-room, I was urged to visit the little church of **St David's Rhulen** *(LD2 3RY)*. Although not on my list, as described by the good lady it seemed worthy of investigation and a little backtracking. It was suggested I ask directions when I arrived at the Hundred House. This forlorn village seemed devoid of all life except for a scrawny woman in a hardware store with almost no goods displayed. A baby was crying in the background while she, on the verge of tears herself, managed to give me no helpful directions at all. After driving back and forth, up and down for a while, I decided to give up my search for this little church only to very nearly miss a tiny little sign to **Rhulen** off to the left – there appears to be little uniform spelling of place names in Wales – so spun off down yet another winding lane, deep between high hedges, up and down hills until, on a valley floor and just past a rare cluster of cottages, I finally came across the tea-room lady's favourite church.

Set back from the track, well screened by several trees, yews and others, it is tiny, whitewashed and essentially C12th. Church notes informed of the original three David churches, this is the only one remaining – the other two, long gone, being Gregrina and Glascwym. The Black Death of 1384 led to economic decay in the area as elsewhere – lots of churches tumbled into disrepair and disappeared. The notes continued: *"late C13th and early C14th attempts to extend were impeded by a huge yew at the east end – thus no window and today no yew. The original roof timbers remain hidden behind plaster ceiling (*what a pity*). Large porch once acted as a meeting room. Font C15th. Founded by Celtic monks, nothing remains of earlier woad and wattle building."* Although it seemed in good repair and the location remote and beautiful, it had an air of neglect, of being forgotten, ignored, so I left feeling rather sad for it.

Which is possibly why I wasn't concentrating and took all sorts of wrong turns until I managed to come across **St Cewydd's, Disserth** *(LD1 6HR)*. So surrounded is the yew encircled churchyard by farm buildings, the church could almost have been taken for one of them had it not been for its crenellated tower. Inside I was struck by the depth of window sills, at least a metre wide, before wandering amongst the C17th family box pews, doors inscribed with their names: *"Mrs Crummer of New Castle"*, *"Mr Crummer of New Hall"* – intriguing! – *Bryn James Watts Esq"* (local resident who improved on Thomas Newcomen's steam engine) *and* simply *"EP 174" amongst them.* This didn't prevent seating squabbles: there was an instance in 1700 when a woman *"claiming a seat in a certain box, first sat on the lap of the woman occupying it, and then pulled her out of the box."* Mrs Crummer, perhaps? The Vestry Book of 1735 lists various expenses such as *"1s for washing the surplys each time, 3s 4d for killing a fox , …….. burial of the parish poor: 6s for a coffin, 6 yards of shrewd 6s, shrewding and washing 2s, parson and clerk 2s, fetching of bier's ale 6d."* The coffin would have been a communal one in those days as the poor would only have 'rested' in it prior to being lowered into the ground. For those who could afford a coffin the dress code for burial was *"for a man, his best hat best cravat, best gloves best girdle or belt best breeches, garters, hose, shoes and buckles, knife, sheath, fur, tobacco box, pocket tongs. For a woman, her best hood and cap, best scarf, best handker and girdle, best apron and purse, best hose and garters, best shoes and buckles."* No mention of a shirt for a man or dress for a woman.

I continued northwards some distance along the A483 to **St Cynilo's, Llanbister** *(LD1 6TN)*, on my list, selected, I suspect, for its proximity to the main road. Though described with some enthusiasm of all things ecclesiastical by eminent knights Simon Jenkins and John Betjamin, I didn't warm to the cavernous interior and austerity of this C13th church. Behind a wall facing the south door is a baptistery, apparently only ever used on four occasions due to a lack of any nearby water source! According to my tape measure – a permanent inhabitant of my handbag – a single oak beam extends the entire 5.6 metres width of the fine screen. I walked outside to find an old lady attacking a patch of tussocky grass with a spade and next to her a tall, wispy sapling in a plastic pot. She declined my offer to help dig a hole and told me, in between sadly ineffectual jabs at the unyielding earth, it was *her* eightieth birthday and *she* was going to plant *her* tree! I do hope a strong man came along to make this possible.

I was so disappointed to find both the remaining two churches I had looked forward to visiting that day were not only closed but no longer in service. **Llanymawddwy** is a remote village in the Berwyn Hills, northeast of the A470. The drive to it was spectacular. Walking up the path to the locked door of **St Tydecho's,** the dilapidation and neglect was immediately apparent. I peered through a cloudy window to an interior festooned with cobwebs, a sitting room made for Miss Haversham. Before retracing my steps a quick glance at a nearby visitor information board noted two giants of yesteryear were buried in the churchyard: one of them, Cawr Mawddwy *"threw a rock from the top of Aran Fawddwy, leaving indentations where his fingers held it. The rock, Maen y Cawr, lies on Ffridd Wenallt"*. Double consonants everywhere!

Even more disappointing, especially as both Simon and John had painted such an exciting picture of this church, was to find **St Mark's, Brithdir** *(LL40 2RN)* similarly closed and no longer in service. I returned to the A470 in quite a grump, not defused by a succession of road works and traffic lights making for a tedious stop start drive to Bettys-y-Coed and my Bed and Breakfast for the next three nights. When making my booking I was unaware this town is such a tourist hub; happily where I was staying was a brisk hill walk away from the centre. Greeted by the cheery lady of the house who, I soon discovered, bustled from dawn to dusk, ever helpful and enthused by her role as hostess. "*All* my guests are *so* interesting" she chirruped next morning while I enjoyed her husband's scrambled eggs, "Now, do tell. What brings *you* to our little town?"

When planning these few days, the tiny island church of **St Cwfan** was the lure to venture as far north as Anglesey. As it is only accessible at low tide I planned my visit for late afternoon so decided to follow the coast road southwest to two very different churches then back track to Bangor. I'm so pleased I took a left fork at

Capel Curig, as suggested by our helpful hostess as this was the high road passing Mount Snowdon and Pen-y-Gwryd Hotel where Edmund Hillary stayed when preparing for his climb up Everest. If the weather had been better the vistas would have been far reaching. High on the pass, below Snowdon, a surprising number of hearty walkers were booting up, ready to ascend the slopes despite the cold and snow.

Soon after driving away from Caernarfon I turned off the coast road towards **St Baglan's, Llanfaglan** *(LL54 5RA)* and the sea. In the village I was directed to the keeper of the church key who pointed in the general direction of sea and church. After a mile or so the lane turned sharp right along the sea front and only then in the distance did St Baglan's become visible in the middle of a large field dotted with brown cows grazing, tucked behind an encircling *llan* of stone wall and tall trees, still bare branches windswept to lean almost horizontal in one direction. What a wonderful location. I hopped over the style and across the field, trying to pretend there were no cows. In days gone by lych gates were useful as an overnight resting place for a coffin, wide enough to provide cover for the deceased as well as the sleeping custodian. This robust stone walled, slate roofed gate directly faces across grass to the even more substantial north porch. Before venturing inside, I wandered about the kempt churchyard still in use for burials though the C13th church itself, Grade 1 listed, is now in the care of The Friends of Friendless Church. The whitewashed interior, original roof beams and trusses which were painted creamy white, are lit by two plain glass windows. There are C18th box pews for the gentry and plank benches for their servants against one of which is an unusual crooked little seven-sided font. At the bottom of a large memorial plaque commemorating a Jones family I noticed mention of Peter who *'gloriously fell leading the forlorn hope at the memorable Battle of Badajos during the Peninsular War.'*

I gleaned what information I could from a book inside the entrance. The stone over the internal door to form a lintel has been dated as C5th or C6th: it is incised with the words *'Fili Loverni Anatemori'* to mark the loss of a son. I was intrigued to read the legend of Baglan's well, filled in long ago. According to folklore the water had healing powers: *bathe the infected area, prick it with a pin which then bend before dropping into the well.* This *'treatment'* was particularly successful in the removal of warts! Two basins of bent pins were found when the well was filled in the C19th! Long after my visit to this wild and windswept corner **St Baglan's** received a famous, permanent visitor: *'On 20 January 2017, the church was the venue for the funeral of Antony Armstrong-Jones, 1st Earl of Snowdon. He was buried in the churchyard where the family has a plot'.*

Reluctant to leave this little delight and such tranquility and quiet I walked back to the stile and sat there, between field and sea, to eat my picnic lunch. Heaven! With time to fill before the tide was right for visiting the island church, I returned to the coast road and drove for some miles to **St Beuno's, Clynnog-Fawr.** Simon found much to admire in this church but as I'm not a student of architecture I found the huge interior somewhat soulless and intimidating. A very small font appeared lost in a sea of surrounding flagstones and

Llanfaglan location

the fourteen misericords disappointed in their uniformity and plain design. Although I hunted for them I didn't come across "*dog tongs for removing obstreperous animals*" as mentioned by Simon. The only item of real interest to me was reading about a young man whose parents were keen supporters of this church. Edgar Christian accompanied his explorer uncle, John Hornby, to the North West Territories of Canada in 1926-27. The intention was to winter in 'the Barren Lands' and depend entirely on hunting caribou for food, storing enough meat to last the winter. Sadly there were no caribou about, resulting in the death of all three from starvation. Throughout this tragic period Edgar, the last to die, kept a diary discovered a year later as he left a note "Look in stove". The Canadian Mounted Police buried all three in situ, their graves marked by simple wooden crosses. This diary was published in Canada under the title *Unflinching*. Recalling how much I had enjoyed *Barrow's Boys* by Fergus Fleming, a riveting account of British attempts to navigate the north-west passage in the C18th, I looked for a secondhand copy of this diary and found two: £27.18 in paperback form, £149.48 hardback. I decided to re-read *Barrow's Boys* instead.

Fast forward over the next few hours. I returned along the coast road to Bangor, crossed to Anglesea and followed the east coast all the way to St Elian's, Llaneilian. It was locked. So I drove on, this time straight across the island towards **Aberfraw.** In the quiet early evening of a long day I parked Ruby above a cove from which the sea had just receded, leaving puddles among the still wet rocks and glistening dark strands of slippery twisted seaweed. To the far side of the cove and lying just within it is a flat, small, almost round island with quite high vertical sides and room for just one small white painted building, **St Cwfan's, church of Llangwyfan.** The medieval church was built on what was once a promontory until erosion caused by centuries of weather and water marooned it on a tiny island protected by a sea wall built in 1893, linked to the mainland at low tide by a causeway. I skirted the cove then walked, eyes cast down, stepping rather gingerly over rocks and seaweed until reaching stone steps leading up on to bouncy tufted grass. What a fabulous setting for a simple place of worship! Of course it was locked but no matter; the whole interior was easily visible through the east window. Outside a wooden bench against the west wall faced the sea and just in front, fringed by grass, is a memorial stone to *Frank Gurney aged 21, drowned 31.07.1861* while trying to save" *papers of value"* off a sailing ship in distress. I sat for some while, sea stretching to the horizon and beyond, all pale greys and blues in the early evening light. For a mad moment I considered lingering until the sea lapped all around this tiny island, to lie down on the grass next to Frank, a tiny bit of insignificance looking up at the wide night sky, isolated from Everything until, as ever, the ebb tide obeyed the moon, reconnecting this spiritual place to the mainland. It was with considerable reluctance I returned to Ruby.

Aberffraw location

Next morning, after a substantial breakfast of scrambled eggs and smoked salmon, I looked forward to visiting **St Gwyddelan's** in the village **Dolwyddelan** *(LL25 0SJ)* on the A470 just south of Betws-y-coed. The photograph in Simon's book is of a little stone church in a rustic setting not far from a river. With this picture in my mind I searched everywhere for such a church: down a farm track, beyond the school and further down the main road then turning off over a Roman bridge towards a hill farm. Returning to the village I even asked the staff in the Spar shop where to find this church. None of the assistants knew. However they suggested, as I was there anyway, I pop into the church all but next door as it was "very sweet, really old and always open." According to a board by the gate, this *was* St Gwyddelan's church! I was astonished. It didn't appear to match the church pictured in Simon's book at all yet, once inside, the interior was just as described in his text. He hadn't mentioned the bright blue carpet on flagstones or a row of tired old bibles though he described much else. I particularly liked something I had never seen before, wooden 'sleigh' sides linking the pews. It was well worth the search and, once I had walked round to the rear of this adorable little C16th building, it became clear from which position the photograph had been taken.

I intended to make a long circular walk in the afternoon but my hostess was determined I wasn't going to miss out on any quirky kirks in *her* area so, deferring to her enthusiasm, I drove north of Betws-y-coed to visit **Gwydir Uchaf** *(LL26 0PN),* a private chapel once connected to Gwydir Castle now in the care of Cadw, historic environment department of the Welsh Assembly. Following instructions, I collected an enormous key from the Castle, crossed the road and walked up into the woods to find the little stone chapel built in 1673. The key unlocked a studded, heavily hinged door. It opened into such a jolly interior my reaction was to smile as I looked about and above. The barrel ceiling, a sort of greeny-blue from end to end, is covered with colourful, quite crudely painted chubby cherubs, flying angels, clouds, stars and, in the very centre, a spreading sun. I hardly noticed the walls wood paneled to sill height, double decker pulpit, few benches and gaily painted western gallery: instead I lay on the flagstones to best enjoy the heaven above me. In 1757 a Dr Pococke was most complimentary, describing a *'very handsome chapel'*. However in 1800 Mr Bingley was dismissive, writing *'parts are decorated with paintings of scriptural figures most miserably executed'*. A distinct difference of opinion! Outside, I followed a path behind the chapel until I came to an unusual holly hedge which starts from a centre point in unbroken rings ever increasing in diameter to make a large circle, a sort of non-maze, the path in between prickly walls a carpet of wild garlic. Curious.

St Rhychwyn's, Llanrhychwyn was quite different. By now I had become used to narrow lanes deep set meandering lanes between dense, winter cropped hedges. Far, far along a lane, high on hills above Gwydir Forest, I glimpsed a low lying stone chapel. I hopped over a stile into a field of grazing, disinterested sheep and entered the *llan* through, of course, a fat stone lych gate. St Rhychwyn's has overlooked the valley since at least late C11th so is probably the oldest of all the churches I visited over those few days. The warm stone exterior didn't appear to have changed at all since that time though the north aisle was added four hundred years after the original south aisle. Dotted about the interior lay all sorts of furniture and items of interest: a bier slung on the wall; desks – the sort with ink wells and bench seats – indicating use as a school room once upon a time; C17th pulpit and rails; C18th altar and settle. According to church notes, an unusual dinky little square font atop two steps next to a column is thought to be one of the oldest in Wales, as is the glass in the east window. When I left I secured the door shut with a forked twig, a novel sort of padlock! A thought: from where does a congregation come of a Sunday? I hadn't noted any sort of dwelling for miles around.

By now sporadic rain had disappeared along with the afternoon. I found **St Mary's, Caerhun**, at the end of a short lane off the B5106 nestled close to the River Conway and surrounded by sheep-filled fields. St Mary's facade is plain, the west door, set in grey stone under a double bell-cote which, according to church notes, was only ever home to a single bell. I pushed open the oak door onto the long central aisle. The length and simplicity of the original C13th nave flanked by some twenty rows of pews within fat white painted stone walls, under dark beams and trusses of the barrel ceiling is handsome if a tad austere. No ornament, other than a medieval holy water stoup just by the entrance, no inferior stained glass to despoil the quiet of this interior. Charming.

Next morning at breakfast I reported back to mine hostess who was delighted I had visited and enjoyed *her* churches. Just before I continued my meandering way towards Shropshire, the man of the house appeared in time for me to compliment him on his scrambled eggs. After four days of seeking rural churches I was pretty much 'churched out' but, taking the view 'one may not pass this way again', I decided not to bypass four more located en route home.

St Michael's, Efenechyd (*LL15 2PP),* is located far along a climbing lane in a surprisingly affluent appearing village in which all the houses appeared freshly painted white and the vicarage boasted imposing wrought iron gates, incongruous in this rural setting. The churchyard however was surprisingly neglected: two groups of at least four ancient tabletop monuments were completely hidden by many years ivy growth. There's a door knocker on the ancient west door: it's unusual to find one at all on a church door let alone one shaped like a wishbone! Inside all is red: the aisle carpet,

Efenechtyd oak font

327

vestry curtain, carpet offcuts as runners along every bench. There are two ancient fonts. The stone one was last used as a drinking bowl for dogs belonging to farmers attending service! A more interesting and rare font dated C16th, still in use, was hewn from a single piece of oak; it has fourteen facets and, despite the rather crude bulbous beading carved round the base, rather beautiful.

Returning to the main road I headed southeast to another chapel once privately owned by the local Salesbury family. Both **Rug Chapel** *(LL21 9BT)* and the church I went on to visit afterwards are now in the care of Cadw. **Rug,** built in 1854-55 and furnished with C17th and C18th pieces, has its own visitor centre and charges a small entrance fee. I don't know what I expected to see when I opened the internal west door but I was immediately reminded of a Swiss chalet although I'm uncertain how colourfully painted are their wood interiors. The wood of this interior is decorated to charming and amusing effect everywhere the eye looked. Pitched roof beams, five trusses, canopied pews, gallery balustrade and supporting beam: all covered with a mélange of leafy and geometric designs. Four painted wooden angels appear to fly off two trusses and, suspended from the very centre of the roof, a surely unique double-tiered wooden candelabrum topped with four little angels facing out and very long 'tear-drops' hanging from beneath each candle. A painted frieze runs along the south and north walls comprising small rectangular panels depicting strange animals in the middle of each one. A 'jolly' Fred is depicted with rounded rib-cage and a weird toothy grin, recumbent beneath another skull and outsize hour-glass. Best of all are the wooden 'sleigh' bench ends linking pews, a set on each side of the aisle. According to notes, the beautifully carved depictions of animals into these joining sides are C17th workmanship. Most of the creatures I recognized – dragons, wyverns, serpents, a pelican in her piety – are subjects often carved into misericords; in addition a cow's face, a fleecy sheep with collar, a donkey, squirrel with small dog and a large dog stamping on a small dog! Compared with the very plain pew sides in St Gwyddelan, Dolwyddelan these are rather grand. Why raised sides at all? Simon suggests they were designed to keep out mud. Could well be.

Rug chapel pew end

Rug was certainly memorable. But so too was the last church I visited. **All Saints, Llangar,** a little way outside the town of Curwen, is inaccessible to cars. I parked Ruby in a layby, crossed the road and set off down a track until I came to a five-bar gate with a sign indicating the church at the end of what had been a drovers' road. Skirting a large patch of mud and cowpats I followed the track up an incline and round a bend before the church came into sight. A grassy path under the lych gate – this one has *two* benches *and* a door! – led up a slope to the south porch of a church glowing white in the sun. Only then did I notice how deep cut into the hillside is the east end: the window is barely a foot off the ground. Fields and river lie beyond the stone walled *llan*, a lovely open vista somewhat lost on those lying under a considerable number of old tabletop gravestones and semi-toppled headstones. But for the presence of a couple of other visitors and Geraint, to enter All Saints was to leave behind the C21st and step back to the days of bows and arrows, illiterate peasants and plain, useful and sparse furnishings. The couple departed almost immediately, and I was left to enjoy and benefit from Geraint's company and thorough knowledge of this little reminder of times medieval. I was so lucky to arrive during the hour or so this volunteer guide spent two or three days a week explaining the history and oddities of his beloved church to any interested visitor. I didn't expect to find as much interest in so unpretentious a church. Geraint wasted no time explaining Fred! So named by the parishioners, Fred is the more than life size skeleton painted on the north wall, there to 'greet' illiterate worshippers entering through the south door. Doom paintings vary considerably. In this one Fred symbolizes death and the baby lying across his pelvis represents new life; between his legs a pick and spade for growing food; in one hand a bow for hunting and in the other an hour-glass, symbol of the brevity of man's time on earth.

Fred is not alone on the wall. All round the church are faint remains of educational paintings all about the church dating from C14th to C17th. Geraint pointed out the only three recognisable depictions of the seven deadly sins: a lion (pride), boar (gluttony) and goat (lechery). Above, the handsome timber roof exposed when remedial work was carried out in the 1970s. On the floor, which slopes towards the altar, old stone flags. The interior is far from empty. Facing the rather grand triple deck pulpit on the south wall is a row of box pews, varying in size and decoration according to the owner's house and standing in the community. At right angles to the wall, next to the pulpit, is a row of basic benches on which servants and farmhands would have sat, most uncomfortably. Geraint said it is thought the origin of the saying *backs to the wall* came from these benches, seats of the lowliest and weakest. Set into a niche in the wall an old tub font. At the east end of the north wall a squint, long blocked up, allowed lepers and other unclean to observe services from a safe distance. Geraint urged me to climb stone steps up to the gallery to see the 'pen' in which musicians were seated around a rare four-sided music stand; outside the 'pen', choristers on benches behind them. Geraint regaled me with the legend of the white deer – a long story! – then pointed out the scratch marks on both sides of the door where hazel wood arrows had been sharpened. Before leaving I persuaded Geraint to have his photograph taken. He stood in front of Fred, stocky, hands thrust deep in the pockets of his windcheater, black beanie hat offset above a single dangling earring, a hint of smile below his glasses, someone to remember. Llangar was a church of great charm with which to end this visit to Wales before crossing into Shropshire to stay once again with Penny and Tim.

* * *

Three or four years before embarking on this 'church crawl' while staying with Penny and Tim, they urged me to slip over the border into Wales and visit a rural church with a tale to tell about a hare! The route would pass by the village of **Melverley, Shropshire** with a church I was keen to visit so I was easily persuaded. Sometimes that special something is to be found in the church, sometimes the church proves to be a poor accessory to its surroundings. Neither **St Peter's** *(SY10 8PJ)* nor its surroundings disappointed. The little church, all black timber and white daub, is mirrored in the River Vyrnwy coursing beneath the bank on which it perches, safely underpinned, just beyond the village streets. Unusually, the west door opens into a small hall from which stairs lead up to the gallery and a door opens into the nave. I climbed the stairs onto boards angled so steeply towards the east wall the childhood nursery rhyme *'There was a crooked man who had a crooked house'* came to mind just as it did when visiting St Michael's, Cwmyoy in Wales. Rafters, down posts, cross beams, floor boards: a spirit level wouldn't know where to start! Downstairs in the nave I looked about, feeling the abundance of oak embrace rather than depress me. How many babies had been sprinkled with water over the Saxon font? How many readings delivered from the 1727 bible chained to its lectern across the aisle from the carved Jacobean pulpit? Church records from 1739 to 1900 listed many special occasions commemorated by His, or Her, Majesty's Special Command. Listed among them the Jacobite Rebellion, the earthquake of 1756, cholera epidemics, the Sikh Rebellion in India and Queen Victoria's safe delivery in childbirth. Also mentioned were crop failure, the Crimean War, thanks for abundant harvest, the Indian Mutiny, Queen Victoria's jubilees and the South African Boer War. On the 17th December 1766, the parish clerk in frivolous mood added this poem following the marriage between one Matthew Dodd and Elinor Foster:

This day I have put a Tye
No man could put it faster
Tween Matthew Dodd, the man of God
And modest Nelly Foster.

I continued my drive west into Wales. The day was glorious, a little jewel among the many drear ones that summer. The near traffic-free road wound towards hills, tree green, scree grey. **Pennant Melangell** *(SY10 0HQ)* is signed left along a narrow lane through deciduous woods before meandering between fields. A mile or so along the way a very small red post box had been strapped to a tree trunk. How often, I wondered, were items posted in let alone collected from it. I decided to leave the car opposite the first dwelling I came to, whitewashed Pennant Cottage, and continue along the lane on foot. A red quad bike bumped over the grass, sheepdog lolloping alongside, disregarded by sheep grazing or lying in the shade of huge trees dotted about. But for the quad bike, the scene, framing the distant stocky church tower crowned with a little wooden bell-turret, was surely unchanged for centuries past. A bend, a cottage, and beyond a rough clearing, a substantial broad stone lych-gate, complete with stone seats, set in a low wall surrounding the circular churchyard in which grow five ancient yew trees, dated to be around two thousand years old. Names on headstones read almost exclusively Davies, Jones, Evans but also harpist Nansi and Tom, her teacher. A sturdy low gate keeps 'lawnmower' sheep from entering the porch but couldn't deter swallows nesting, rather messily, in one corner. Inside the wooden door, just above head height, hangs a candelabrum over a metre wide: it resembles a cartwheel with eight turned spokes, each one a candle holder, and below them a deep hoop around which is painted the names of two churchwardens; Robert James, Robert Jones.

St Melangell's church is charming. Beyond the pitch roof of the nave and C15th rood screen, is a barrel ceiling above the chancel. An arch opens into the recently restored simple apsidal chancel with lancet window and cobbled floor, furnished only with a single seat and kneeler, perfect for quiet reflection. The church is permeated with the tale of the Melangell hare. The legend is attributed to the year 604 when the hounds of a hunting prince chased a hare into a thicket where – lucky hare! – St Melangell, virgin hermit, happened to be at prayer. To elude capture the quick thinking hare hid under her garment and has been protected in the area ever since. The hare is everywhere. It is just visible peeping from the skirts of the female effigy, stitched into a single purple hassock, carved crouching and painted red in the frieze on the rood screen and depicted variously in four beautifully worked stone carvings placed along a wall ledge. They are so inviting to the touch, I wondered how many visitors had been tempted to take one home! The church's *piéce de resistance* is a C12th shrine to St Melangell, hare held in her arms, flanked by two ancient recumbent effigies, a man and a woman. A Welsh language bible with an illustrated frontispiece lay open on the lectern, a green ribbon marking a page showing the Lords Prayer in fourteen languages against a green and tan elaborately decorated background. Nearby there is a bi-lingual bible printed in 1852. A hand written note told us this bible had first been '*presented to Richard Oswald Richards by his father on attaining his seventh birthday, August 27th 1891*' and was thereafter '*left to me (who?) in 1959 by the Reverend Harold Stanley Richards, and is now given to Howard Edwards of Ealing, London on the First Sunday in Advent 1986*'. I popped upstairs to the tower room where boards displayed local history. There was also a collage illustrating a mix of cities and countries from which visitors had come including South Africa, Zimbabwe *and* Sun City but *not* Botswana.

Before retracing steps to my car, I walked on the lane a little further until I came to a field with no less than eleven curious elderly rams, all of which came close to inspect my foreign body! One rather magnificent specimen sported horns so curly, so spreading they reminded me of Jimmy Edwards' moustache! Visiting Pennant Melangell was sort of equivalent to dipping one's toes in the sea whereas my subsequent Welsh wander was more of a leisurely and most enjoyable swim.

* * *

Some years later I returned to Wales for the third time during the month of May when the gods smiled for a whole week of glorious sunshine and warmth and the countryside was wearing its best clothes. Driving was a simple pleasure: following near empty roads, sunken lanes between high ragged hedges or tunneling under arching tree boughs. The waysides and banks were a-dazzle with flowers in paint-box colours: wild garlic, campion, bluebell, cow parsley, celandine, speedwell, cowslip, ox-eye daisy. As before I followed a linear route from chapel to chapel, not always with success, staying in three different bed-and-breakfast venues along the way.

After a comfortable night north of Carmarthen and hostess Anne's excellent breakfast I set off to the village of Bosherton *(SA71 5DN)* on the Pembrokeshire coast, excited to be visiting the romantic chapel of **St Govan** nestled under and into the cliff on land owned by the M.O.D. Unfortunately I found the red flag up, barrier down, preventing access during army exercises. Thwarted, I strolled down a path lined with exuberant rhododendrons, passing several lily ponds to a wide cove, low tide sand glistening, reminiscent of beaches I had walked or ridden in the Cape, South Africa. I perched awhile on a rock while a sprinkle of visitors walked barefoot along the waters edge. Determined to visit the simple place of worship hewn from rock in the C15th, I decided to leave the house very early next morning, return to Bosherton then drive back in time for breakfast. The post dawn sky was grey, the breeze playful and the parking area by the cliff deserted. Not another soul in sight. Perfect. I made my way to and down steep stone steps to the 'back' door of a narrow building, atop the pitched stone tiled roof of which a crude structure which may once have housed a bell. Inside to a space 20 x 12 ft enclosed by rough hewn walls, mud floor, stone shelf-cum-altar and steps up to a space under a tiny high window into what was probably the cell of **St Govan,** hermit of the C6th. The outlook from a larger window in the chapel is between rocky cliffs to churning grey sea beyond. I was so lucky to spend a while in this romantic, spiritual edifice on the cliffs without another human being to intrude on its magic.

Later that day it was disappointing to find **The Holy Cross, Mwnt** *(SA43 1QH)* locked. White painted stone under grey slate, this ancient place of worship for sailors and pilgrims, nestled below a hummock off the coastal path, used to be open day and night; now closed but for services held in the summer months, Christmas and Easter. Deciding to make the best of being there, I climbed up and around the hill behind the church following a narrow stony track way above the sea. I abandoned all attempts to find the next church on my itinerary – even the local builder and postman hadn't heard of it! – so continued north to Aberaeron where I stretched my legs along the sea wall, had coffee overlooking the harbour. The road continued north, loosely following the coast, on to Dolgellau, very near to my base for the next two nights. The Dyfi Valley is part of the Mach Loop, used for low level flying practice – flash noise from screaming jet engines is an almost daily occurrence. For my landlady and her husband, migrants from proximity to Heathrow, this was peace!

Next morning after a particularly good breakfast I headed up the valley towards the coastal town of Criccieth. I looked forward to seeing a complete set of Georgian furniture in **St Cynhaerarn's, Ynyscynhaearn.** Taking a brisk walk along a farm track towards the ancient silhouette visible amongst a small clump of trees growing above marshland outside the town, I overtook rusty brown cows and a very tall woman walking a very small dog to be confronted with yet another locked door. It seems much has changed in the few years since my first Welsh crawl: then all was open, now much is locked.

Despite a post code and explicit directions from a number of local folk, I never did find **St Leslyn's, Llandegwning** *(LL53 8PS),* apparently near Llanglan, well down the peninsular. Lured as I had been by John Betjeman's description – "*engaging dolls' house church circa 1840, it has a two-stage octagonal round tower, conical spire and all is painted white inside except the green-grained box pews*" – this was a further disappointment. My spirits lifted as I drove further west. Turning off the main road, a narrow lane led to the highest point above Aberdaron from where the view over countryside, beaches and sea, all brilliant under the sun, was stupendous. Overlooking this vista is **St Maelrhys, LLanfaelrhys** *(LL53 8AN)*, a simple chapel built of local rubble stone in a sparsely populated graveyard surrounded by a dry stonewall. At last, an open door! I spent a quiet moment in the cool dark before a descent of many bends into Aberdaron. Once parked in the seaside town I relaxed sitting outside one of several pubs, nursing a long cool drink before walking the beach from end to end.

My bed for the next two nights lay over the border near Kington, Shropshire. Nearby is **St Michael the Archangel, Llanyblodwel** *(SY0 9DW)*. This little church is perched on a slope overlooking fields and a river. Little remained of its Norman origin by the time John Parker, eccentric vicar and self-styled architect, persuaded parishioners to stump up for restoration work 1845-60, carried out to his designs. As a result a tower and octagonal spire replaced a stumpy bell housing, and the highly decorated, quirky interior is full of interest. Of particular interest to me was an unusual dark oak chair – its high back curved forward to form a small canopy from which two rounded spindles dropped onto each chair arm – and in the porch, carved in relief on a rectangular slab, the Melangell hare chased by a dog. The church notes describe the legend of the hare I first came across at Pennant Melangell. I continued via Welshpool, following narrow hill lanes through hilly farmland to **All Saints, Trelystar**, black and white, long and low, alone in a large sloping field, fenced in with six ancient yew trees. The only church in Wales built in the C15th wholly of timber, subsequently encased in brick and timber. The arch braced roof is original, the altar rail Jacobean and the east widow the work of one Charles Clutterbuck. Great name.

Despite clear if contradictory directions from two locals, I was no nearer to finding **St Michael's, Llanfihangel Helygen** *(LD1 6EB0),* until a visiting sales rep insisted on walking me to the open door of a rather wonderful farmhouse. He hollered for Farmer Robert whose directions led me straight to this simple church. A cottage amongst trees, with deep brownstone walls, ancient roof arch braces and a touching wall plaque, memorial to a boy soldier killed in the Great War.

My last day in Wales was full of interest. **St Michael's, Cascob** *(LD8 2NW)* south of Knighton, was memorable only for its location in deep countryside, two sheep acting as lawnmowers and the detailed Cascob Abracacadabra charm hanging on the wall '*to protect the church from dragons*' – written in English not Welsh, would dragons have been deterred?! As the crow flies from Cascob yet some distance through the valley, I found and was enchanted by **St David's, Colva** *(HR5 3RA),* the one church referenced by Reverend Francis Kilvert (1840-79 in his enchanting diaries describing his love of countryside. Allegedly one of the highest churches in Wales it stands remote on the Radnor hills, surrounded by yew trees. Inside a handwritten notice to visitors: '*Welcome to St David's Colva. Help yourself to a nice hot cup of Tea or Coffee. Rest awhile and feel refreshed. Take in the fresh air and admire the scenery*'. Charming. As was the interior: thick walls patched with mould, vases of drooping wild flowers and rows of school benches serving as pews. Outside the surface of a tabletop gravestone served to lay out and prepare my picnic lunch which I then ate sitting on a bench, absorbing the view at leisure. I remembered to raise my mug to toast Prince Harry and Megan whose wedding was taking place at the time.

The last church, **St Mary's, Pilleth** *(LD7 1LP,)* was the king of this Welsh wander. Not far from Presteign, St Mary, white painted and visible from the road far below, is in a glorious position high on Bryn Glas hillside, site of a bloody battle on the 22nd June 1402 when the outnumbered forces of Owain Glyndwr, Prince of Wales were victorious against an English army led by the acting Earl of Marches, cousin of King Henry 1V. After battle this C13th church was damaged by fire, as it was again in 1894 when a chimney set fire to the roof. This was finally restored in 1905. In medieval times pilgrims were drawn to a holy well next to the tower as the water was thought to have healing properties, especially for eyes. The white painted interior is unadorned, peaceful, imbued with a sense of days long gone. I sat for a while on a modern wooden bench with a view of surrounding countryside little changed over six centuries and pondered the advice inscribed on the backrest. *Don't cry because it's over – Smile because it happened.*

St Mary, Pilleth

I had one more building to visit in the centre of Presteigne (*LD8 2AD*) Over breakfast that morning my hostess had enthused about the **Judges Lodgings** in the recently restored Shire Hall. The grand Victorian building has apartments for the comfort of Judges while staying in town to hear cases in the in-house courtroom and, below stairs, a wondrous rabbit warren of kitchens, pantries and general storage rooms. Not only is every item setting the scene true to the times but so is the lighting, which adds to the mid C19th feel, especially so in the gas lit basement rooms. It was an excellent ending to my springtime wander round Wales.

* * *

I've enjoyed two further visits to Wales, both in good company. During a family holiday based in Tenby I was more than happy not to pass through a single church door. Apart from ice creams in a cone, the obligatory meal of fish and chips and messing about on the beach, the highlight for all of us was a short sea trip across to Skomer Island, sea bird paradise and nesting burrows for Charlie Chaplin in avian form, the puffin.

* * *

Driving up from Bath, this time as a passenger in fellow Dawdler Rupert's car, we made a considerable detour to St David, the smallest city in Britain and the western tip of Pembrokeshire before joining the Dorset Dawdlers in a village near the other Newport where we had rented a house as a base from where we spent four days following the north coastal path. Only because of its cathedral does St David purport to be a city; it really is little more than a charming village by the sea. A short walk from the car and there before us, beyond an apron of lawn, was the full length of this magnificent cathedral and, from close by the west door, a pedestrian bridge over a stream led to the towering ruins of the C14th Bishop's Palace, a still majestic example of a medieval ecclesiastical palace. It is a truly spectacular scene. Over the following hour or so Rupert and I wandered separately through the cathedral and cloisters before meeting up in the ruins. There was so much to absorb. I particularly loved the painted roofs and the almost hidden cloisters around a small square of grass. A kindly steward gave me permission to peek at and photograph the misericords, not one of an angel, king or even a pelican in her piety. Printed in gold letters above some of them is the name of whose seat it is: *Arch:Brecon* above four worried men in a coracle; *Cancellarius* above a bishop with wings; an alarming scene of one weird creature eating another is beneath the seat for *P:Curfatis*; *Thefaurius* above a dragon with tail between its legs; *P:Aurea* above a fun scene of a duck man and dog woman in the kitchen; above the head of a fox is *Vicr.Epifcop*; a monster has the head of a stuggling man in his mouth beneath *P:Cludeu*; *P:Llan:Dewi* above a tubby owl while underneath *Archd:Cardign* a scene of five pigs eating a dog; finally a snoozing man beneath *P:Caer-Farchell*. Three misericords do not seem to be person specific: two men dancing, two men in loin cloths under a cauldron and snakes entwined.

Rupert and I agreed the detour was well taken.

* * *

Cloisters, St David's Cathedral

Index (town, dedication)

Hough on the Hill (Lincs)	All Saints	283
Hythe (Kent)	St Leonard	12,134
Houghton-on-Hill (Norfolk)	St Mary the Virgin	194,195
Hubberholme (Yorks)	St Michael & All Saints	167
Huccaby (Devon)	St Rafael	122
Idsworth (Hants)	St Hubert	77
Iken (Suffolk)	St Botolph	252
Imber Village (Wilts)		27
Isle Abbotts (Somerset)	St Mary's	2
Isleham (Cambs)	St Andrew	184
Ivychurch (Kent)	St George	128
Ixworth (Suffolk)	All Saints	292
Jevington (E.Sussex)	St Andrews	60
Judges Lodgings (Wales)		340
Kedington (Suffolk)	St Peter & St Paul	184
Kempley (Glos)	St Mary	207
Kemsing (Kent)	St Mary	132
Keswick (Norfolk)	All Saints	200
Kidlington (Oxon)	St Mary the Virgin	143
Kilpeck (Heres)	St Mary & St David	210
King Somborne (Hants)	St Peter & St Paul	87
Kingerby (Lincs)	St Peter	290
Kingston (Dorset)	St James	22
Kingston St Mary (Somerset)		16
Kingston near Lewes (E.Sussex)	St Pancras	60
Kinwarton Dovecote (Waks)		273
Kirkby Underdale (Yorks)	All Saints	171
Kirkstead(Lincs)	St Leonard	240
Knapton (Norfolk)	t Peter & St Paul	242
Lakenheath (Norfolk)	St Mary the Virgin	193,249
Langham (Dorset)	St George	106
Langley Chapel (Shrops)		214
Lastingham (N.Yorks)	St Mary	160
Lavenham (Suffolk)	St Peter & St Paul	183
Leckford (Hants)	St Nicholas	89,90
Ledbury (Heres)	St Michael	204
Lichfield Cathedral		276
Lincoln Cathedral		237
Little Rollright (Oxon)	St Philip	142
Little Snoring (Norfolk)	St Andrew	186
Little Somborne (Hants)	All Saints	86
Little Washbourne	St Mary	227
Little Witchingham (Norfolk)	St Faith	201
Llanafaur Fawr (Powys)	St Afan	315
Llanbister (Powys)	St Cynilo	318
Llanfaelrhys (Wales)	St Maelrhys	337
Llanfaglan (Caernarfon)	St Baglan	320
Llanfair Kilgeddin (Mons)	St Mary	306.307
LLanfihangel Helygen (Wales)	St Michael	338

Llangar (Denbighs)	All Saints	330
Llanrhychwyn (Denbighs)	St Rhychwyn	326
Llanyblodwel (Wales)	St Michael the Archangel	337
Llanymawaddwy (Gwynedd)	St Tydecho	319
Long Melford (Suffolk)	Holy Trinity	108,183
Long Sutton (Somerset)	Holy Trinity	7
Lower Kingswood	Church of the Wisdom of God	67,68
Lud's Church (Staffs)		257,258
Lullington (E. Sussex)	The Good Shepherd	50
Lyddington (Rutland)	St Andrew	232
Lyndhurst (Hants)	St Michael & All Saints	81
Markby (Lincs)	St Peter	239
Martock (Somerset)	All Saints	7
Mells(Somerset)	St Andrew	8
Melton Constable (Norfolk)	St Peter	241
Melverley (Shrops)	St Peter	331
Mevesyn Ridware (Staffs)	St Nicholas	277,278,279
Midhopestone (Yorks)	St James	165
Mildenhall (Cambs)	St Mary & St Andrew	184
Milton Abbey (Dorset)		24
Minstead (Hants)	All Saints	81
Minsterley (Shrops)	Holy Trinity	85
Misericords		216,217,218
Moreton (Dorset)	St Nicholas	18
Morston(Norfolk)	All Saints	243
Morton-on-Hill (Norfolk)	St Margaret	201
Mottisfont (Hants)	St Andrew	87
Muchelney Abbey (Somerset)		5
Much Marcle (Heres)	St Bartholomew	206
Mwnt (Wales)	Holy Cross	336
Mylor (Cornwall)	St Mylor	103,104
Nately Scures (Hants)	St Swithun	94
North Chideock (Dorset)	RC Church of Our Lady Queen	21
North Marden (W. Sussex)	St Mary	41
Northumberlandia		260
Norwich Cathedral		244
Oare (Somerset)	St Mary	5
Odda's Chapel (Gloucs)		224,225
Old Bewick (Northumberland)	Holy Trinity	262
Old Dilton (Wilts)	St Mary	221
Old Kea (Cornwall)	St Kea	104,105
Old Romney (Kent)	St Clement	128
Orford Keep (Suffolk)		299
Ottery St Mary (Devon)		107
Painswick (Gloucs)	St Mary	223
Parham (Sussex)	St Peter	56
Patrishow (Powys)	St Issui	311,312
Patrixbourne (Kent)	St Mary	130
Pennant Melangell (Powys)	St Melangell	333,334

Pilleth (Wales)	St Mary	339
Playden (E. Sussex)	St Michael	126
Portland (Dorset)	St George	36,37
Princetown (Devon)	St Michael & All Angels	123
Puxton (Somerset)	St Saviour	16
Pyecombe (E. Sussex)	Church of Transfiguration	60
Quarley (Hants)	St Michael the Archangel	91
Radley (Oxon)	St James the Great	145
Ramsholt (Suffolk)	All Saints	296,297,298
Ranworth (Norfolk)	St Helen	196,197
Ratlinghope (Shrops)	St Margaret	214
Reepham (Norfolk)		202
Rhulen (Powys)	St David	316
Ripon Cathedral (Yorks)		153
Ripple (Worces)	St Mary	212
Rollesby (Norfolk)	St George	202
Rothwell(Northants)	Holy Trinity	134,135,289
Rug (Denbighs)	Chapel	328,329
St Anthony-in-Roseland (Corn)		101
St Bartholomew (Chichester)		47
St Cross (Hants)	Alms Houses & church	96
St David's Cathedral (Wales)		341
St Endelion (Cornwall)	St Endelienta	102
St Enodoc (Cornwall)		102,103
St Govan (Wales)		335
St John's Chapel (Chichester)		47
St Just-in-Roseland (Cornwall)		100
St Magnus-the-Martyr (London)		174
St Mary Aldermary (London)		175
St Mary-at-Hill (London)		175
St Mary's Hospice (W.Sussex)		47
St Michael Paternoster (London)		176
St Stephen Walbrook (London)		175
Salle (Norfolk)	St Peter & St Paul	186,202
Sampford Courtney (Devon)	St Andrew	107
Sandford (Devon)	St Swithun	114
Sapiston (Suffolk)	St Andrew	293
Saxted (Suffolk)	All Saints	295
Saxton (Yorks)	Mary's Chapel, Lead	168
Selborne (Hants)	St Mary	78
Selham (W. Sussex)	St James	46
Selworthy (Somerset)	All Saints	3
Sherborne Abbey(Dorset)		24,25
Shere (Surrey)	St James	72
Sherrington (Wilts)	St Cosmas & St Damian	219
Shimpling (Norfolk)	St George	294,295
Shobdon (Heres)	St John the Evangelist	211
Shoreham (Kent)	St Peter & St Paul	132
Shorthampton (Oxon)	All Saints	142

Waddingworth(Lincs)	St Margaret	240
Walpole St Peter (Norfolk)		187
Wareham (Dorset)	St Martin	21
Warminghurst (E.Sussex)	The Holy Sepulchre	49
Warkleigh (Devon)	St John	118
Waterperry (Oxon)	St Mary the Virgin	147
Watts Chapel (Surrey)		66
Wells Cathedral (Somerset)		9
Welton (Yorks)	St Helen	173
Wensley (E. Yorks)	Holy Trinity	156
West Grinstead (Sussex)	St George	51,52
West Markham (Notts)	All Saints	283
West Somerton (Norfolk)	St Mary	198
West Stoke (W. Sussex)	St Andrew	44
West Tisted (Hants)	St Mary Magdelene	76
Whalley (Lancs)	St Mary	257
Wheatfield (Oxon)	St Andrew	148
Whitby (N. Yorks)	St Mary	169,161
Widford (Oxon)	St Oswold	140
Wigganholt (Sussex)	no dedication	56
Willingdon Dovecote & Stables		285
Wilmington (E. Sussex)	St Mary & St Peter	50
Wimborne Minster (Dorset)		24,25
Winchelsea (E. Sussex)	St Thomas the Apostle	125
Wickham (Berks)	St Swithun	137
Wingham (Kent)	St Mary	129
Winterborne Tomson(Dorset)	St Andrew	28
Wirksworth (Derbys)	St Mary	189
Withyham (Sussex)	St Michael & All Angels	53
Woodhorn Museum (Northumberland)		266
Worthing (Norfolk)	St Margaret	202
Worth Matravers	St Aldhem	24
Wrabness (Essex)	All Saints	269
Wyndham Oak		22
Yelford (Oxon)	St Nicholas & St Swithun	139